1996

Episodes in Five Poetic Trac

Episodes

IN FIVE POETIC TRADITIONS

The Sonnet
The Pastoral Elegy
The Ballad
The Ode
Masks and Voices

R. G. BARNES
POMONA COLLEGE

CHANDLER PUBLISHING COMPANY
An Intext Publisher
SAN FRANCISCO SCRANTON LONDON TORONTO

Library of Congress Cataloging in Publication Data

Barnes, Richard G 1932- comp.
Episodes in five poetic traditions.

1. Poetry—Collections. I. Title.
PN6101.B27 808.81 70-178297
ISBN 0-8102-0460-6

International Standard Book Number 0-8102-0460-6
Library of Congress Card Catalog Number 70-178297

Printed in the United States of America

This list of previously published and copyrighted materials continues on the following page or pages.

The list of previously published and copyrighted materials on this page is a continuation of the copyright notice that begins on the verso of the title page of this book.

Robin Blaser. Pindar's Seventh Olympic Hymn. Reprinted from Caterpillar Magazine with the permission of Mr. Blaser.

John Clare, several poems. "Written in Prison," "Well, Honest John," "To the Snipe." From the book *Selected Poems* by John Clare. Edited by J. W. Tibble and Anne Tibble. Everyman's Library edition. Published by E. P. Dutton & Co., Inc. and used with their permission. Published by J. M. Dent & Sons Ltd. and used with their permission. "Sudden Shower," "Signs of Winter," "Gipsies." From *Selected Poems of John Clare,* edited by Jason Reeves, published 1954 by William Heinemann, Ltd.

Tom Clark. "Sonnet" (Five A.M. on East Fourteenth . . .) from *Stones* by Tom Clark. Copyright © 1969 by Tom Clark. All rights reserved.

Samuel Taylor Coleridge. "The Rime of the Ancient Mariner" and "Dejection." From *The Poems of Samuel Taylor Coleridge* edited by E. H. Coleridge 1912. By permission of the Clarendon Press, Oxford.

Gregory Corso. "Zizi's Lament," from *Gasoline.* Copyright © 1958 by Gregory Corso. Reprinted by permission of City Lights Books.

Robert Creeley. "The Friends" is reprinted by permission of Charles Scribner's Sons from *Pieces* by Robert Creeley. Copyright © 1969 Robert Creeley. "Not Now" and "I Know a Man" are reprinted by permission of Charles Scribner's Sons from *For Love* by Robert Creeley. Copyright © 1962 Robert Creeley.

E. E. Cummings. Several poems: "the Cambridge ladies who live in furnished souls." Copyright, 1923, 1951, by E. E. Cummings. Reprinted from his volume, *Poems 1923-1954* by permission of Harcourt Brace Jovanovich, Inc. "unnoticed woman from whose kind large flesh," "O It's Nice To Get Up In,the slipshod mucous kiss," "the dirty colours of her kiss have just." Copyright, 1925, by E. E. Cummings. Reprinted from his volume, *Poems 1923-1954* by permission of Harcourt Brace Jovanovich, Inc. "Thou in whose swordgreat story shine the deeds." Copyright, 1925, 1953 by E. E. Cummings. Reprinted from his volume, *Poems 1923-1954* by permission of Harcourt Brace Jovanovich, Inc. " 'next to of course god america i." Copyright, 1926, by Horace Liveright; renewed, 1954, by E. E. Cummings. Reprinted from *Poems 1923-1954* by E. E. Cummings by permission of Harcourt Brace Jovanovich, Inc. "Space being(don't forget to remember) Curved," "helves surling out of eakspeasies per(reel)hapsingly." Copyright, 1951, 1959, by E. E. Cummings. Reprinted from his volume, *Poems 1923-1954* by permission of Harcourt Brace Jovanovich, Inc. "nothing false and possible is love." Copyright, 1944, by E. E. Cummings. Reprinted from his volume, *Poems 1923-1954* by permission of Harcourt Brace Jovanovich, Inc.

John Dryden. "Virgil's Tenth Pastoral, or Gallus." From *The Poems of John Dryden* edited by James Kinsley Volume 2 1958. By permission of the Clarendon Press, Oxford.

Robert Duncan. "A Poem Beginning with a Line by Pindar." Reprinted by permission of Grove Press, Inc. Copyright © 1960 by Robert Duncan.

T. S. Eliot. "The Love Song of J. Alfred Prufrock," "Let us go then, you and I." From *Collected Poems 1909-1962* by T. S. Eliot, copyright, 1936, by Harcourt Brace Jovanovich, Inc.; copyright © 1963, 1964, by T. S. Eliot. Reprinted by permission of the publishers. Reprinted by permission of Faber and Faber Ltd. from *Collected Poems 1909-1962* for sale in Canada.

Robert Frost. "A Servant to Servants," "After Apple-Picking." From *The Poetry of Robert Frost* edited by Edward Connery Lathem. Copyright 1930, 1939, © 1969 by Holt, Rinehart and Winston, Inc. Copyright © 1958 by Robert Frost. Copyright © 1967 by Lesley Frost Ballantine. Reprinted by permission of Holt, Rinehart and Winston, Inc.

This list of previously published and copyrighted materials continues on the following page or pages.

This list of previously published and copyrighted materials continues on the following page or pages.

This list of previously published and copyrighted materials continues on the following page or pages.

Contents

Preface

THIS IS A BOOK *for use, a teaching anthology, and its use accounts in part for its form,—though I am bound to admit my affection for it as an artefact and as a "witness." It was put together to answer a very specific pedagogical need, the introduction to poetry course whose emphasis is on close and detailed reading of everything that is intelligible in the poem, tone, diction, imagery, prosody and so on. To these may be added the poet's tacit assertion of his place relative to a tradition, that movement of allegiance or rebellion, of awareness or ignorance, that play of expectations that is always part of the transaction. What it actually means, at some certain time, to write a poem in some certain form, is also intelligible. Thoughts cross over. A language is being spoken. Hence these* Episodes, *materials for the biographies of five kinds of poetry over the centuries.*

The reason there are five is a pretty reason: because there aren't six. Arbitrary practical and aesthetic reasons have kept the book the size and shape it is. I haven't found room for poems in foreign languages, even originals of translations; the translations then are ones I think stand on their own as poems in English. I have also left out good specimens for taxonomy that I don't actually care for as poems: Shelley's Adonais *is perhaps the most distinguished member of this large group, but also Tom Clark's "sonnet" that is a clinical description, in prose, of what happens to a woman's body during orgasm, copied out in fourteen verses; it illustrates a point but it's not here. On the other hand, I confess I have especially sought poems that speak to each other over the years: Tom Clark out early in the New York morning, his feelings affected by the antique ghost of William Wordsworth on Westminster bridge. I thought this anthology would be the one that could get along without "My Galley Chargèd with Forgetfulness," but John Berryman put it back in. If I thought anyone would take this book, these episodes, for the whole story, I should no doubt avoid such tidy congruities, because I don't myself have, nor wish to cause anyone else to have, an idea of all English poetry glued together by a Tradition. I no longer believe in Mr. Eliot's mystical edifice of "monuments" which must be studied with "great labour," thank heaven he excluded everything but "the literature of Europe since Homer," an ideal order whose relations, proportions and values are readjusted every time a new "(a really new)" work is added: "and the poet who is aware of this will be aware of great difficulties and responsibilities." We can all be glad those old days are gone forever. For us, here, in America, the glue is gone and the wind blows through everything. Denise Levertov has a bad memory, can Mnemosyne still be the mother of the Muses? Seriously, projective verse, American verse in general as it lives now, happens in real time. Mr. Eliot's Chinese jar is shattered. I have recently been scolded by Robert Bly for teaching in an "English" department. I claim that this book is a fresh look back, at these five kinds of poetry, from where we are now, as they matter to us now. I don't really think anyone will find it too tidy; I have not brought order out of chaos. Looking closely, we see that everything is chaos still.*

In every case I have consulted the original versions, where possible, and the best scholarly editions of the earlier poets. Somewhat reluctantly I have modernized spelling except where I thought such a change would actually introduce a false meaning or sound. Punctuation, I have left mainly alone on the grounds that its use was to indicate rhythms of speech or thought, not the grammar-rules of more recent respectability; and that the "irregularities" thus remaining would be tolerated (along with so much else) in the work of a poet writing today.

I owe Andrew Hoyem a special debt for his gracious help with the design and the cover. Anne Woltmann and Susan Nowers were both patient and reliable in preparing the manuscript. My wife, Mary, wrote most of the footnotes, helped with the textual editing, did all the work getting permissions, and brought a fresh judgment to many a choice. It seems out of place to thank her in her own book.

Episodes in Five Poetic Traditions

to the memory of

W. R. RODGERS

The Sonnet

THE EARLIEST SONNETS were written in Sicily during the thirteenth century by a group of poets influenced by the troubadours both in the use of rhymed stanza forms and in their subject matter. There were always other uses, but from the beginning sonnets were mainly supposed to be about the emotions of the noble, devout, and sensitive heart afflicted by passionate love, and to be written by the lover himself modestly answering that description. "If you have so earth-creeping a mind that it cannot lift itself up to look to the sky of poetry," Sir Philip Sidney warns the reader of his *Defense,* "thus much curse I must send you in the behalf of all poets: that while you live, you live in love, and never get favor for [your] lacking skill of a sonnet." Who lost his own heart loving, and read Petrarch (as Petrarch must be read to be understood) for his life.

Sidney's *Astrophel and Stella* is one of the first, best, and most influential sonnet sequences in English, and more developed as a literary form than many it inspired. If you are in love, you may write sonnets to gain favor or just to show how you feel; then, later, if you like them, you may allow them to be published. I think this fairly describes Spenser's or Shakespeare's, or John Berryman's procedure. Being a by-product of a real series of events, the sequence will have a certain narrative interest even though the intention in each sonnet is not at all to tell a story, but in fact almost the opposite: to describe emotional states that are of more interest than the biographical accidents that provoked them because they themselves, these emotional states, are to the lover unchanging truth; and while they are quite incommensurable with anything the ungentle heart could ever feel, there is no attempt to distinguish between one lover and the next so long as he qualifies as noble. Sidney's innovation was the persona Astrophel, a character not individualized but dramatically objectified; so that while the details of his own life enter freely into the poems—Stella from "Aurora's court" or Essex, the savage play on the name "Rich," Astrophel's father bridling the unruly Irish, and so on—they are imagined as dramatic monologues.

The great spate of sonneteering that followed the publication of *Astrophel and Stella* in 1591 would have been enough to make anything go out of style: if the bad wouldn't discourage you from writing sonnets, the terribly good might. There are, of course, dissenting voices, satires, travesties, of which Davies's "Gulling Sonnets" are the best—though it is doubtful whether they are as funny as what Barnabe Barnes produced apparently in all seriousness. As the seventeenth century wore on the sonnet came to seem old-fashioned, arbitrary and pretentious, the form to which an Oronte, in Molière's *Misanthrope,* would commit his ingregious sentiments. Ben Jonson and Thomas Campion both objected to the quatorzain on neoclassical grounds, independently using the nearly inevitable comparison to Procrustes's bed where the occupant was racked out or chopped off to fit. One new development was the adaptation of the form, along with some of its traditional sentiments and imagery, to devotional poetry; I think the name of Donne's "Holy Sonnets" was still probably meant as oxymoron (though there had been earlier devotional sonnets including a whole "*Divine Century*" of them by the unconscious Barnabe Barnes in 1595). Milton, following Tasso's example, composed a few "heroic sonnets," as they are called; in his hands it became a new form, a trumpet to blow soul-animating strains, but alas, too few. For more than a century after Milton there is hardly a sonnet in English worth the reading. Indeed, it was partly out of perversity that the Romantic poets started writing them again, just because the Augustans hadn't.

What has happened to the sonnet since then these pages can only begin to show, but it's half the history. There is some use after all in having a literary form that has been obsolete, and known to be so, not just for decades like the novel, but for centuries.

Francis Petrarch 1304–1374

from IN VITA DI MADONNA LAURA

156

My galley chargèd with forgetfulness,
Thoroùgh sharp seas in winter nights doth pass
'Tween rock and rock; and eke mine enemy, alas,
That is my lord, steereth with cruelness;
And every oar, a thought in readiness,
As though that death were light in such a case.
An endless wind doth tear the sail apace
Of forcèd sighs, and trusty fearfulness.
A rain of tears, a cloud of dark disdain,
Hath done the wearied cords great hinderance;
Wreathèd with error, and eke with ignorance,
The stars be hid that led me to this pain;
Drownèd is reason that should me consort,
And I remain, despairing of the port.

109

The long love that in my thought doth harbour,
And in mine heart doth keep his residence,
Into my face presseth with bold pretence,
And therein campeth spreading his banner.
She that me learns to love and suffer,
And wills that my trust, and lust's negligence,
Be reigned by reason, shame, and reverence,
With his hardiness takes displeasure.
Wherewithall unto the heart's forest he fleeth,
Leaving his enterprise with pain and cry,
And there him hideth, and not appeareth:

In Vita di Madonna Laura, a sequence of 227 sonnets.

156 Translated by Sir Thomas Wyatt 1503-1542. 156:3 also 15: 12 *The stars:* The Italian original makes clear what he means: her eyes ("Celansi i duo mei dolci usati segni;").

109 Translated by Sir Thomas Wyatt. Another translation of the same sonnet follows.

What may I do when my master feareth?
But in the field with him to live and die:
For good is the life, ending faithfully.

109

Love that liveth and reigneth in my thought,
That built his seat within my captive breast;
Clad in the arms wherein with me he fought,
Oft in my face he doth his banner rest.
She that me taught to love and suffer pain,
My doubtful hope, and eke my hot desire
With shamefast cloak to shadow and refrain,
Her smiling grace converteth straight to ire.
And coward Love then to the heart apace
Taketh his flight, whereas he lurks, and plains
His purpose lost, and dare not shew his face.
For my Lord's guilt thus faultless bide I pains;
Yet from my Lord shall not my foot remove:
Sweet is his death that takes his end by love.

62

Father of heaven, after squandered days
after the nights spent raving
in wild heart-scorching desire
dreaming of features so fair, so much to my undoing,
may it please thee that I turn by thy illumination
to the other life, and to more handsome enterprises,
so that my adversary, his nets stretched
being empty, may come to shame.
The eleventh year is turning, Lord,
since I came under the pitiless yoke
that towards the more downcast becomes more cruel.
Have mercy upon my unworthy grief
lead back my wand'ring thoughts to better places
remind me how this day thou wert on the cross.

109 Translated by Henry Howard, Earl of Surrey 1517?-1547. 109: 10 complains

62 Translated by R. G. Barnes 1932—.

157

A white doe appeared to me over green
grass, gold antlered, between
two rivulets, in a laurel's shade
as the sun rose early in the spring season:
so pleasing and so proud a sight
that following her I left all enterprise
like a miser drawing near to treasure
weariness lightened by delight.
"Dare no one touch me," she wore inscribed
round her fair neck in diamond, in topaz,
"for I am Caesar's who has set me free."
The sun wheeled quickly to mid day;
my eyes insatiate, worn out from gazing,
I fell, in the water; she vanished.

157

Whoso list to hunt, I know where is an hind,
But as for me, alas, I may no more:
The vain travail hath wearied me so sore.
I am of them that furthest come behind;
Yet may I by no means my wearied mind
Draw from the deer; but as she fleeth afore
Fainting I follow; I leave off therefore,
Since in a net I seek to hold the wind.
Who list her hunt, I put him out of doubt,
As well as I, may spend his time in vain:
And graven with diamonds in letters plain,
There is written her fair neck round about;
Noli me tangere, for Caesar's I am,
And wild for to hold, though I seem tame.

157 Translated by R. G. Barnes. Another translation of the same sonnet follows. 157:9 *Dare no one touch me* alludes to an old legend about a hart found 300 years after Caesar's death, wearing a collar inscribed with the motto: NOLI ME TANGERE : CAESARIS SUM.

157 Adapted by Sir Thomas Wyatt. 157:1 desires

Sir Thomas Wyatt 1503–1542

TO RAIL OR JEST, YE KNOW I USE IT NOT

To rail or jest, ye know I use it not;
    Though that such cause sometime in folks I find.
    And though to change ye list to set your mind,
    Love it who list, in faith I like it not.
And if ye were to me, as ye are not,
    I would be loth to see you so unkind:
    But since your fault must needs be so by kind,
    Though I hate it I pray you love it not.
Things of great weight I never thought to crave,
    This is but small; of right deny it not:
    Your feigning ways, as yet forget them not.
But like reward let other Lovers have;
    That is to say, for service true and fast,
    Too long delays, and changing at the last.

3 like   7 nature

Sir Philip Sidney 1554–1586

from ASTROPHEL AND STELLA *1591*

I

Loving in truth, and fain in verse my love to show,
    That she (dear she) might take some pleasure of my
        pain;
Pleasure might cause her read, reading might make her know,
    Knowledge might pity win, and pity grace obtain,
I sought fit words to paint the blackest face of woe,
    Studying inventions fine, her wits to entertain:
Oft turning others' leaves, to see if thence would flow
    Some fresh and fruitful showers upon my sun-burn'd
        brain.

But words came halting forth, wanting invention's stay;
    Invention's Nature's child, fled step-dame Study's
        blows,
And other's feet still seem'd but strangers in my way.
    Thus, great with child to speak, and helpless in my
        throes,
Biting my truant pen, beating myself for spite,
Fool! said my Muse to me, look in thy heart, and write.

14

    Alas have I not pain enough my friend,
Upon whose breast a fiercer gripe doth tire
Than did on him who first stole down the fire,
    While Love on me doth all his quiver spend;
But with your rhubarb words you must contend,
    To grieve me worse, in saying, that Desire
    Doth plunge my well-form'd soul even in the mire
Of sinful thoughts, which do in ruin end?

Astrophel and Stella, a sequence of 108 sonnets and 11 songs.
1 The twelve-syllable line of this sonnet imitates the alexandrine of Ronsard. 1:1 eager
14:2 vulture doth tear

If that be sin which doth the manners frame,
Well staid with truth in word, and faith of deed,
Ready of wit, and fearing nought but shame;
If that be sin, which in fix'd hearts doth breed
A loathing of all loose unchastity,
Then love is sin, and let me sinful be.

20

Fly, fly, my friends, I have my death wound; fly,
See there that boy, that murdering boy I say,
Who, like a thief, hid in dark bush doth lie,
Till bloody bullet get him wrongful prey.
So tyrant he no fitter place could spy,
Nor so fair level in so secret stay,
As that sweet black which veils the heav'nly eye;
There himself with his shot he close doth lay.

Poor passenger, pass now thereby I did,
And staid pleas'd with the prospect of the place;
While that black hue from me the bad guest hid:
But straight I saw motions of lightning grace,
And then descried the glistering of his dart:
But ere I could fly thence, it pierc'd my heart.

24

Rich fools there be, whose base and filthy heart
Lies hatching still the goods wherein they flow:
And damning their own selves to Tantal's smart,
Wealth breeding want, more blest, more wretched grow;
Yet to those fools heav'n doth such wit impart,
As what their hands do hold, their heads do know,
And knowing, love, and loving, lay apart,
As sacred things, far from all dangers show.

14:9 builds character

20:6 aim

24:1 *Rich fools:* Penelope Devereux, Sidney's Stella, rejected his suit and married a certain Lord Rich. 24:3 *Tantal's smart:* the punishment of Tantalus.

But that Rich fool, who by blind Fortune's lot,
The richest gem of love and life enjoys,
And can with foul abuse such beauties blot;
Let him, depriv'd of sweet but unfelt joys,
(Exil'd for aye from those high treasures, which
He knows not) grow in only folly Rich.

30

Whether the Turkish new-moon minded be
To fill his horns this year on Christian coast;
How Poles' right king means, without leave of host
To warm with ill-made fire cold Muscovy;
If French can yet three parts in one agree;
What now the Dutch in their full diets boast;
How Holland hearts, now so good towns be lost,
Trust in the shade of pleasant *Orange* tree?

How Ulster likes of that same golden bit,
Wherewith my father once made it half tame;
If in the Scottish court be weltring yet;
These questions busy wits to me do frame;
I, cumber'd with good manners, answer do,
But know not how, for still I think of you.

31

With how sad steps, O moon, thou climb'st the skies,
How silently, and with how wan a face,
What, may it be, that ev'n in heav'nly place
That busy archer his sharp arrows tries?

24:13 ever

30:3–4 *Poles' right king:* King Stephen, who in 1580-1581 invaded Russia; *ill-made fire* is obscure, but perhaps means cannon shot. 30:5 *Three parts:* the Huguenots, Catholics, and moderates. 30:6 *Full diets:* refers to the Diet of the Holy Roman Empire held at Augsburg, 1576-1582. 30:8 *Orange tree:* William of Orange, king of Holland, who lost "so good towns" to the Spaniards. 30:10 *My father:* Sir Henry Sidney was three times Lord Deputy of Ireland. 30:11 *weltring:* unrest among various factions who sought the Scottish rule before and after 1568 when Mary Stuart, Queen of Scots, was held captive in England because of her claim to the English throne.

Sure, if that long-with-Love-acquainted eyes
Can judge of love, thou feel'st a lover's case;
I read it in thy looks, thy languish'd grace,
To me that feel the like, thy state descries.

Then, ev'n of fellowship, O moon, tell me,
Is constant love deem'd there but want of wit?
Are beauties there as proud as here they be?
Do they above love to be lov'd, and yet
Those lovers scorn, whom that Love doth possess?
Do they call Virtue there ungratefulness?

34

Come, let me write, and to what end? to ease
A burthen'd heart; how can words ease, which are
The glasses of thy daily vexing care?
Oft cruel fights, well pictur'd forth, do please;
Art not asham'd to publish thy disease?
Nay, that may breed my fame, it is so rare:
But will not wise men think thy words fond ware?
Then be they close, and so none shall displease.

What idler thing than speak, and not be heard?
What harder thing than smart, and not to speak?
Peace, foolish wit, with wit my wit is marr'd.
Thus write I while I doubt to write, and wreak
My harms on ink's poor loss, perhaps some find
Stella's great powers, that so confuse my mind.

37

My mouth doth water, and my breast doth swell,
My tongue doth itch, my thoughts in labour be;
Listen then Lordings with good ear to me,
For of my life I must a riddle tell.
Toward Aurora's Court a Nymph doth dwell,

34:3 mirrors 34:7 foolish 34:8 secret 37:5 *nymph:* Penelope Devereux, "Stella," was the daughter of the Earl of Essex, literally, the land of the East Saxons. *Aurora* = dawn, hence east. Penelope married Lord Rich.

Rich in all beauties which man's eye can see;
Beauties so far from reach of words, that we
Abase her praise, saying she doth excel:

Rich in the treasure of deserv'd renown,
Rich in the riches of a royal heart,
Rich in those gifts which give th' eternal crown:
Who though most rich in these and ev'ry part,
Which make the patents of true worldly bliss,
Hath no misfortune, but that Rich she is.

71

Who will in fairest book of Nature know,
How Virtue may best lodg'd in beauty be,
Let him but learn of Love to read in thee,
Stella, those fair lines, which true goodness show:
There shall he find all vices' overthrow
Not by rude force, but sweetest sovereignty
Of reason, from whose light those night-birds fly;
That inward sun in thine eyes shineth so.

And not content to be Perfection's heir
Thyself, dost strive all minds that way to move,
Who mark in thee what is in thee most fair.
So while thy beauty draws the heart to love,
As fast thy Virtue bends that love to good:
"But, ah," Desire still cries, "give me some food."

83

Good brother Philip, I have borne you long,
I was content you should in favour creep,
While craftily you seem'd your cut to keep,
As though that fair soft hand did you great wrong,
I bare (with envy) yet I bare your song

71:7 *night-birds:* emblems of vice and error
83:1 *Good brother Philip:* Apparently a name for pet sparrows, recalling at once the one Skelton wrote the dirge for and the one Claudia played with while Catullus ate his heart out. 83:3 to nurse some hurt

When in her neck, you did love ditties peep;
Nay, more fool I, oft suffer'd you to sleep,
In lilys' nest, where Love's self lies along.

What, doth high place ambitious thoughts augment?
Is sauciness reward of courtesy?
Cannot such grace your silly self content,
But you must needs with those lips billing be?
And through those lips drink nectar from that tongue;
Leave that, Sir Phip, lest off your neck be wrung.

THOU BLIND MAN'S MARK, THOU FOOL'S SELF-CHOSEN SNARE

Thou blind man's mark, thou fool's self-chosen snare,
Fond fancy's scum, and dregs of scatter'd thought,
Band of all evils, cradle of causeless care,
Thou web of will whose end is never wrought;
Desire, desire I have too dearly bought,
With price of mangled mind thy worthless ware;
Too long, too long asleep thou hast me brought,
Who shouldst my mind to higher things prepare.

But yet in vain thou hast my ruin sought,
In vain thou mad'st me to vain things aspire,
In vain thou kindlest all thy smoky fire:
For Virtue hath this better lesson taught,
Within myself to seek my only hire:
Desiring nought but how to kill Desire.

From *Certain Sonnets,* in *The Countess of Pembroke's Arcadia* 1598.
2 foolish

Edmund Spenser 1552?–1599

from AMORETTI AND EPITHALAMION *1595*

18

The rolling wheel that runneth often round,
The hardest steel, in tract of time doth tear:
And drizzling drops that often do redound,
The firmest flint doth in continuance wear.
Yet cannot I, with many a dropping tear
And long entreaty, soften her hard heart:
That she will once vouchsafe my plaint to hear,
Or look with pity on my painful smart,
But when I plead, she bids me play my part;
And when I weep, she says tears are but water,
And when I sigh, she says I know the art;
And when I wail she turns herself to laughter.
    So do I weep, and wail, and plead in vain,
    Whiles she as steel and flint doth still remain.

67

Like as a huntsman after weary chase,
Seeing the game from him escaped away,
Sits down to rest him in some shady place,
With panting hounds beguilèd of their prey:
So after long pursuit and vain assay,
When I all weary had the chase forsook,
The gentle deer returned the selfsame way,
Thinking to quench her thirst at the next brook:
There she beholding me with milder look,
Sought not to fly, but fearless still did bide;
Till I in hand her yet half trembling took,
And with her own good-will her firmly tied.
    Strange thing me seemed to see a beast so wild,
    So goodly won with her own will beguiled.

Amoretti and Epithalamion, a sequence of 88 sonnets and the great wedding ode (see page 261 of this book).

68

Most glorious Lord of life, that on this day,
Didst make thy triumph over death and sin;
And having harrowed hell, didst bring away
Captivity thence captive us to win:
This joyous day, dear Lord, with joy begin,
And grant that we for whom thou diddest die,
Being with thy dear blood clean washed from sin,
May live for ever in felicity.
And that thy love we weighing worthily,
May likewise love thee for the same again;
And for thy sake that all like dear didst buy,
With love may one another entertain.
So let us love, dear love, like as we ought:
Love is the lesson which the Lord us taught.

Samuel Daniel c. 1562–1619

from DELIA *1592*

51

Care-charmer sleep, son of the sable night,
    Brother to death, in silent darkness born,
    Relieve my languish, and restore the light;
    With dark forgetting of my care return,
And let the day be time enough to mourn
    The shipwreck of my ill-adventur'd youth;
    Let waking eyes suffice to wail their scorn,
    Without the torment of the night's untruth.
Cease, dreams, the images of day-desires,
    To model forth the passions of the morrow;
    Never let rising sun approve you liars,
    To add more grief to aggravate my sorrow;
Still let me sleep, embracing clouds in vain,
And never wake to feel the day's disdain.

Delia, a sequence of 50 sonnets and an ode.

Michael Drayton 1563–1631

from IDEA'S MIRROR *1594*

6

How many paltry, foolish, painted things
That now in coaches trouble every street,
Shall be forgotten, whom no poet sings,
Ere they be well wrapp'd in their winding-sheet!
Where I to thee eternity shall give,
When nothing else remaineth of these days,
And Queens hereafter shall be glad to live
Upon the alms of thy superfluous praise.
Virgins and matrons reading these my rhymes,
Shall be so much delighted with thy story,
That they shall grieve they liv'd not in these times
To have seen thee, their sex's only glory:
  So shalt thou fly above the vulgar throng,
  Still to survive in my immortal song.

61

Since there's no help, come let us kiss and part,
Nay, I have done, you get no more of me,
And I am glad, yea, glad with all my heart,
That thus so cleanly I myself can free;
Shake hands for ever, cancel all our vows,
And when we meet at any time again,
Be it not seen in either of our brows
That we one jot of former love retain;
Now at the last gasp of Love's latest breath,
When, his pulse failing, passion speechless lies,
When Faith is kneeling by his bed of death,
And Innocence is closing up his eyes,
  Now if thou would'st, when all have given him over,
  From death to life thou might'st him yet recover.

Idea's Mirror, a sequence of 51 sonnets published in 1594; enlarged to 59 sonnets in *Idea* 1599; to 67 sonnets in *Idea's Mirror* 1602; reduced to 64 sonnets in 1619.

Barnabe Barnes 1569?–1609

from PARTHENOPHIL AND PARTHENOPHE *1593*

18

Write! write! help! help, sweet Muse! and never cease!
In endless labours, pens and paper tire!
Until I purchase my long wished Desire.
Brains, with my Reason, never rest in peace!
Waste breathless words! and breathful sighs increase!
Till of my woes, remorseful, you espy her;
Till she with me, be burnt in equal fire.
I never will, from labour, wits release!
My senses never shall in quiet rest;
Till thou be pitiful, and love alike!
And if thou never pity my distresses;
Thy cruelty, with endless force shall strike
Upon my wits, to ceaseless writs addrest!
My cares, in hope of some revenge, this lesses.

21

Yea, but uncertain hopes are Anchors feeble,
When such faint-hearted pilots guide my ships,
Of all my fortune's Ballast with hard pebble,
Whose doubtful voyage proves not worth two chips.
If when but one dark cloud shall dim the sky,
The Cables of hope's happiness be cut;
When bark, with thoughts-drowned mariners shall lie,
Prest for the whirlpool of grief's endless glut.
If well thou mean, PARTHENOPHE! then ravish
Mine heart, with doubtless hope of mutual love!
If otherwise; then let thy tongue run lavish!
For this, or that, am I resolved to prove!

Parthenophil and Parthenophe, a sequence of 105 sonnets, 26 madrigals, 5 sestinas, 22 elegies, 20 odes, and 3 canzone, with 6 dedicatory sonnets by the author and an envoy.

And both, or either ecstasy shall move
Me! ravished, end with surfeit of relief;
Or senseless, daunted, die with sudden grief.

63

JOVE for EUROPA's love, took shape of Bull;
And for CALISTO, played DIANA's part:
And in a golden shower, he fillèd full
The lap of DANAE, with celestial art.
Would I were changed but to my Mistress' gloves,
That those white lovely fingers I might hide!
That I might kiss those hands, which mine heart loves!
Or else that chain of pearl (her neck's vain pride)
Made proud with her neck's veins, that I might fold
About that lovely neck, and her paps tickle!
Or her to compass, like a belt of gold!
Or that sweet wine, which down her throat doth trickle,
To kiss her lips, and lie next at her heart,
Run through her veins, and pass by Pleasure's part!

Sir John Davies 1569–1626

from GULLING SONNETS

I

The Lover under burden of his Mistress' love
Which like to Aetna did his heart oppress:
Did give such piteous groans that he did move
The heav'ns at length to pity his distress
But for the Fates in their high Court above
Forbad to make the grievous burthen less.
The gracious powers did all conspire to prove
If miracle this mischief might redress;
Therefore regarding that the load was such
As no man might with one man's might sustain
And that mild patience imported much
To him that should endure an endless pain:
By their decree he soon transformèd was
Into a patient burden-bearing Ass.

5

Mine Eye, mine ear, my will, my wit, my heart
Did see, did hear, did like, discern, did love:
Her face, her speech, her fashion, judgement, art,
Which did charm, please, delight, confound, and move.
Then fancy, humor, love, conceit, and thought
Did so draw, force, entice, persuade, devise,
That she was won, mov'd, carried, compast, wrought
To think me kind, true, comely, valiant, wise;
That heaven, earth, hell, my folly and her pride
Did work, contrive, labor, conspire, and swear
To make me scorn'd, vile, cast off, base, defied
With her my love, my light, my life, my dear:
So that my heart, my wit, will, ear, and eye
Doth grieve, lament, sorrow, despair and die.

Gulling Sonnets, a sequence of 9 sonnets, not published until 1873.
1:7 to test
5:5 concept

8

My case is this, I love Zepheria bright,
Of her I hold my heart by fealty:
Which I discharge to her perpetually,
Yet she thereof will never me acquite.
For now supposing I withhold her right
She hath distrained my heart to satisfy
The duty which I never did deny,
And far away impounds it with despite;
I labor therefore justly to repleve
My heart which she unjustly doth impound
But quick conceit which now is love's high Shrieve
Returns it as eloigned, not to be found:
Then which the law affords I only crave
Her heart for mine in withernam to have.

8 Compare the imagery in this to Shakespeare's sonnet 30. 8:9 *repleve:* seek to regain by legal action; replevin. 8:11 *Shrieve:* sheriff. 8:12 *eloigned:* removed out of the jurisdiction of a sheriff or count. 8:14 *withernam:* legal term meaning illegal or forbidden distraint.

William Shakespeare 1564–1616

from SONNETS 1609

19

Devouring Time blunt thou the lion's paws,
And make the earth devour her own sweet brood,
Pluck the keen teeth from the fierce tiger's jaws,
And burn the long-liv'd phœnix in her blood,
Make glad and sorry seasons as thou fleetst,
And do whate'er thou wilt swift-footed Time
To the wide world and all her fading sweets;
But I forbid thee one most heinous crime:
O carve not with thy hours my love's fair brow,
Nor draw no lines there with thine antique pen;
Him in thy course untainted do allow
For beauty's pattern to succeeding men.
    Yet do thy worst old Time despite thy wrong,
    My love shall in my verse ever live young.

29

When in disgrace with fortune and men's eyes,
I all alone beweep my outcast state,
And trouble deaf heaven with my bootless cries,
And look upon myself and curse my fate,
Wishing me like to one more rich in hope,
Featur'd like him, like him with friends possess'd,
Desiring this man's art, and that man's scope,
With what I most enjoy contented least;
Yet in these thoughts myself almost despising,
Haply I think on thee; and then my state,
Like to the lark at break of day arising
From sullen earth, sings hymns at heaven's gate;
    For thy sweet love remember'd such wealth brings
    That then I scorn to change my state with kings.

Sonnets, a sequence of 154 sonnets.
29:3 vain

30

When to the sessions of sweet silent thought
I summon up remembrance of things past,
I sigh the lack of many a thing I sought,
And with old woes new wail my dear time's waste:
Then can I drown an eye, unus'd to flow,
For precious friends hid in death's dateless night,
And weep afresh love's long since cancell'd woe,
And moan th'expense of many a vanish'd sight:
Then can I grieve at grievances foregone,
And heavily from woe to woe tell o'er
The sad account of fore-bemoanèd moan,
Which I new pay as if not paid before.
    But if the while I think on thee, dear friend,
    All losses are restor'd and sorrows end.

55

Not marble, nor the gilded monuments
Of princes shall outlive this powerful rhyme;
But you shall shine more bright in these contents
Than unswept stone besmear'd with sluttish time.
When wasteful war shall statues overturn,
And broils root out the work of masonry,
Nor Mars his sword nor war's quick fire shall burn
The living record of your memory.
'Gainst death and all-oblivious enmity
Shall you pace forth, your praise shall still find room
Even in the eyes of all posterity
That wear this world out to the ending doom.
    So, till the judgement that yourself arise,
    You live in this, and dwell in lovers' eyes.

60

Like as the waves make towards the pebbled shore,
So do our minutes hasten to their end,
Each changing place with that which goes before,
In sequent toil all forwards do contend.

55:12 Last Judgment

Nativity, once in the main of light,
Crawls to maturity, wherewith being crown'd,
Crooked eclipses 'gainst his glory fight,
And Time that gave, doth now his gift confound.
Time doth transfix the flourish set on youth
And delves the parallels in beauty's brow,
Feeds on the rarities of nature's truth,
And nothing stands but for his scythe to mow:
    And yet to times in hope, my verse shall stand
    Praising thy worth, despite his cruel hand.

65

Since brass, nor stone, nor earth, nor boundless sea,
But sad mortality o'er-sways their power,
How with this rage shall beauty hold a plea,
Whose action is no stronger than a flower?
O how shall summer's honey breath hold out
Against the wrackful siege of battering days,
When rocks impregnable are not so stout,
Nor gates of steel so strong, but Time decays?
O fearful meditation, where alack,
Shall Time's best jewel from Time's chest lie hid?
Or what strong hand can hold his swift foot back?
Or who his spoil of beauty can forbid?
    O none, unless this miracle have might,
    That in black ink my love may still shine bright.

71

No longer mourn for me when I am dead
Than you shall hear the surly sullen bell
Give warning to the world that I am fled
From this vile world, with vilest worms to dwell:
Nay if you read this line, remember not
The hand that writ it, for I love you so
That I in your sweet thoughts would be forgot
If thinking on me then should make you woe.
O if, I say, you look upon this verse

60:5 broad expanse   60:10 wrinkles   60:13 future times

When I perhaps compounded am with clay,
Do not so much as my poor name rehearse;
But let your love even with my life decay,
    Lest the wise world should look into your moan,
    And mock you with me after I am gone.

73

That time of year thou mayst in me behold
When yellow leaves, or none, or few, do hang
Upon those boughs which shake against the cold,
Bare ruin'd choirs, where late the sweet birds sang.
In me thou see'st the twilight of such day
As after sunset fadeth in the west,
Which by and by black night doth take away,
Death's second self that seals up all in rest.
In me thou see'st the glowing of such fire,
That on the ashes of his youth doth lie,
As the death-bed, whereon it must expire
Consum'd with that which it was nourish'd by.
    This thou perceiv'st, which makes thy love more strong,
    To love that well which thou must leave ere long.

94

They that have power to hurt, and will do none,
That do not do the thing, they most do show,
Who, moving others, are themselves as stone,
Unmovèd, cold, and to temptation slow;
They rightly do inherit heaven's graces,
And husband nature's riches from expense;
They are the lords, and owners of their faces,
Others, but stewards of their excellence.
The summer's flower is to the summer sweet,
Though to itself, it only live and die,
But if that flower with base infection meet,
The basest weed outbraves his dignity:
    For sweetest things turn sourest by their deeds;
    Lilies that fester smell far worse than weeds.

94:6 expenditure   94:12 excels

116

Let me not to the marriage of true minds
Admit impediments, love is not love
Which alters when it alteration finds,
Or bends with the remover to remove:
O no, it is an ever-fixèd mark
That looks on tempests and is never shaken:
It is the star to every wandering bark,
Whose worth's unknown, although his height be taken.
Love's not Time's fool, though rosy lips and cheeks
Within his bending sickle's compass come,
Love alters not with his brief hours and weeks,
But bears it out even to the edge of doom:
    If this be error and upon me proved,
    I never writ, nor no man ever loved.

128

How oft when thou, my music, music play'st,
Upon that blessèd wood whose motion sounds
With thy sweet fingers, when thou gently sway'st
The wiry concord that mine ear confounds,
Do I envy those jacks that nimble leap
To kiss the tender inward of thy hand,
Whilst my poor lips, which should that harvest reap,
At the wood's boldness by thee blushing stand.
To be so tickled they would change their state
And situation with those dancing chips,
O'er whom thy fingers walk with gentle gait,
Making dead wood more blest than living lips.
    Since saucy jacks so happy are in this,
    Give them thy fingers, me thy lips to kiss.

129

Th'expense of spirit in a waste of shame
Is lust in action, and till action, lust
Is perjur'd, murth'rous, bloody, full of blame,
Savage, extreme, rude, cruel, not to trust,
Enjoy'd no sooner but despisèd straight,
Past reason hunted, and no sooner had

Past reason hated as a swallow'd bait,
On purpose laid to make the taker mad.
Mad in pursuit and in possession so,
Had, having, and in quest to have, extreme;
A bliss in proof, and prov'd, a very woe;
Before, a joy propos'd; behind, a dream.
All this the world well knows; yet none knows well
To shun the heaven that leads men to this hell.

130

My mistress' eyes are nothing like the sun,
Coral is far more red than her lips' red,
If snow be white, why then her breasts are dun;
If hairs be wires, black wires grow on her head.
I have seen roses damask'd, red and white,
But no such roses see I in her cheeks;
And in some perfumes is there more delight
Than in the breath that from my mistress reeks.
I love to hear her speak, yet well I know,
That music hath a far more pleasing sound:
I grant I never saw a goddess go;
My mistress when she walks treads on the ground:
And yet by heaven I think my love as rare,
As any she belied with false compare.

135

Whoever hath her wish, thou hast thy Will,
And Will to boot, and Will in overplus,
More than enough am I that vex thee still,
To thy sweet will making addition thus.
Wilt thou whose will is large and spacious,
Not once vouchsafe to hide my will in thine,
Shall will in others seem right gracious,
And in my will no fair acceptance shine:
The sea all water, yet receives rain still,
And in abundance addeth to his store

129:11 in the experience
130:5 variegated 130:11 walk

So thou being rich in Will add to thy Will,
One will of mine, to make thy large Will more.
    Let no unkind, no fair beseechers kill,
    Think all but one, and me in that one Will.

136

If thy soul check thee that I come so near,
Swear to thy blind soul that I was thy Will,
And will, thy soul knows, is admitted there;
Thus far for love my love-suit, sweet, fulfil.
Will, will fulfil the treasure of thy love,
Ay, fill it full with wills, and my will one,
In things of great receipt with ease we prove
Among a number one is reckon'd none:
Then in the number let me pass untold,
Though in thy stores' account I one must be,
For nothing hold me, so it please thee hold
That nothing me, a something sweet to thee:
    Make but my name thy love and love that still,
    And then thou lov'st me, for my name is Will.

138

When my love swears that she is made of truth,
I do believe her, though I know she lies,
That she might think me some untutor'd youth,
Unlearnèd in the world's false subtleties.
Thus vainly thinking that she thinks me young,
Although she knows my days are past the best,
Simply I credit her false-speaking tongue:
On both sides thus is simple truth suppress'd.
But wherefore says she not she is unjust?
And wherefore say not I that I am old?
O, love's best habit is in seeming trust,
And age in love loves not to have years told:
    Therefore I lie with her, and she with me,
    And in our faults by lies we flatter'd be.

136:7 size

144

Two loves I have of comfort and despair,
Which like two spirits do suggest me still:
The better angel is a man right fair,
The worser spirit a woman colour'd ill.
To win me soon to hell, my female evil
Tempteth my better angel from my side,
And would corrupt my saint to be a devil,
Wooing his purity with her foul pride.
And whether that my angel be turn'd fiend
Suspect I may, yet not directly tell,
But being both from me, both to each friend,
I guess one angel in another's hell:
    Yet this shall I ne'er know, but live in doubt,
    Till my bad angel fire my good one out.

146

Poor soul the centre of my sinful earth,
Thrall to these rebel powers that thee array,
Why dost thou pine within and suffer dearth,
Painting thy outward walls so costly gay?
Why so large cost, having so short a lease,
Dost thou upon thy fading mansion spend?
Shall worms, inheritors of this excess,
Eat up thy charge? is this thy body's end?
Then soul live thou upon thy servant's loss,
And let that pine to aggravate thy store;
Buy terms divine in selling hours of dross;
Within be fed, without be rich no more:
    So shalt thou feed on Death, that feeds on men,
    And Death once dead, there's no more dying then.

144:2 tempt   144:14 *fire:* drive away with fire

John Donne 1572–1631

from DIVINE POEMS *1633*: HOLY SONNETS

7

At the round earth's imagin'd corners, blow
Your trumpets, angels, and arise, arise
From death, you numberless infinities
Of souls, and to your scatter'd bodies go
All whom the flood did, and fire shall o'erthrow,
All whom war, dearth, age, agues, tyrannies,
Despair, law, chance, hath slain, and you whose eyes
Shall behold God, and never taste death's woe.
But let them sleep, Lord, and me mourn a space,
For if above all these my sins abound,
'Tis late to ask abundance of thy grace
When we are there; here on this lowly ground
Teach me how to repent; for that's as good
As if thou'dst seal'd my pardon, with thy blood.

9

If poisonous minerals, and if that tree
Whose fruit threw death on else immortal us,
If lecherous goats, if serpents envious
Cannot be damn'd; alas; why should I be?
Why should intent or reason, born in me,
Make sins, else equal, in me, more heinous?
And mercy being easy, and glorious
To God, in his stern wrath, why threatens he?
But who am I, that dare dispute with thee?
O God, O! of thine only worthy blood,
And my tears, make a heavenly Lethean flood,
And drown in it my sins' black memory.
That thou remember them, some claim as debt,
I think it mercy, if thou wilt forget.

Divine Poems: Holy Sonnets, a sequence of 19 sonnets.

10

Death be not proud, though some have callèd thee
Mighty and dreadful, for thou art not so,
For, those, whom thou think'st thou dost overthrow
Die not, poor Death, nor yet canst thou kill me.
From rest and sleep, which but thy pictures be,
Much pleasure, then from thee, much more must flow,
And soonest our best men with thee do go,
Rest of their bones and soul's delivery.
Thou'rt slave to Fate, chance, kings, and desperate men,
And dost with poison, war, and sickness dwell,
And poppy,'or charms can make us sleep as well,
And better than thy stroke; why swell'st thou then?
One short sleep past, we wake eternally,
And death shall be no more, Death thou shalt die.

14

Batter my heart, three person'd God; for, you
As yet but knock, breathe, shine, and seek to mend;
That I may rise, and stand, o'erthrow me,'and bend
Your force, to break, blow, burn, and make me new.
I, like an usurp'd town, to'another due,
Labor to'admit you, but O, to no end,
Reason your viceroy in me, me should defend,
But is captiv'd, and proves weak or untrue.
Yet dearly'I love you'and would be lovèd fain,
But am betroth'd unto your enemy,
Divorce me,'untie, or break that knot again,
Take me to you, imprison me, for I
Except y'enthrall me, never shall be free,
Nor ever chaste, except you ravish me.

10:11 Donne uses the apostrophe between two syllables that are meant to be scanned as one.

George Herbert 1593–1633

THE HOLDFAST

I threat'ned to observe the strict decree
Of my dear God with all my power and might.
But I was told by one, it could not be;
Yet I might trust in God to be my light.
Then will I trust, said I, in him alone.
Nay, ev'n to trust in him, was also his:
We must confess that nothing is our own.
Then I confess that he my succour is:
But to have nought is ours, not to confess
That we have nought, I stood amaz'd at this,
Much troubled, till I heard a friend express,
That all things were more ours by being his.
What Adam had, and forfeited for all,
Christ keepeth now, who cannot fail or fall.

SIN

Lord, with what care hast Thou begirt us round!
Parents first season us: then schoolmasters
Deliver us to laws; they send us bound
To rules of reason, holy messengers,
Pulpits and Sundays, sorrow dogging sin,
Afflictions sorted, anguish of all sizes,
Fine nets and stratagems to catch us in,
Bibles laid open, millions of surprises,
Blessings beforehand, ties of gratefulness,
The sound of glory ringing in our ears;
Without, our shame; within, our consciences;
Angels and grace, eternal hopes and fears.
Yet all these fences and their whole array
One cunning bosom-sin blows quite away.

From *The Temple* 1633 (five poems).

PRAYER (I)

Prayer the Church's banquet, Angel's age,
 God's breath in man returning to his birth,
 The soul in paraphrase, heart in pilgrimage,
The Christian plummet sounding heav'n and earth;
Engine against th'Almighty, sinner's tower,
 Reversèd thunder, Christ-side-piercing spear,
 The six-days world transposing in an hour,
A kind of tune, which all things hear and fear;
Softness, and peace, and joy, and love, and bliss,
 Exalted Manna, gladness of the best,
 Heaven in ordinary, man well dressed,
The milky way, the bird of Paradise,
 Church-bells beyond the stars heard, the soul's blood,
 The land of spices; something understood.

THE HOLY SCRIPTURES (I)

Oh Book! infinite sweetness! let my heart
 Suck ev'ry letter, and a honey gain,
 Precious for any grief in any part;
To clear the breast, to mollify all pain.
Thou art all health, health thriving till it make
 A full eternity: thou art a mass
 Of strange delights, where we may wish and take.
Ladies, look here; this is the thankful glass,
That mends the looker's eyes: this is the well
 That washes what it shows. Who can endear
 Thy praise too much? thou art heav'n's Lidger here,
Working against the states of death and hell.
 Thou art joy's handsel: heav'n lies flat in thee,
 Subject to ev'ry mounter's bended knee.

Prayer: 5 device
The Holy Scriptures: 11 ambassador 13 first gift, earnest money

THE ANSWER

My comforts drop and melt away like snow:
I shake my head, and all the thoughts and ends,
Which my fierce youth did bandy, fall and flow
Like leaves about me: or like summer friends,
Flies of estates and sun-shine. But to all,
Who think me eager, hot, and undertaking,
But in my prosecutions slack and small;
As a young exhalation, newly waking,
Scorns his first bed of dirt, and means the sky;
But cooling by the way, grows pursy and slow,
And settling to a cloud, doth live and die
In that dark state of tears: to all, that so
    Show me, and set me, I have one reply,
    Which they that know the rest, know more than I.

John Milton 1608–1674

11. ON THE DETRACTION WHICH FOLLOWED UPON MY WRITING CERTAIN TREATISES

A book was writ of late called *Tetrachordon,*
And woven close, both matter, form, and style;
The subject new: it walked the town a while,
Numbering good intellects; now seldom pored on.
Cries the stall-reader, "Bless us! what a word on
A title-page is this!"; and some in file
Stand spelling false, while one might walk to Mile-
End Green. Why, is it harder, sirs, than *Gordon,*
Colkitto, or *Macdonnel,* or *Galasp?*
Those rugged names to our like mouths grow sleek
That would have made Quintilian stare and gasp.
Thy age, like ours, O soul of Sir John Cheek,
Hated not learning worse than toad or asp,
When thou taught'st Cambridge and King Edward Greek.

16. TO THE LORD GENERAL CROMWELL, MAY 1652

Cromwell, our chief of men, who through a cloud
Not of war only, but detractions rude,
Guided by faith and matchless fortitude,
To peace and truth thy glorious way has ploughed,
And on the neck of crownèd Fortune proud
Hast reared God's trophies, and his work pursued,

From *Poems, etc.* 1673, except sonnet 16, which because of its controversial nature was withheld from publication until 1695.

11:1 *Tetrachordon:* Milton's third divorce tract, so named because it was based on the four chief passages in Scripture which deal with divorce. 11:7 misreading 11:12 *Sir John Cheek* (or Cheke): 1514-1557, tutor to Prince Edward, was an advocate of pure English.

16:1 *Oliver Cromwell* succeeded Thomas Fairfax as commander-in-chief of the Parliamentary army. 16:5 Charles I was executed in 1649.

While Darwen stream, with blood of Scots imbrued,
And Dunbar field, resounds thy praises loud,
And Worcester's laureate wreath: yet much remains
To conquer still; Peace hath her victories
No less renowned than War: new foes arise,
Threatening to bind our souls with secular chains.
Help us to save free conscience from the paw
Of hireling wolves, whose Gospel is their maw.

18. ON THE LATE MASSACRE IN PIEDMONT

Avenge O Lord thy slaughtered saints, whose bones
Lie scattered on the Alpine mountains cold,
Even them who kept thy truth so pure of old,
When all our fathers worshiped stocks and stones,
Forget not: in thy book record their groans
Who were thy sheep and in their ancient fold
Slain by the bloody Piemontese, that rolled
Mother with infant down the rocks. Their moans
The vales redoubled to the hills, and they
To Heav'n. Their martyred blood and ashes sow
O'er all th' Italian fields, where still doth sway
The triple Tyrant; that from these may grow
A hundredfold, who, having learnt thy way
Early may fly the Babylonian woe.

16:7–9 *Darwen, Dunbar,* and *Worcester:* sites of Cromwell's victories.
18 *On the Late Massacre:* In April 1655, the Duke of Savoy's troops attacked the Protestant sect of Waldensians in the Piedmont in Northern Italy, as a result of which some 1700 members of the sect were killed. They had existed as a sect since the twelfth century, first within the Catholic church, later as excommunicated heretics. 18:4 idols 18:12 *triple Tyrant:* the Pope, whose tiara has three crowns. 18:14 *Babylonian woe:* the destruction of Babylon referred to in Revelations 12. Protestants identified Babyon, city of worldly luxury and sin, allegorically with the Catholic Church, which they believed would be destroyed according to the prophecy in Revelations.

19. ON HIS BLINDNESS

When I consider how my light is spent
    Ere half my days in this dark world and wide,
    And that one talent which is death to hide
    Lodged with me useless, though my soul more bent
To serve therewith my Maker, and present
    My true account, lest He returning chide,
    "Doth God exact day-labour, light denied?"
    I fondly ask. But Patience, to prevent
That murmur, soon replies, "God doth not need
    Either man's work or his own gifts. Who best
    Bear his mild yoke, they serve him best. His state
Is kingly: thousands at his bidding speed,
    And post o'er land and ocean without rest;
    They also serve who only stand and wait."

23. ON HIS DECEASED WIFE

Methought I saw my late espousèd saint
    Brought to me like Alcestis from the grave,
    Whom Jove's great son to her glad husband gave,
    Rescued from Death by force, though pale and faint.
Mine, as whom washed from spot of child-bed taint
    Purification in the Old Law did save,
    And such as yet once more I trust to have
    Full sight of her in Heaven without restraint,
Came vested all in white, pure as her mind.
    Her face was veiled; yet to my fancied sight
    Love, sweetness, goodness, in her person shined
So clear as in no face with more delight.
    But, oh! as to embrace me she inclined,
    I waked, she fled, and day brought back my night.

19:3 *talent:* See the Parable of the Talents, Matthew 15:14-30. 19:8 foolishly

23.2 *Alcestis* was brought back from the dead to her husband by Hercules. 23:5 Refers to an Old Testament (or Old Law) rite in which

Juana de Asbaje 1651–1695

"CRIMSON LUTE THAT COMEST IN THE DAWN" . . .

Crimson lute that comest in the dawn
with doleful ditty to thy cherished mate
and in the amber of the nutrient rose
stainest coral red thy golden beak.

Gentle goldfinch, birdling born to sorrow,
that scarce didst glimpse the lovely break of day
when, at the first note of thy melody,
thou wast by death received, by song abandoned.

In life there is no sure lot, verily;
with thine own voice thou callest on the hunter
that he fail not to strike thee with his shaft.

Oh dreaded destiny and yet pursued!
Oh passing belief that thine own life should be,
rather than silent, privy to thy death!

"GREEN ENRAVISHMENT OF HUMAN LIFE"...

Green enravishment of human life,
smiling frenzy of demented hope,
inextricable dream of them that wake
and, as a dream, of riches destitute.

Spirit of the world, robust old age,
imagination of decrepit vigour,
longing for the happy ones' to-day
and for the unhappy ones' to-morrow.

a woman, after a certain period following childbirth, brings an offering to the temple that she may be purified. Leviticus 12.
Translated by Samuel Beckett 1906—.

Let those who, with green glasses spectacled,
see all things sicklied o'er with their desire,
questing for thy light pursue thy shadow:

but I, more mindful of my destiny,
imprison my two eyes in my two hands
and see no other thing than it I touch.

William Wordsworth 1770–1850

THE WORLD IS TOO MUCH WITH US; LATE AND SOON

The world is too much with us; late and soon,
Getting and spending, we lay waste our powers:
Little we see in Nature that is ours;
We have given our hearts away, a sordid boon!
This Sea that bares her bosom to the moon;
The winds that will be howling at all hours,
And are up-gathered now like sleeping flowers;
For this, for everything, we are out of tune;
It moves us not.—Great God! I'd rather be
A Pagan suckled in a creed outworn;
So might I, standing on this pleasant lea,
Have glimpses that would make me less forlorn;
Have sight of Proteus rising from the sea;
Or hear old Triton blow his wreathèd horn.

IT IS A BEAUTEOUS EVENING, CALM AND FREE

It is a beauteous evening, calm and free,
The holy time is quiet as a Nun
Breathless with adoration; the broad sun
Is sinking down in its tranquillity;
The gentleness of heaven broods o'er the Sea:
Listen! the mighty Being is awake,
And doth with his eternal motion make
A sound like thunder—everlastingly.
Dear Child! dear Girl! that walkest with me here,
If thou appear untouched by solemn thought,
Thy nature is not therefore less divine:
Thou liest in Abraham's bosom all the year;
And worshipp'st at the Temple's inner shrine,
God being with thee when we know it not.

From *Poems, in Two Volumes* 1807 (four poems).

COMPOSED UPON WESTMINSTER BRIDGE, SEPTEMBER 3, 1802

Earth has not anything to show more fair:
Dull would he be of soul who could pass by
A sight so touching in its majesty:
This City now doth, like a garment, wear
The beauty of the morning; silent, bare,
Ships, towers, domes, theatres, and temples lie
Open unto the fields, and to the sky;
All bright and glittering in the smokeless air.
Never did sun more beautifully steep
In his first splendour, valley, rock, or hill;
Ne'er saw I, never felt, a calm so deep!
The river glideth at his own sweet will:
Dear God! the very houses seem asleep;
And all that mighty heart is lying still!

LONDON, 1802

Milton! thou shouldst be living at this hour:
England hath need of thee: she is a fen
Of stagnant waters: altar, sword, and pen,
Fireside, the heroic wealth of hall and bower,
Have forfeited their ancient English dower
Of inward happiness. We are selfish men;
Oh! raise us up, return to us again;
And give us manners, virtue, freedom, power.
Thy soul was like a Star, and dwelt apart;
Thou hadst a voice whose sound was like the sea:
Pure as the naked heavens, majestic, free,
So didst thou travel on life's common way,
In cheerful godliness; and yet thy heart
The lowliest duties on herself did lay.

SCORN NOT THE SONNET; CRITIC, YOU HAVE FROWNED

Scorn not the Sonnet; Critic, you have frowned,
Mindless of its just honours; with this key
Shakspeare unlocked his heart; the melody
Of this small lute gave ease to Petrarch's wound;
A thousand times this pipe did Tasso sound;
With it Camöens soothed an exile's grief;
The Sonnet glittered a gay myrtle leaf
Amid the cypress with which Dante crowned
His visionary brow: a glow-worm lamp,
It cheered mild Spenser, called from Faery-land
To struggle through dark ways; and, when a damp
Fell round the path of Milton, in his hand
The Thing became a trumpet; whence he blew
Soul-animating strains—alas, too few!

From *Collected Poems* 1827.

Samuel Taylor Coleridge 1772–1834

SONNET II. TO SIMPLICITY

Oh I do love thee, meek SIMPLICITY!
For of thy lays the lulling simpleness
Goes to my heart, and soothes each small distress,
Distress tho' small, yet haply great to me.
'Tis true on Lady Fortune's gentlest pad
I amble on; and yet I know not why
So sad I am! but should a friend and I
Frown, pout and part, then I am *very* sad.
And then with sonnets and with sympathy
My dreamy bosom's mystic woes I pall;
Now of my false friend plaining plaintively,
Now raving at mankind in general;
But whether sad or fierce, 'tis simple all,
All very simple, meek SIMPLICITY!

"Sonnets Attempted in the Manner of Contemporary Writers," from *Biographia Literaria* 1817. First published in *The Monthly Magazine* under the pseudonym "Nehemiah Higginbotham," November, 1797.
11:5 horse

SONNET III. ON A RUINED HOUSE IN A ROMANTIC COUNTRY

And this reft house is that, the which he built,
Lamented Jack! and here his malt he pil'd,
Cautious in vain! these rats, that squeak so wild,
Squeak not unconscious of their father's guilt.
Did he not see her gleaming thro' the glade!
Belike 'twas she, the maiden all forlorn.
What tho' she milk no cow with crumpled horn,
Yet, *aye* she haunts the dale where *erst* she stray'd:
And *aye,* beside her stalks her amorous knight!
Still on his thighs their wonted brogues are worn,
And thro' those brogues, still tatter'd and betorn,
His hindward charms gleam an unearthly white.
Ah! thus thro' broken clouds at night's high Noon
Peeps in fair fragments forth the full-orb'd harvest-moon!

III:8 always; before

Percy Bysshe Shelley 1792–1822

OZYMANDIAS

I met a traveller from an antique land
Who said: Two vast and trunkless legs of stone
Stand in the desert . . . Near them, on the sand,
Half sunk, a shattered vizage lies, whose frown,
And wrinkled lip, and sneer of cold command,
Tell that its sculptor well those passions read
Which yet survive, stamped on these lifeless things,
The hand that mocked them, and the heart that fed:
And on the pedestal these words appear:
"My name is Ozymandias, king of kings:
Look on my works, ye Mighty, and despair!"
Nothing beside remains. Round the decay
Of that colossal wreck, boundless and bare
The lone and level sands stretch far away.

From *The Examiner,* January, 1818.
Ozymandias: Rameses II of Egypt, thirteenth century B.C.

John Keats 1795–1821

ON THE GRASSHOPPER AND CRICKET

The poetry of earth is never dead:
    When all the birds are faint with the hot sun,
    And hide in cooling trees, a voice will run
From hedge to hedge about the new-mown mead;
That is the Grasshopper's—he takes the lead
    In summer luxury,—he has never done
    With his delights; for when tired out with fun
He rests at ease beneath some pleasant weed.
The poetry of earth is ceasing never:
    On a lone winter evening, when the frost
        Has wrought a silence, from the stove there shrills
The Cricket's song, in warmth increasing ever,
    And seems to one in drowsiness half lost,
        The Grasshopper's among some grassy hills.

From *Poems* 1817.

John Clare 1793–1864

SUDDEN SHOWER

Black grows the southern sky, betokening rain,
And humming hive-bees homeward hurry by:
They feel the change; so let us shun the grain,
And take the broad road while our feet are dry.
Ay, there some dropples moistened on my face,
And pattered on my hat—'tis coming nigh!
Let's look about, and find a sheltering place.
The little things around, like you and I,
Are hurrying through the grass to shun the shower.
Here stoops an ash-tree—hark! the wind gets high,
But never mind; this ivy, for an hour,
Rain as it may, will keep us dryly here:
That little wren knows well his sheltering bower,
Nor leaves his dry house though we come so near.

GIPSIES

The snow falls deep; the forest lies alone;
The boy goes hasty for his load of brakes,
Then thinks upon the fire and hurries back;
The gipsy knocks his hands and tucks them up,
And seeks his squalid camp, half hid in snow,
Beneath the oak which breaks away the wind,
And bushes close in snow like hovel warm;
There tainted mutton wastes upon the coals,
And the half-wasted dog squats close and rubs,
Then feels the heat too strong, and goes aloof;
He watches well, but none a bit can spare,
And vainly waits the morsel thrown away.
'Tis thus they live—a picture to the place,
A quiet, pilfering, unprotected race.

From *The Rural Muse* 1835 (three poems).

SIGNS OF WINTER

The cat runs races with her tail. The dog
Leaps o'er the orchard hedge and knarls the grass.
The swine run round and grunt and play with straw,
Snatching out hasty mouthfuls from the stack.
Sudden upon the elm-tree tops the crow
Unceremonious visit pays and croaks,
Then swops away. From mossy barn the owl
Bobs hasty out—wheels round and, scared as soon,
As hastily retires. The ducks grow wild
And from the muddy pond fly up and wheel
A circle round the village and soon, tired,
Plunge in the pond again. The maids in haste
Snatch from the orchard hedge the mizzled clothes
And laughing hurry in to keep them dry.

WELL, HONEST JOHN

Well, honest John, how fare you now at home?
The spring is come, and birds are building nests;
The old cock-robin to the sty is come,
With olive feathers and its ruddy breast;
And the old cock, with wattles and red comb,
Struts with the hens, and seems to like some best,
Then crows, and looks about for little crumbs,
Swept out by little folks an hour ago;
The pigs sleep in the sty; the bookman comes—
The little boy lets home-close nesting go,
And pockets tops and taws, where daisies blow,
To look at the new number just laid down,
With lots of pictures, and good stories too,
And Jack the Giant-killer's high renown.

2 chews 13 misted over

From *John Clare: Poems Chiefly from Manuscript* 1920, ed. Edmund Blunden and Alan Porter.

WRITTEN IN PRISON

I envy e'en the fly its gleams of joy
In the green woods; from being but a boy
Among the vulgar and the lowly bred,
I envied e'en the hare her grassy bed.
Inured to strife and hardships from a child,
I traced with lonely step the desert wild;
Sighed o'er bird pleasures, but no nest destroyed;
With pleasure felt the singing they enjoyed;
Saw nature smile on all and shed no tears,
A slave through ages, though a child in years
The mockery and scorn of those more old,
An Aesop in the world's extended fold.
The fly I envy settling in the sun
On the green leaf, and wish my goal was won.

From *The Poems of John Clare* 1935, ed. J. W. Tibble.

Gérard de Nerval 1808–1855

SPOOK SHEEP

I am gloomy; I am the Widower; I belong to the band of the Inconsolables.
I am the Prince of Acquitaine seated solitarily and arbitrarily in his lightning-struck tower.
The light of my life has gone out.
A star-studded lute belongs to me in the heavens.
An invisible member of my constellation is the black sun of *Melancholia.*

You who have given comfort in the darkness of my supraterrestrial grave, give back to me please also Posilipo, the Mediterranean, the *flower* which used to warm my now sunless, desolate heart, and the arbor of vines with roses entwined.

Am I Amor or Phoebus? Am I ——— or ——— ?
The only clue is red on my forehead from the kiss of a Queen.
In the grotto where the siren swims I've had a dream.
Twice I've crossed the Acheron and returned.
I've played on Orpheus' lyre such sounds as might modulate a saint's sighs and a faery's cries, turn by turn.

In the shadow of glorious deeds, of wealth and earthly honor, of special dispensation from the gods, and of a long chain of loves, I rescue from among the list of my accomplishments solely the ability to sing this sad song.

From *Les Chimeres.* Translated by Andrew Hoyem 1935—: *Chimeras* 1966 (two poems).

GOLDEN

"everything is alive"
Pythagoras

Man, free-thinker, think you yourself alone possessed of thought?
From this world bursting with life helter-skelter, you order the forces of the universe about as if drafting a foreign legion of toy soldiers.

Each beast is a free Spirit worthy of respect.
Every flower is a soul opening out to Nature.
Even in metal dwells the mystery of Love.
"Everything is alive" and holds powers over you.

In a blank wall you may well fear the blindness which sees through you and sees you through.
All matter is saturated with the Word regardless of ears and whether or not you put them and it to true and false uses.

The meanest being may be and often is a god's disguise.
Just as an infant's eyelids are sealed over fresh Vision, late angels' aged ghosts are healed within the surface of stones.

Edward Lear 1812–1888

COLD ARE THE CRABS

Cold are the crabs that crawl on yonder hills,
Colder the cucumbers that grow beneath,
And colder still the brazen chops that wreathe
    The tedious gloom of philosophic pills!
For when the tardy film of nectar fills
The ample bowls of demons and of men,
There lurks the feeble mouse, the homely hen,
    And there the porcupine with all her quills.
Yet much remains—to weave a solemn strain
That lingering sadly—slowly dies away,
Daily departing with departing day.
A pea-green gamut on a distant plain
When wily walruses in congress meet—
    Such such is life—

From *Teapots and Quails and Other New Nonsenses* 1953.

George Meredith 1828–1909

LUCIFER IN STARLIGHT

ON a starred night Prince Lucifer uprose.
Tired of his dark dominion swung the fiend
Above the rolling ball in cloud part screened,
Where sinners hugged their spectre of repose.
Poor prey to his hot fit of pride were those.
And now upon his western wing he leaned,
Now his huge bulk o'er Afric's sands careened,
Now the black planet shadowed Arctic snows.
Soaring through wider zones that pricked his scars
With memory of the old revolt from Awe,
He reached a middle height, and at the stars,
Which are the brain of heaven, he looked, and sank.
Around the ancient track marched, rank on rank,
The army of unalterable law.

from MODERN LOVE *1862*

I

BY this he knew she wept with waking eyes:
That, at his hand's light quiver by her head,
The strange low sobs that shook their common bed
Were called into her with a sharp surprise,
And strangled mute, like little gaping snakes,
Dreadfully venomous to him. She lay
Stone-still, and the long darkness flowed away
With muffled pulses. Then, as midnight makes
Her giant heart of Memory and Tears
Drink the pale drug of silence, and so beat
Sleep's heavy measure, they from head to feet
Were moveless, looking through their dead black years,
By vain regret scrawled over the blank wall.

"Lucifer . . ." is from *Poems and Lyrics of the Joy of the Earth* 1883.
Modern Love, a novel in 50 sonnets.

Like sculptured effigies they might be seen
Upon their marriage-tomb, the sword between;
Each wishing for the sword that severs all.

XV

I think she sleeps: it must be sleep, when low
Hangs that abandoned arm toward the floor;
The face turned with it. Now make fast the door.
Sleep on: it is your husband, not your foe!
The Poet's black stage-lion of wronged love
Frights not our modern dames:—well if he did!
Now I will pour new light upon that lid,
Full-sloping like the breasts beneath. "Sweet dove,
Your sleep is pure. Nay, pardon: I disturb.
I do not? good!" Her waking infant-stare
Grows woman to the burden my hands bear:
Her own handwriting to me when no curb
Was left on Passion's tongue. She trembles through;
A woman's tremble—the whole instrument:—
I show another letter lately sent.
The words are very like: the name is new.

XVII

At dinner, she is hostess, I am host.
Went the feast ever cheerfuller? She keeps
The Topic over intellectual deeps
In buoyancy afloat. They see no ghost.
With sparkling surface-eyes we ply the ball:
It is in truth a most contagious game:
HIDING THE SKELETON, shall be its name.
Such play as this, the devils might appal!
But here's the greater wonder; in that we,
Enamoured of an acting nought can tire,
Each other, like true hypocrites, admire;
Warm-lighted looks, Love's ephemeridae
Shoot gaily o'er the dishes and the wine.
We waken envy of our happy lot.
Fast, sweet, and golden, shows the marriage-knot.
Dear guests, you now have seen Love's corpse-light shine.

Gerard Manley Hopkins 1844–1889

GOD'S GRANDEUR

The world is charged with the grandeur of God.
    It will flame out, like shining from shook foil;
    It gathers to a greatness, like the ooze of oil
Crushed. Why do men then now not reck his rod?
Generations have trod, have trod, have trod;
    And all is seared with trade; bleared, smeared with toil;
    And wears man's smudge and shares man's smell: the soil
Is bare now, nor can foot feel, being shod.

And for all this, nature is never spent;
    There lives the dearest freshness deep down things;
And though the last lights off the black West went
    Oh, morning, at the brown brink eastward, springs—
Because the Holy Ghost over the bent
    World broods with warm breast and with ah! bright wings.

THE WINDHOVER:

To Christ our Lord

I caught this morning morning's minion, king-
    dom of daylight's dauphin, dapple-dawn-drawn Falcon,
        in his riding
    Of the rolling level underneath him steady air, and striding
High there, how he rung upon the rein of a wimpling wing
In his ecstasy! then off, off forth on swing,
    As a skate's heel sweeps smooth on a bow-bend: the hurl
        and gliding
    Rebuffed the big wind. My heart in hiding
Stirred for a bird,—the achieve of, the mastery of the thing!

From *Collected Poems* 1918 (six poems).
4 rippling

Brute beauty and valour and act, oh, air, pride, plume, here
        Buckle! AND the fire that breaks from thee then, a billion
Times told lovelier, more dangerous, O my chevalier!

        No wonder of it: shéer plód makes plough down sillion
Shine, and blue-bleak embers, ah my dear,
        Fall, gall themselves, and gash gold-vermilion.

DUNS SCOTUS'S OXFORD

Towery city and branchy between towers;
Cuckoo-echoing, bell-swarmèd, lark-charmèd, rook-racked,
        river-rounded;
The dapple-eared lily below thee; that country and town did
Once encounter in, here coped and poisèd powers;

Thou hast a base and brickish skirt there, sours
That neighbour-nature thy grey beauty is grounded
Best in; graceless growth, thou hast confounded
Rural rural keeping—folk, flocks, and flowers.

Yet ah! this air I gather and I release
He lived on; these weeds and waters, these walls are what
He haunted who of all men most sways my spirits to peace;

Of realty the rarest-veinèd unraveller; a not
Rivalled insight, be rival Italy or Greece;
Who fired France for Mary without spot.

12 furrow

Duns Scotus: a scholastic philosopher (1265?-1308?) who was professor of divinity at Oxford in 1301, and is said to have been a "regent" at the University of Paris.

FELIX RANDAL

Felix Randal the farrier, O he is dead then? my duty all ended,
Who have watched his mould of man, big-boned and hardy-
handsome
Pining, pining, till time when reason rambled in it and some
Fatal four disorders, fleshed there, all contended?

Sickness broke him. Impatient he cursed at first, but mended
Being anointed and all; though a heavenlier heart began some
Months earlier, since I had our sweet reprieve and ransom
Tendered to him. Ah well, God rest him all road ever he
offended!

This seeing the sick endears them to us, us too it endears.
My tongue had taught thee comfort, touch had quenched thy
tears,
Thy tears that touched my heart, child, Felix, poor Felix
Randal;

How far from then forethought of, all thy more boisterous
years,
When thou at the random grim forge, powerful amidst peers,
Didst fettle for the great grey drayhorse his bright and batter-
ing sandal!

PIED BEAUTY

Glory be to God for dappled things—
For skies of couple-colour as a brinded cow;
For rose-moles all in stipple upon trout that swim;

1 blacksmith 8 *all road* (West Midlands dialect): in every way 14 shoe

Pied Beauty: Hopkins called this a *curtal* sonnet; instead of an eight-line and six-line division it has six lines and four lines, plus "a halfline tailpiece."

2 streaked

Fresh-firecoal chestnut-falls; finches' wings;
Landscape plotted and pieced—fold, fallow, and plough;
And áll trádes, their gear and tackle and trim.

All things counter, original, spare, strange;
Whatever is fickle, freckled (who knows how?)
With swift, slow; sweet, sour; adazzle, dim;
He fathers-forth whose beauty is past change:
Praise him.

THAT NATURE IS A HERACLITEAN FIRE AND OF THE COMFORT OF THE RESURRECTION

Cloud-puffball, torn tufts, tossed pillows | flaunt forth, then chevy on an air-
built thoroughfare: heaven-roysterers, in gay-gangs | they throng; they glitter in marches.
Down roughcast, down dazzling whitewash, | wherever an elm arches.
Shivelights and shadowtackle in long | lashes lace, lance, and pair.
Delightfully the bright wind boisterous | ropes, wrestles, beats earth bare
Of yestertempest's creases; | in pool and rut peel parches
Squandering ooze to squeezed | dough, crust, dust; stanches, starches
Squadroned masks and manmarks | treadmire toil there
Footfretted in it. Million-fuelèd, | nature's bonfire burns on.
But quench her bonniest, dearest | to her, her clearest-selvèd spark
Man, how fast his firedint, | his mark on mind, is gone!

That Nature . . . : Heraclitus, pre-Socratic philosopher, taught that the world began and will end in fire, which he believed was the primary element. Hopkins called this a "sonnet with two codas." Most readers count three.

2 scamper 4 *Shivelights and shadowtackle:* splinters of light and shadows in unusual shapes.

Both are in an unfathomable, all is in an enormous dark
Drowned. O pity and indig ' nation! Manshape, that shone
Sheer off, disseveral, a star, ' death blots black out; nor mark
Is any of him at all so stark
But vastness blurs and time ' beats level. Enough! the Resurrection,
A heart's-clarion! Away grief's gasping, ' joyless days, dejection.
Across my foundering deck shone
A beacon an, eternal beam. ' Flesh fade, and mortal trash
Fall to the residuary worm; ' world's wildfire, leave but ash:
In a flash, at a trumpet crash,
I am all at once what Christ is, ' since he was what I am, and
This Jack, joke, poor potsherd, ' patch, matchwood, immortal diamond,
Is immortal diamond.

William Butler Yeats 1865–1939

THE FASCINATION OF WHAT'S DIFFICULT

The fascination of what's difficult
Has dried the sap out of my veins, and rent
Spontaneous joy and natural content
Out of my heart. There's something ails our colt
That must, as if it had not holy blood
Nor on Olympus leaped from cloud to cloud,
Shiver under the lash, strain, sweat and jolt
As though it dragged road-metal. My curse on plays
That have to be set up in fifty ways,
On the day's war with every knave and dolt,
Theatre business, management of men.
I swear before the dawn comes round again
I'll find the stable and pull out the bolt.

From *The Green Helmet and Other Poems* 1910.

LEDA AND THE SWAN

A sudden blow: the great wings beating still
Above the staggering girl, her thighs caressed
By the dark webs, her nape caught in his bill,
He holds her helpless breast upon his breast.

How can those terrified vague fingers push
The feathered glory from her loosening thighs?
And how can body, laid in that white rush,
But feel the strange heart beating where it lies?

A shudder in the loins engenders there
The broken wall, the burning roof and tower
And Agamemnon dead.
                                        Being so caught up,
So mastered by the brute blood of the air,
Did she put on his knowledge with his power
Before the indifferent beak could let her drop?

From *The Tower* 1928.

Enrique Gonzáles Martínez 1871–1952

WRING THE SWAN'S NECK

Wring the swan's neck who with deceiving plumage
inscribes his whiteness on the azure stream;
he merely vaunts his grace and nothing feels
of nature's voice or of the soul of things.

Every form eschew and every language
whose processes with deep life's inner rhythm
are out of harmony . . . and greatly worship
life, and let life understand your homage.

See the sapient owl who from Olympus
spreads his wings, leaving Athene's lap,
and stays his silent flight on yonder tree.

His grace is not the swan's, but his unquiet
pupil, boring into the gloom, interprets
the secret book of the nocturnal still.

Translated by Samuel Beckett 1906—.

e e cummings 1894–1962

THE CAMBRIDGE LADIES WHO LIVE IN FURNISHED SOULS

the Cambridge ladies who live in furnished souls
are unbeautiful and have comfortable minds
(also, with the church's protestant blessings
daughters, unscented shapeless spirited)
they believe in Christ and Longfellow, both dead,
are invariably interested in so many things—
at the present writing one still finds
delighted fingers knitting for the is it Poles?
perhaps. While permanent faces coyly bandy
scandal of Mrs. N and Professor D
. . . . the Cambridge ladies do not care, above
Cambridge if sometimes in its box of
sky lavender and cornerless, the
moon rattles like a fragment of angry candy

UNNOTICED WOMAN FROM WHOSE KIND LARGE FLESH

unnoticed woman from whose kind large flesh

i turn to the cruel-littleness of cold
(when battling street-lamps fail upon the gold
dawn, where teeth of slowturning streets mesh

in a frieze of smoking Face Bluish-old

and choked pat of going soles on flat
pavements with icy cries of this and that
stumbling in gloom, bad laughters, smiles unbold)

From *Tulips and Chimneys* 1923.
From & 1935 (three poems).

also, tomorrow the daily papers will feature
Peace And Good Will, and Mary with one lung
extended to the pumping Child, and " 'Twas
the night before Christmas when all through the house not a
    creature
was stirring, not even a mouse. The stockings were hung
by the chimney with care in hopes that Saint Nicholas"

O IT'S NICE TO GET UP IN,THE SLIPSHOD MUCOUS KISS

O It's Nice To Get Up In,the slipshod mucous kiss
of her riant belly's fooling bore
—When The Sun Begins To(with a phrasing crease
of hot subliminal lips,as if a score
of youngest angels suddenly should stretch neat necks
just to see how always squirms
the skilful mystery of Hell)me suddenly

grips in chuckles of supreme sex.

In The Good Old Summer Time.
My gorgeous bullet in tickling intuitive flight
aches,just,simply,into,her.   Thirsty
stirring.   (Must be summer.   Hush.   Worms.)
But It's Nicer To Lie In Bed
                                        —eh?   I'm

not.   Again.   Hush.   God.   Please hold.   Tight

THE DIRTY COLOURS OF HER KISS HAVE JUST

the dirty colours of her kiss have just
throttled
          my seeing blood,her heart's chatter

riveted a weeping skyscraper

in me

      i bite on the eyes' brittle crust
(only feeling the belly's merry thrust
Boost my huge passion like a business

and the Y her legs panting as they press

proffers its omelet of fluffy lust)
at six exactly
               the alarm tore

two slits in her cheeks. A brain peered at the dawn.
she got up

            with a gashing yellow yawn
and tottered to a glass bumping things.
she picked wearily something from the floor

Her hair was mussed,and she coughed while tying strings

THOU IN WHOSE SWORDGREAT STORY SHINE THE DEEDS

Thou in whose swordgreat story shine the deeds
of history her heroes, sounds the tread
of those vast armies of the marching dead,

From *XLI Poems* 1925.

with standards and the neighing of great steeds
moving to war across the smiling meads;
thou by whose page we break the precious bread
of dear communion with the past, and wed
to valor, battle with heroic breeds;

thou, Froissart, for that thou didst love the pen
while others wrote in steel, accept all praise
of after ages, and of hungering days
for whom the old glories move, the old trumpets cry;
who gavest as one of those immortal men
his life that his fair city might not die.

"NEXT TO OF COURSE GOD AMERICA I

"next to of course god america i
love you land of the pilgrims' and so forth oh
say can you see by the dawn's early my
country 'tis of centuries come and go
and are no more what of it we should worry
in every language even deafanddumb
they sons acclaim your glorious name by gorry
by jingo by gee by gosh by gum
why talk of beauty what could be more beaut-
iful than these heroic happy dead
who rushed like lions to the roaring slaughter
they did not stop to think they died instead
then shall the voice of liberty be mute?"

He spoke. And drank rapidly a glass of water

From *is 5* 1926.

SPACE BEING(DON'T FORGET TO REMEMBER)CURVED

Space being(don't forget to remember)Curved
(and that reminds me who said o yes Frost
Something there is which isn't fond of walls)

an electromagnetic(now I've lost
the)Einstein expanded Newton's law preserved
conTinuum(but we read that beFore)

of Course life being just a Reflex you
know since Everything is Relative or

to sum it All Up god being Dead(not to

mention inTerred)
                                        LONG LIVE that Upwardlooking
Serene Illustrious and Beatific
Lord of Creation,MAN:
                                                  at a least crooking
of Whose compassionate digit,earth's most terrific

quadruped swoons into billiardBalls!

HELVES SURLING OUT OF EAKSPEASIES PER(REEL)HAPSINGLY

helves surling out of eakspeasies per(reel)hapsingly
proregress heandshe-ingly people
trickle curselaughgroping shrieks bubble
squirmwrithed staggerful unstrolls collaps ingly
flash a of-faceness stuck thumblike into pie
is traffic this recalls hat gestures bud

From *W*[*ViVa*] 1931 (two poems).

plumptumbling hand voices Eye Doangivuh sud-
denly immense impotently Eye Doancare Eye
And How replies the upsquirtingly careens
the to collide flatfooting with Wushyuhname
a girl-flops to the Geddup curb leans
carefully spewing into her own Shush Shame

as(out from behind Nowhere)creeps the deep thing
everybody sometimes calls morning

NOTHING FALSE AND POSSIBLE IS LOVE

nothing false and possible is love
(who's imagined,therefore limitless)
love's to giving as to keeping's give;
as yes is to if,love is to yes

must's a schoolroom in the month of may:
life's the deathboard where all now turns when
(love's a universe beyond obey
or command,reality or un-)

proudly depths above why's first because
(faith's last doubt and humbly heights below)
kneeling, we—true lovers—pray that us
will ourselves continue to outgrow

all whose mosts if you have known and i've
only we our least begin to guess

From *1x1* 1944.

Dylan Thomas 1914–1953

ALTARWISE BY OWL-LIGHT

I

Altarwise by owl-light in the half-way house
The gentleman lay graveward with his furies;
Abaddon in the hangnail cracked from Adam,
And, from his fork, a dog among the fairies,
The atlas-eater with a jaw for news,
Bit out the mandrake with to-morrow's scream.
Then, penny-eyed, that gentleman of wounds,
Old cock from nowheres and the heaven's egg,
With bones unbuttoned to the half-way winds,
Hatched from the windy salvage on one leg,
Scraped at my cradle in a walking word
That night of time under the Christward shelter:
I am the long world's gentleman, he said,
And share my bed with Capricorn and Cancer.

III

First there was the lamb on knocking knees
And three dead seasons on a climbing grave
That Adam's wether in the flock of horns,
Butt of the tree-tailed worm that mounted Eve,
Horned down with skullfoot and the skull of toes
On thunderous pavements in the garden time;
Rip of the vaults, I took my marrow-ladle
Out of the wrinkled undertaker's van,
And, Rip Van Winkle from a timeless cradle,
Dipped me breast-deep in the descended bone;
The black ram, shuffling of the year, old winter,
Alone alive among his mutton fold,
We rung our weathering changes on the ladder,
Said the antipodes, and twice spring chimed.

Altarwise by Owl-Light, a sequence of 10 sonnets. From *Collected Poems* 1939.

I:3 *Abaddon:* Hebrew for "destruction"; the bottomless pit.

V

And from the windy West came two-gunned Gabriel,
From Jesu's sleeve trumped up the king of spots,
The sheath-decked jacks, queen with a shuffled heart;
Said the fake gentleman in suit of spades,
Black-tongued and tipsy from salvation's bottle.
Rose my Byzantine Adam in the night.
For loss of blood I fell on Ishmael's plain,
Under the milky mushrooms slew my hunger,
A climbing sea from Asia had me down
And Jonah's Moby snatched me by the hair,
Cross-stroked salt Adam to the frozen angel
Pin-legged on pole-hills with a black medusa
By waste seas where the white bear quoted Virgil
And sirens singing from our lady's sea-straw.

VII

This was the crucifixion on the mountain,
Time's nerve in vinegar, the gallow grave
As tarred with blood as the bright thorns I wept;
The world's my wound, God's Mary in her grief,
Bent like three trees and bird-papped through her shift,
With pins for teardrops is the long wound's woman.
This was the sky, Jack Christ, each minstrel angle
Drove in the heaven-driven of the nails
Till the three-coloured rainbow from my nipples
From pole to pole leapt round the snail-waked world.
I by the tree of thieves, all glory's sawbones,
Unsex the skeleton this mountain minute,
And by this blowclock witness of the sun
Suffer the heaven's children through my heartbeat.

V:1 *Gabriel:* archangel and special messenger of God, he announced to Mary that she would give birth to Jesus. Luke 1:26. V:7 *Ishmael:* the son of Abraham by his wife Sarah's handmaiden. When Sarah had her own child, Isaac, she insisted that Ishmael be cast out to roam the wilderness. Genesis 12.

X

Let the tale's sailor from a Christian voyage
Atlaswise hold half-way off the dummy bay
Time's ship-racked gospel on the globe I balance:
So shall winged harbours through the rockbirds' eyes
Spot the blown word, and on the seas I image
December's thorn screwed in a brow of holly.
Let the first Peter from a rainbow's quayrail
Ask the tall fish swept from the bible east,
What rhubarb man peeled in her foam-blue channel
Has sown a flying garden round that sea-ghost?
Green as beginning, let the garden diving
Soar, with its two bark towers, to that Day
When the worm builds with the gold straws of venom
My nest of mercies in the rude, red tree.

William Carlos Williams 1883–1963

SONNET IN SEARCH OF AN AUTHOR

Nude bodies like peeled logs
sometimes give off a sweetest
odor, man and woman

under the trees in full excess
matching the cushion of

aromatic pine-drift fallen
threaded with trailing woodbine
a sonnet might be made of it

Might be made of it! odor of excess
odor of pine needles, odor of
peeled logs, odor of no odor
other than trailing woodbine that

has no odor, odor of a nude woman
sometimes, odor of a man.

From *Pictures from Brueghel and Other Poems* 1962.

John Berryman 1914–1972

from BERRYMAN'S SONNETS *1967*

13

I lift—lift you five States away your glass,
Wide of this bar you never graced, where none
Ever I know came, where what work is done
Even by these men I know not, where a brass
Police-car sign peers in, wet strange cars pass,
Soiled hangs the rag of day out over this town,
A juke-box brains air where I drink alone,
The spruce barkeep sports a toupee alas—

My glass I lift at six o'clock, my darling,
As you plotted . . Chinese couples shift in bed,
We shared today not even filthy weather,
Beasts in the hills their tigerish love are snarling,
Suddenly they clash, I blow my short ash red,
Grey eyes light! and we have our drink together.

15

What was Ashore, then? . . Cargoed with Forget,
My ship runs down a midnight winter storm
Between whirlpool and rock, and my white love's form
Gleams at the wheel, her hair streams. When we met
Seaward, Thought frank & guilty to each oar set
Hands careless of port as of the waters' harm.
Endless a wet wind wears my sail, dark swarm
Endless of sighs and veering hopes, love's fret.

Rain of tears, real, mist of imagined scorn,
No rest accords the fraying shrouds, all thwart
Already with mistakes, foresight so short.
Muffled in capes of waves my clear sighs, torn,
Hitherto most clear,—Loyalty and Art.
And I begin now to despair of port.

(AFTER PETRARCH & WYATT)

Berryman's Sonnets, written in the 1940's; a sequence of 115 sonnets.

71

Our Sunday morning when dawn-priests were applying
Wafer and wine to the human wound, we laid
Ourselves to cure ourselves down: I'm afraid
Our vestments wanted, but Francis' friends were crying
In the nave of pines, sun-satisfied, and flying
Subtle as angels about the barricade
Boughs made over us, deep in a bed half made
Needle-soft, half the sea of our simultaneous dying.

"Death is the mother of beauty." Awry no leaf
Shivering with delight, we die to be well . .
Careless with sleepy love, so long unloving.
What if our convalescence must be brief
As we are, the matin meet the passing bell? . .
About our pines our sister, wind, is moving.

103

A "broken heart" . . but *can* a heart break, now?
Lovers have stood bareheaded in love's "storm"
Three thousand years, changed by their mistress' "charm",
Fitted their "torment" to a passive bow,
Suffered the "darts" under a knitted brow,
And has one heart *broken* for all this "harm"?
An arm is something definite. My arm
Is acting—I hardly know to tell you how.

It aches . . well, after fifteen minutes of
Serving, I can't serve more, it's not my arm,
A piece of pain joined to me, helpless dumb thing.
After four months of work-destroying love
(An hour, I still don't lift it: I feel real alarm:
Weeks of this,—no doctor finds a thing),
        not much; and not all. Still, this is something.

71:13 death knell
103:6 grief

Ted Berrigan 1934—

from THE SONNETS *1964*

XV

In Joe Brainard's collage its white arrow
He is not in it, the hungry dead doctor.
Of Marilyn Monroe, her white teeth white-
I am truly horribly upset because Marilyn
and ate King Korn popcorn," he wrote in his
of glass in Joe Brainard's collage
Doctor, but they say "I LOVE YOU"
and the sonnet is not dead.
takes the eyes away from the gray words,
Diary. The black heart beside the fifteen pieces
Monroe died, so I went to a matinee B-movie
washed by Joe's throbbing hands. "Today
What is in it is sixteen ripped pictures
does not point to William Carlos Williams.

XXXVIII

Sleep half sleep half silence and with reasons
For you I starred in the movie
Made on the site
Of Benedict Arnold's triumph, Ticonderoga, and
I shall increase from this
As I am a cowboy and you imaginary
Ripeness begins corrupting every tree
Each strong morning   A man signs a shovel
And so he digs   It hurts   and so
We get our feet wet in air   we love our lineage
Ourselves   Music, salve, pills, kleenex, lunch
And the promise never to truckle   A man
Breaks his arm and so he sleeps   he digs
In sleep half silence and with reason

LI

Summer so histrionic, marvelous dirty days
is not genuine it shines forth from the faces
littered with soup, cigarette butts, the heavy
is a correspondent the innocence of childhood
sadness graying the faces of virgins aching
and everything comes before their eyes
to be fucked, we fondle their snatches but they
that the angels have supereminent wisdom is shown
they weep and get solemn etcetera
from thought for all things come to them gratuitously
by their speech it flows directly and spontaneously
and O I am afraid! but later they'll be eyeing the butts of the studs
in the street rain flushing the gutters bringing from Memphis
Gus Cannon gulping, "I called myself Banjo Joe!"

LII

for Richard White

It is a human universe: & I
is a correspondent The innocence of childhood
is not genuine it shines forth from the faces
The poem upon the page is as massive as Anne's thighs
Belly to hot belly we have laid
baffling combustions
are everywhere graying the faces of virgins
aching to be fucked we fondle their snatches
and O, I am afraid! The poem upon the page
will not kneel for everything comes to it
gratuitously like Gertrude Stein to Radcliffe
Gus Cannon to say "I called myself Banjo Joe!"
O wet kisses, death on earth, lovely fucking in the poem upon the page,
you have kept up with the times, and I am glad!

LXVIII

I am closing my window. Tears silence the wind.
and the rust on the bolt in my door
Mud on the first day (night, rather
littered with soup, cigarette butts, the heavy
getting used to using each other
my dream a drink with Ira Hayes we discuss the code of the
west
I think I was thinking when I was ahead
To the big promise of emptiness
This excitement to be all of night, Henry!
Three ciphers and a faint fakir. And he walks.
White lake trembles down to green goings on
Of the interminably frolicsome gushing summer showers
Everything turning in this light to stones
Which owe their presence to our sleeping hands

Tom Clark 1941—

SONNET

Five A.M. on East Fourteenth I'm out to eat
The holiday littered city by my feet a jewel
In the mire of the night waits for the light
Getting and spending and day's taxi cry   The playful

Waves of the East River move toward their date
With eternity down the street, the slate sky
In Tompkins Square Park prepares for the break
Through of lean horses of morning   I

Move through these streets like a lamplighter
Touch ragged faces with laughter by my knowledge
Of tragic color on a pavement at the edge
Of the city   Softly in the deep East River water

Of dreams in which my long hair flows
Slow waves move   Of my beginnings, pauses

From *Stones* 1969.

The Pastoral Elegy

"I first bucked hay when I was seventeen.
I thought, that day I started,
I sure would hate to do this all my life.
And dammit, that's just what
I've gone and done."

FACILE NOTIONS OF "simplicity," rusticity, the comfort or discomfort of the low and sure estate, the "artificial" as opposed to the "natural," while obvious enough, tend to obfuscity. "Of course, I grant you, to concede a point, you do knock across a simple soul once in a blue moon." One touch either of condescension or envy and you (along with so many others) have missed the point. Why Spenser's legend of Sir Calidore, the virtue courtesy, should take place not in the courts but among shepherds; why Pan and Adonis should have led Virgil to the prophetic writings of Asian mystery cults.

Theocritus was in fact from Sicily but he began writing his pastorals in Alexandria. The portion of his first idyll translated here is an exercise in *descriptio,* an imitation of the eighteenth Iliad that charms by its exquisite diminution of scale. Virgil believed that a young poet should learn by writing pastorals before going on to the epic, a program of apprenticeship that

I first bucked hay . . . : Gary Snyder, "Hay for the Horses," from *Riprap and Cold Mountain Poems.*

Of course, I grant you . . . : Mr. Bloom has failed to grasp Stephen's point, that the soul, being a single substance, is incorruptible, "*corruptio per se* and *corruptio per accidens* both being excluded by court etiquette."

was undertaken by the most ambitious English poets from Spenser on down at least to Keats. The various forms of pastoral lyric—the complaint, singing match, elegy, blazon, and palinode—are all set pieces each with its traditional subject, proper attitudes, and rhetorical furniture. All this is to say that Cain slays Abel and though cursed as a vagabond, is marked, to be protected, by the Lord.

In the moral interpretation Abel, who followed his sheep, stands for the contemplative life, pure instinct, intuition apposed to the active Cain, who tilled the soil; typologically his sacrifice, which God accepted, and his death, by his brother's hand, prefigure Christ crucified. So the Christian poet recovers the archetypal meaning of the ancient pastoral, with its rural Pan and (in the elegy) its lament for a mortal favored as poet or lover by the gods. And the great commonplaces of the pastoral elegy—the procession of mourners, the presence of a muse, the refrain, the assertion that grief has interrupted the processes of nature or the expression of wonder that it has not, flower symbolism, accusations against death, the digression against contemporary abuses, the final consolation of mourners or the apotheosis of the dead—live on after the shepherds, with their oaten pipes, are gone.

to Keats:

. . . first the realm I'll pass
Of Flora, and old Pan: sleep in the grass,
Feed upon apples red, and strawberries,
And choose each pleasure that my fancy sees;
Catch the white-handed nymphs in shady places, . . .
And can I ever bid these joys farewell?
Yes, I must pass them for a nobler life,
Where I may find the agonies, the strife
Of human hearts: for lo! I see afar,
O'er sailing the blue cragginess, a car
And steeds with streamy manes— . . .
—"Sleep and Poetry," ll. 101-105, 122-127, from *Poems* 1817

Theocritus (3rd Century B.C.)

IDYL I

THYRSIS

The whisper of the wind in
    that pine-tree,
        goat-herd,
is sweet as the murmur of live water;
    likewise
        your flutenotes. After Pan
you shall bear away second prize.
    And if he
        take the goat,
with the horns,
    the she-goat
        is yours: but if
he choose the she-goat,
    the kid will fall
        to your lot.
And the flesh of the kid
    is dainty
        before they begin milking them.

GOAT-HERD

Your song is sweeter,
    shepherd,
        than the music

From *Idyls,* translated by William Carlos Williams 1883-1963.

Dr. Williams did not translate *The Afflictions of Daphnis* (l. 54), which amounts to ninety verses or so and describes the death of a musical neat-herd whose attractions were irresistible to girl, nymph, or god, but who defied love; in anger Aphrodite afflicted him with a terrible passion which, he still resisting, broke his heart. Dying, he returned his pipes to Pan and prayed for chaos.

6 *Pan:* originally a local Arcadian god; hence, in poetry, a god of shepherds.

of the water as it plashes
from the high face
of that rock!
If the Muses
choose the young ewe
you shall receive
a stall-fed lamb
as your reward,
but if
they prefer the lamb
you
shall have the ewe for
second prize.

THYRSIS

Will you not, goat-herd,
in the Nymph's name
take your place on this
sloping knoll
among the tamarisks
and pipe for me
while I tend my sheep.

GOAT-HERD

No, shepherd,
nothing doing;
it's not for us
to be heard during the noon hush.
We dread Pan,
who for a fact
is stretched out somewhere,
dog tired from the chase;
his mood is bitter,
anger ready at his nostrils.
But, Thyrsis,
since you are good at
singing of *The Afflictions of Daphnis,*
and have most deeply
meditated the pastoral mode,

come here,
let us sit down,
under this elm
facing Priapus and the fountain fairies,
here where the shepherds come
to try themselves out
by the oak trees.
Ah! may you sing
as you sang that day
facing Chromis out of Libya,
I will let you milk, yes,
three times over,
a goat that is the mother of twins
and even when
she has sucked her kids
her milk fills
two pails. I will give besides,
new made, a two-eared bowl
of ivy-wood,
rubbed with beeswax
that smacks still
of the knife of the carver.
Round its upper edges
winds the ivy, ivy
flecked with yellow flowers
and about it
is twisted
a tendril joyful with the saffron fruit.
Within,
is limned a girl,
as fair a thing as the gods have made,
dressed in a sweeping
gown.
Her hair
is confined in a snood.
Beside her

60 *Priapus:* a rustic fertility god; here, a carving that decorates the fountain.

two fair-haired youths
with alternate speech
are contending
but her heart is
untouched.
Now,
she glances at one,
smiling,
and now, lightly
she flings the other a thought,
while their eyes,
by reason of love's
long vigils, are heavy
but their labors
all in vain.
In addition
there is fashioned there
an ancient fisherman
and a rock,
a rugged rock,
on which
with might and main
the old man poises a great net
for the cast
as one who puts his whole heart into it.
One would say
that he was fishing
with the full strength of his limbs
so big do his muscles stand out
about the neck.
Gray haired though he be,
he has the strength
of a young man.
Now, separated
from the sea-broken old man
by a narrow interval
is a vineyard,
heavy
with fire-red clusters,

and on a rude wall
sits a small boy
guarding them.
Round him
two she-foxes are skulking.
One
goes the length of the vine-rows
to eat the grapes
while the other
brings all her cunning to bear,
by what has been set down,
vowing
she will never quit the lad
until
she leaves him bare
and breakfastless.
But the boy
is plaiting a pretty
cage of locust stalks and asphodel,
fitting in the reeds
and cares less for his scrip
and the vines
than he takes delight
in his plaiting.
All about the cup
is draped the mild acanthus,
a miracle of varied work,
a thing for you to marvel at.
I paid
a Caledonian ferry man
a goat and a great white
cream-cheese
for the bowl.
It is still virgin to me,
its lip has never touched mine.
To gain my desire,
I would gladly
give this cup
if you, my friend,

will sing for me
    that delightful song.
        I hold nothing back.
Begin, my friend,
    for you cannot,
        you may be sure,
take your song,
    which drives all things out of mind,
        with you to the other world.

Bion (3rd or 2nd Century B.C.)

LAMENT FOR ADONIS

Wail, wail, Ah for Adonis! He is lost to us, lovely Adonis!
Lost is lovely Adonis! The Loves respond with lamenting.

Nay, no longer in robes of purple recline, Aphrodite:
Wake from thy sleep, sad queen, black-stoled, rain blows on
thy bosom;
Cry to the listening world, *He is lost to us, lovely Adonis!*
Wail, wail, Ah for Adonis! The Loves respond with
lamenting.

Lovely Adonis is lying, sore hurt in his thigh, on the mountains,
Hurt in his thigh with the tusk, while grief consumes
Aphrodite:
Slowly he drops toward death, and the black blood drips from
his fair flesh,
Down from his snow-white skin; his eyes wax dull 'neath the
eyelids,
Yea and the rose hath failed his lips, and around them the
kisses
Die and wither, the kisses that Kupris will not relinquish:
Still, though he lives no longer, a kiss consoles Aphrodite;
But he knows not, Adonis, she kissed him while he was dying.
Wail, wail, Ah for Adonis! The Loves respond with
lamenting.

Cruel, cruel the wound in the thigh that preys on Adonis:
But in her heart Cytherea hath yet worse wounds to afflict her.

Translated by John Addington Symonds 1810-1893.

NOTE: These are English hexameters scanned like the Latin and Greek: each of the first four feet may be a dactyl or a spondee; the fifth must be a dactyl; the last may be a spondee or a trochee.

3 *Aphrodite:* "foam-born"; other names for Venus are *Kupris* (l.12), because of her ancient cult on Cyprus; *Cytherea* (l.17), because she was born from the sea near the island of Cythera.

Round him his dear hounds bay, they howl in their grief to the heavens;
Nymphs of the woodlands wail: but she, the Queen Aphrodite,
Loosing her locks to the air, roams far and wide through the forest,
Drowned in grief, disheveled, unsandaled, and as she flies onward,
Briars stab at her feet and cull the blood of the goddess.
She with shrill lamentation thro' glen and thro' glade is carried,
Calling her Syrian lord, demanding him back, and demanding.
But where he lies, dark blood wells up and encircles the navel;
Blood from the gushing thighs empurples the breast; and the snow-white
Flank that was once so fair, is now dyed red for Adonis.
  Wail, wail, Ah, Cytherea! The Loves respond with lamenting.

She then hath lost her lord, and with him hath lost her celestial
Beauty; for fair was he, and fair, while he lived, Aphrodite:
Now in his death her beauty hath died. *Ah, Ah, Cytherea!*
All the mountains lament, and the oaks moan, *Ah for Adonis*
Streams as they murmur and flow complain of thy griefs, Aphrodite:
Yea and the springs on the hills, in the woods, weep tears for Adonis:
Flowers of the field for woe flush crimson red; and Cythêra,
Through the dells and the glens, shrills loud the dirge of her anguish:
Woe, woe, Ah, Cytherea! He is lost to us, lovely Adonis!
Echo repeats the groan: *Lost, lost, is lovely Adonis!*
Kupris, who but bewailed thy pangs of a love overwhelming?

She, when she saw, when she knew the unstanchable wound of Adonis,
When she beheld the red blood on his pale thigh's withering blossom,
Spreading her arms full wide, she moaned out: "Stay, my Adonis!
Stay, ill-fated Adonis! that I once more may approach thee!

Clasp thee close to my breast, and these lips mingle with thy lips!
Rouse for a moment, Adonis, and kiss me again for the last time;
Kiss me as long as the kiss can live on the lips of a lover;
Till from thy inmost soul to my mouth and down to my marrow
Thy life-breath shall run, and I quaff the wine of thy philter,
Draining the draught of thy love: that kiss will I treasure, Adonis,
E'en as it were thyself; since thou, ill-starred, art departing.
Fleeing me far, O Adonis, to Acheron faring, the sad realm
Ruled by a stern savage king: while I, the unhappy, the luckless,
I live; goddess am I, and I may not follow or find thee.
Persephone, take thou my lord, my lover; I know thee
Stronger far than myself: all fair things drift to thy dwelling.
I meanwhile am accursed, possessed with insatiable sorrow,
Weeping my dead, my Adonis who died, and am shaken and shattered.
Diest thou then, my desired? and desire like a dream hath escaped me.
Widowed is now Cytherea; the Loves in her halls are abandoned;
Perished with thee is my girdle. Ah, why wouldst thou hunt, overbold one?
Being so beautiful, why wast thou mad to fight with a wild beast?"
Thus then Kupris mourned; and the Loves respond with lamenting:
Wail, wail, Ah for Adonis! He is lost to us, lovely Adonis!
Tears the Paphian shed, drop by drop for the drops of Adonis'
Blood; and on earth each drop, as it fell, grew into a blossom:
Roses sprang from the blood, and the tears gave birth to the wind-flower.
Wail, wail, Ah, Cytherea! He is lost to us, lovely Adonis!

Wail, wail, Ah for Adonis! He is lost to us, lovely Adonis!

Now in the oak-woods cease to lament for thy lord, Aphrodite.
No proper couch is this which the wild leaves strew for Adonis.
Let him thy own bed share, Cytherea, the corpse of Adonis;
E'en as a corpse he is fair, fair corpse as fallen aslumber,
Now lay him soft to sleep, sleep well in the wool of the bedclothes,
Where with thee through the night in holy dreams he commingled,
Stretched on a couch all gold, that yearns for him stark though he now be.
Shower on him garlands, flowers: all fair things died in his dying;
Yea, as he faded away, so shrivel and wither the blossoms.
Syrian spikenard scatter, anoint him with myrrh and with unguents:
Perish perfumes all, since he, thy perfume, is perished.
Wail, wail, Ah for Adonis! The Loves respond with lamenting.

Lapped in his purple robes is the delicate form of Adonis.
Round him weeping Loves complain and moan in their anguish,
Clipping their locks for Adonis: and one of them treads on his arrows,
One of them breaks his bow, and one sets heel on the quiver;
One hath loosed for Adonis the lachet of sandals, and some bring
Water to pour in an urn; one laves the wound in his white thigh;
One from behind with his wings keeps fanning dainty Adonis.
Wail, wail, Ah for Adonis! The Loves respond with lamenting.

Wail, wail, Ah, Cytherea! The Loves respond with lamenting.
Every torch at the doors hath been quenched by thy hand, Hymenaeus;

90 *Hymenaeus:* god of marriage.

Every bridal wreath hath been torn to shreds; and no longer,
Hymen, Hymen, no more is the song, but a new song of sorrow,
Woe, woe! and Ah for Adonis! resounds in lieu of the bridesong.
This the Graces are shrilling, the son of Cinyras hymning,
Lost is lovely Adonis! in loud antiphonal accents.
Woe, woe! sharply repeat, far more than the praises of Paiôn,
Woe! and *Ah for Adonis!* The Muses who wail for Adonis,
Chaunt their charms to Adonis.—But he lists not their singing;
Not that he wills not to hear, but the Maiden doth not release him.
Cease from moans, Cytherea, to-day refrain from the death-songs:
Thou must lament him again, and again shed tears in a new year.

94 *Cinyras:* Adonis's father, a mythical king of Cyprus. 96 *Paiôn:* originally the name of the physician of the gods, Paiôn (or Paean) came to mean "deliverer from evil" and was finally applied to Apollo and became also the name of the song dedicated to him.

Virgil 70–19 B.C.

THE TENTH PASTORAL. OR, GALLUS

THE ARGUMENT. Gallus *a great Patron of Virgil, and an excellent Poet, was very deeply in Love with one* Citheris, *whom he calls* Lycoris; *and who had forsaken him for the Company of a Souldier. The Poet therefore supposes his Friend* Gallus *retir'd in his heighth of Melancholy into the Solitudes of* Arcadia, (*the celebrated Scene of Pastorals;*) *where he represents him in a very languishing Condition, with all the Rural Deities about him, pitying his hard Usage, and condoling his Misfortune.*

Thy sacred Succour, *Arethusa,* bring,
To crown my Labour: 'tis the last I sing.
Which proud *Lycoris* may with Pity view;
The Muse is mournful, tho' the Numbers few.
Refuse me not a Verse, to Grief and *Gallus* due.
So may thy Silver Streams beneath the Tide,
Unmix'd with briny Seas, securely glide.
Sing then, my *Gallus,* and his hopeless Vows;
Sing, while my Cattle crop the tender Browze.
The vocal Grove shall answer to the Sound,
And Echo, from the Vales, the tuneful Voice rebound.
What Lawns or Woods withheld you from his Aid,
Ye Nymphs, when *Gallus* was to Love betray'd;
To Love, unpity'd by the cruel Maid?
Not steepy *Pindus* cou'd retard your Course,
Nor cleft *Parnassus,* nor th' *Aonian* Source:

Translated by John Dryden 1631-1700.

NOTE: In Virgil's Fifth Eclogue, Mopsus laments the death of the shepherd Daphnis, and Menalcas (l. 29) proclaims his divinity, so it better illustrates some of the furniture of the pastoral elegy than this erotic complaint which I have chosen instead because I think it the better poem. The two bereavements are not so different from each other as you might think if you were lucky enough not to know them.

1 *Arethusa:* spring in Sicily associated with the birthplace of Theocritus. The nymph of the Sicilian river does duty as the Muse for a pastoral poem. 4 *Numbers:* verses. 15–16 *Pindus, Parnassus:* sacred mountains; *Aonian Source:* the fountain Aganippe in Boeotia.

Nothing that owns the Muses cou'd suspend
Your Aid to *Gallus, Gallus* is their Friend.
For him the lofty Laurel stands in Tears;
And hung with humid Pearls the lowly Shrub appears.
Maenalian Pines the Godlike Swain bemoan;
When spread beneath a Rock he sigh'd alone;
And cold *Lycaeus* wept from every dropping Stone.
The Sheep surround their Shepherd, as he lyes:
Blush not, sweet Poet, nor the name despise:
Along the Streams his Flock *Adonis* fed;
And yet the Queen of Beauty blest his Bed.
The Swains and tardy Neat-herds came, and last
Menalcas, wet with beating Winter Mast.
Wond'ring, they ask'd from whence arose thy Flame;
Yet, more amaz'd, thy own *Apollo* came.
Flush'd were his Cheeks, and glowing were his Eyes:
Is she thy Care, is she thy Care, he cries?
Thy false *Lycoris* flies thy Love and thee;
And for thy Rival tempts the raging Sea,
The Forms of horrid War, and Heav'ns Inclemency.
Sylvanus came: his Brows a Country Crown
Of Fennel, and of nodding Lillies, drown.
Great *Pan* arriv'd; and we beheld him too,
His Cheeks and Temples of Vermilion Hue.
Why, *Gallus*, this immod'rate Grief, he cry'd:
Think'st thou that Love with Tears is satisfi'd?
The Meads are sooner drunk with Morning Dews;
The Bees with flow'ry Shrubs, the Goats with Brouze.
Unmov'd, and with dejected Eyes, he mourn'd:
He paus'd, and then these broken Words return'd.
'Tis past; and Pity gives me no Relief:
But you, *Arcadian* Swains, shall sing my Grief:
And on your Hills, my last Complaints renew;

17 *owns:* acknowledges. 21 *Maenalian Pines:* on Mt. Maenalus in Arcadia, sacred to Pan. 23 *Lycaeus:* mountain in S. Arcadia, parts of which were sacred to Apollo and Pan. 29 *Menalcas:* a shepherd's name traditional in pastoral poetry, as are the shepherdesses Phyllis and Amyntas in l. 55. *Mast:* fodder.

So sad a Song is onely worthy you.
How light wou'd lye the Turf upon my Breast,
If you my Suff'rings in your Songs exprest?
Ah! that your Birth and Bus'ness had been mine;
To penn the Sheep, and press the swelling Vine!
Had *Phyllis* or *Amyntas* caus'd my Pain,
Or any Nymph, or Shepherd on the Plain,
Tho *Phyllis* brown, tho black *Amyntas* were,
Are Violets not sweet, because not fair?
Beneath the Sallows, and the shady Vine,
My Loves had mix'd their pliant Limbs with mine;
Phyllis with Myrtle Wreaths had crown'd my Hair,
And soft *Amyntas* sung away my Care.
Come, see what Pleasures in our Plains abound;
The Woods, the Fountains, and the flow'ry ground.
As you are beauteous, were you half so true,
Here cou'd I live, and love, and dye with only you.
Now I to fighting Fields am sent afar,
And strive in Winter Camps with toils of War;
While you, (alas, that I shou'd find it so!)
To shun my sight, your Native Soil forgo,
And climb the frozen *Alps*, and tread th' eternal Snow.
Ye Frosts and Snows her tender Body spare,
Those are not Limbs for Ysicles to tear.
For me, the Wilds and Desarts are my Choice;
The Muses, once my Care; my once harmonious Voice.
There will I sing, forsaken and alone,
The Rocks and hollow Caves shall echo to my Moan.
The Rind of ev'ry Plant her Name shall know;
And as the Rind extends, the Love shall grow.
Then on *Arcadian* Mountains will I chase
(Mix'd with the Woodland Nymphs) the Salvage Race.
Nor Cold shall hinder me, with Horns and Hounds,
To thrid the Thickets, or to leap the Mounds.
And now methinks o're steepy Rocks I go;
And rush through sounding Woods, and bend the *Parthian* Bow:
As if with Sports my Sufferings I could ease,
Or by my Pains the God of Love appease.
My Frenzy changes, I delight no more

On Mountain tops, to chace the tusky Boar;
No Game but hopeless Love my thoughts pursue:
Once more ye Nymphs, and Songs, and sounding Woods adieu.
Love alters not for us, his hard Decrees,
Not tho beneath the *Thracian* Clime we freeze;
Or *Italy's* indulgent Heav'n forgo;
And in mid-Winter tread *Sithonian* Snow.
Or when the Barks of Elms are scorch'd, we keep
On *Meroes* burning Plains the *Lybian* Sheep.
In Hell, and Earth, and Seas, and Heav'n above,
Love conquers all; and we must yield to Love.
My Muses, here your sacred Raptures end:
The Verse was what I ow'd my suff'ring Friend.
This while I sung, my Sorrows I deceiv'd,
And bending Osiers into Baskets weav'd.
The Song, because inspir'd by you, shall shine:
And *Gallus* will approve, because 'tis mine.
Gallus, for whom my holy Flames renew,
Each hour, and ev'ry moment rise in view:
As Alders, in the Spring, their Boles extend;
And heave so fiercely, that the Bark they rend.
Now let us rise, for hoarseness oft invades
The Singer's Voice, who sings beneath the Shades.
From Juniper, unwholsom Dews distill,
That blast the sooty Corn; the with'ring Herbage kill;
Away, my Goats, away: for you have browz'd your fill.

95 *Sithonian Snow:* the Sithonian peninsula was at one time part of Thrace. 97 *Meroe:* ancient capital of Ethiopia.

Edmund Spenser 1552?–1599

NOVEMBER

ARGUMENT: *In this xi aeglogue he bewaileth the death of some maiden of great blood, whom he called Dido. The personage is secret, and to me altogether unknown, albe of himself I often required the same. This aeglogue is made in imitation of Marot his song, which he made upon the death of Lois the French queen; but far passing his reach, and in mine opinion all other the aeglogues of this book.*

THENOT COLIN

THENOT

Colin my dear when shall it please thee sing,
As thou were wont, songs of some jouissance?
Thy Muse too long slumb'reth in sorrowing,
Lullèd asleep through love's misgovernance.
Now somewhat sing, whose endless sovenance
Among the shepherds swains may aye remain,
Whether thee list thy lovèd lass advance,
Or honor Pan with hymns of higher vein.

COLIN

Thenot, now nis the time of merimake,
Nor Pan to hery, nor with love to play:
Sik mirth in May is meetest for to make,
Or summer shade under the cockèd hay.
But now sad Winter welkèd hath the day,
And Phoebus weary of his yearly task,
Ystabled hath his steeds in lowly lay,

November: From *The Shepherd's Calendar* 1579.

The Argument, or summary, of the poem is written by "E. K.," possibly Edmund Kirk, who was a friend of Spenser. *Aeglogue* is a form of *eclogue,* which in Greek simply meant selection and was applied as a name to many kinds of poetry. Through tradition, however, it has come specifically to refer to pastoral poetry.

2 merriment 5 remembrance 7 desire . . . praise 9 is not 10 praise 11 such . . . most fitting 13 clouded 14 god of the Sun 15 field

And taken up his inn in Fishes' hask.
Thilk solein season sadder plight doth ask:
And loatheth sik delights as thou dost praise:
The mournful Muse in mirth now list ne mask,
As she was wont in youngth and summer days:
But if thou algate lust light virelays,
And looser songs of love to underfong
Who but thyself deserves sik Poet's praise?
Relieve thy Oaten pipes that sleepen long.

THENOT

The Nightingale is sovereign of song,
Before him sits the Titmouse silent be:
And I unfit to thrust in skilful throng,
Should Colin make judge of my foolery?
Nay, better learn of hem that learnèd be,
And han be watered at the Muses' well:
The kindly dew drops from the higher tree,
And wets the little plants that lowly dwell.
But if sad winter's wrath and season chill,
Accord not with thy Muse's merriment:
To sadder times thou may'st attune thy quill,
And sing of sorrow and death's dreariment.
For dead is Dido, dead alas and drent,
Dido! the great shepherd his daughter sheen.
The fairest May she ever was that went,
Her like she has not left behind I ween:
And if thou wilt bewail my woeful tene:
I shall thee give yond Cosset for thy pain:
And if thy rhymes as round and rueful been

16 *inn:* abode; *Fishes' hask:* a wicker basket. In his gloss, E. K. says, "the sun, reigneth that is, in the sign Pisces all November," which is, of course, wrong, as E. K. often is. 17 This gloomy 19 does not delight in playing 20 youth 21 nevertheless desire 22 undertake 24 revive 26 it befit 29 them 30 have been 35 pipe 37 drowned 38 fair 39 maiden 40 think 41 sorrow 42 lamb 43 are

As those that did thy Rosalind complain,
Much greater gifts for guerdon thou shalt gain,
Than Kid or Cosset, which I thee bynempt:
Then up I say, thou jolly shepherd swain,
Let not my small demand be so contempt.

COLIN

Thenot to that I choose thou dost me tempt,
But ah too well I wot my humble vein,
And how my rhymes been rugged and unkempt;
Yet as I con, my conning I will strain.

Up, then Melpomene thou mournful'st Muse of nine,
Such cause of mourning never hadst afore;
Up grisly ghosts and up my rueful ryme,
Matter of mirth now shalt thou have no more.
For dead she is, that mirth thee made of yore.
  Dido my dear alas is dead,
  Dead and lieth wrapt in lead:
    O heavy herse,
Let streaming tears be pourèd out in store;
    O careful verse.

Shepherds, that by your flocks on Kentish downs abide,
Wail ye this woeful waste of Nature's wark;
Wail we the wight, whose presence was our pride;
Wail we the wight, whose absence is our cark.
The sun of all the world is dim and dark:
  The earth now lacks her wonted light,
  And all we dwell in deadly night,
    O heavy herse
Break we our pipes, that shrilled as loud as Lark,
    O careful verse.

44 *complain:* The complaint is the song of a shepherd forsaken by his mistress. Thenot alludes to the January aeglogue of the *Shepherd's Calendar,* when Colin complained of his loss of Rosalind. 46 promised 48 scorned 50 know 52 am able . . . ability 53 *Melpomene:* Muse of tragedy. 60 *herse:* "the solemn obsequy in funerals."—E. K. 62 sorrowful 64 work 65 creature 66 care

Why do we longer live, (ah why live we so long)
Whose better days Death hath shut up in woe?
The fairest flower our girlond all among
Is faded quite, and into dust ygo.
Sing now ye shepherds' daughters, sing no mo
  The songs that Colin made in her praise,
  But into weeping turn your wanton lays,
    O heavy herse,
Now is time to die. Nay time was long ygo:
    O careful verse.

Whence is it, that the flow'ret of the field doth fade,
And lieth buried long in Winter's bale;
Yet, soon as Spring his mantle hath displayed,
It flow'reth fresh, as it should never fail?
But thing on earth that is of most avail,
  As virtue's branch and beauty's bud,
  Reliven not for any good.
    O heavy herse,
The branch once dead, the bud eke needs must quail,
    O careful verse.

She while she was, (that was, a woeful word to sayn)
For beauty's praise and pleasance had no peer:
So well she couth the shepherds entertain,
With cakes and cracknels and such country cheer.
Ne would she scorn the simple shepherd's swain;
  For she would call hem often heame
  And give hem curds and clouted Cream.
    O heavy herse,
Als Colin Clout she would not once disdain.
    O careful verse.

But now sik happy cheer is turned to heavy chance,
Such pleasance now displaced by dolour's dint:

76 gone 89 revive 91 also . . . die 93 say 95 knew how to 96 light crisp biscuits 98 them . . . home 99 curdled 101 also 103 misfortune

All Music sleeps, where Death doth lead the dance,
And shepherds' wonted solace is extinct.
The blue in black, the green in gray is tinct,
  The gaudy girlonds deck her grave,
  The faded flowers her corse embrave.
    O heavy herse,
Mourn now my Muse, now mourn with tears besprint
    O careful verse.

O thou great shepherd Lobbin, how great is thy grief,
Where been the nosegays that she dight for thee:
The coloured chaplets wrought with a chief,
The knotted rush-rings, and gilt rosemary?
For she deemèd no thing too dear for thee.
  Ah they been all yclad in clay,
  One bitter blast blew all away.
    O heavy herse,
Thereof nought remains but the memory.
    O careful verse.

Ay me that dreary Death should strike so mortal stroke,
That can undo Dame Nature's kindly course:
The faded locks fall from the lofty oak,
The floods do gasp, for drièd is their source,
And floods of tears flow in their stead perforce
  The mantled meadows mourn,
  Their sundry colours turn.
    O heavy herse,
The heavens do melt in tears without remorse.
    O careful verse.

The feeble flocks in field refuse their former food,
And hang their heads, as they would learn to weep:
The beasts in forest wail as they were wood,
Except the Wolves, that chase the wand'ring sheep:

107 stained 109 beautify 111 sprinkled 114 made 115 *chaplets . . . chief:* probably garlands made so that one special flower was prominent. 124 natural 135 mad

Now she is gone that safely did hem keep,
  The Turtle on the barèd branch
  Laments the wound that Death did launch.
    O heavy herse,
And Philomel her song with tears doth steep.
    O careful verse.

The water Nymphs, that wont with her to sing and dance,
And for her girlond Olive branches bear,
Now baleful boughs of Cypress doen advance;
The Muses, that were wont green bays to wear,
Now bringen bitter Elder branches sere,
  The fatal sisters eke repent
  Her vital thread so soon was spent.
    O heavy herse,
Mourn now my Muse, now mourn with heavy cheer.
    O careful verse.

O trustless state of earthly things, and slipper hope
Of mortal men, that swink and sweat for nought,
And shooting wide, do miss the markèd scope:
Now have I learned (a lesson dearly bought)
That nis on earth assurance to be sought:
  For what might be in earthly mould,
  That did her buried body hold,
    O heavy herse,
Yet saw I on the bier when it was brought.
    O careful verse.

But maugre Death, and dreaded sisters' deadly spite,
And gates of hell, and fiery furies' force,
She hath the bonds broke of eternal night,
Her soul unbodied on the burdenous corse.
Why then weeps Lobbin so without remorse?
  O Lobb, thy loss no longer lament,

138 turtledove 141 the nightingale 145 bring forward 148 the three Fates 151 countenance 153 slippery 154 work 163 in spite of . . . the Fates 166 corpse

Dido nis dead, but into heaven hent.
O happy herse,
Cease now, my Muse, now cease thy sorrow's source,
O joyful verse.

Why wail we then? why weary we the Gods with plaints,
As if some evil were to her betight?
She reigns a goddess now among the saints,
That whilom was the saint of shepherds' light:
And is installèd now in heaven's height.
I see thee blessèd soul, I see,
Walk in Elysian fields so free.
O happy herse,
Might I once come to thee (O that I might)
O joyful verse.

Unwise and wretched men, to weet what's good or ill,
We deem of death as doom of ill desert;
But knew we fools, what it us brings until,
Die would we daily, once it to expert.
No danger there the shepherd can astert;
Fair fields and pleasant lays there been,
The fields aye fresh, the grass aye green:
O happy herse,
Make haste ye shepherds, thither to revert,
O joyful verse.

Dido is gone afore (whose turn shall be the next?)
There lives she with the blessèd Gods in bliss,
There drinks she Nectar with Ambrosia mixt,
And joys enjoys, that mortal men do miss.
The honour now of highest gods she is,
That whilom was poor shepherds' pride,
While here on earth she did abide.

169 taken 174 happened 176 once 183 know 184 *We deem . . . desert:* We think of death as a punishment for doing wrong. 186 experience 187 *shepherd . . . astert:* can startle the shepherd. 189 always

O happy herse,
Cease now my song, my woe now wasted is,
O joyful verse.

THENOT

Ay frank shepherd, how been thy verses meint
With doleful pleasance, so as I ne wot
Whether rejoice, or weep for great constraint?
Thine be the cosset, well hast thou it got.
Up Colin up, enough thou mournèd hast,
Now gins to mizzle, hie we homeward fast.

Colin's Emblem.

La mort ny mord.

201 ended 203 mingled 208 drizzle *La mort ny mord:* Death bites not.

John Milton 1608–1674

LYCIDAS

In this Monody the Author bewails a learned Friend, unfortunately drown'd in his Passage from Chester *on the* Irish *Seas, 1637. And by occasion foretells the ruin of our corrupted Clergy then in their height.*

Yet once more, O ye Laurels, and once more
Ye Myrtles brown, with Ivy never sere,
I come to pluck your Berries harsh and crude,
And with forc'd fingers rude,
Shatter your leaves before the mellowing year.
Bitter constraint, and sad occasion dear,
Compels me to disturb your season due:
For *Lycidas* is dead, dead ere his prime,
Young *Lycidas,* and hath not left his peer:
Who would not sing for *Lycidas?* he well knew
Himself to sing, and build the lofty rhyme.
He must not float upon his wat'ry bier
Unwept, and welter to the parching wind,
Without the meed of some melodious tear.
  Begin then, Sisters of the sacred well,
That from beneath the seat of *Jove* doth spring,
Begin, and somewhat loudly sweep the string.
Hence with denial vain, and coy excuse,
So may some gentle Muse
With lucky words favour my destin'd Urn,
And as he passes turn,
And bid fair peace be to my sable shroud.
For we were nurst upon the self-same hill,
Fed the same flock; by fountain, shade, and rill.
  Together both, ere the high Lawns appear'd
Under the opening eye-lids of the morn,

Lycidas. From *Obsequies to the Memory of Mr. Edward King* 1638. *learned Friend:* Edward King, a student with Milton at Cambridge.

3 unripened 6 costly 13 toss about 14 reward 15 *sacred well:* the Pierian spring at the base of Mt. Olympus is sacred to the Muses. 22 black

We drove afield, and both together heard
What time the Gray-fly winds her sultry horn,
Batt'ning our flocks with the fresh dews of night,
Oft till the Star that rose, at Ev'ning, bright,
Toward Heav'n's descent had slop'd his westering wheel.
Mean while the Rural ditties were not mute,
Temper'd to th'Oaten Flute,
Rough *Satyrs* danc'd, and *Fauns* with clov'n heel,
From the glad sound would not be absent long,
And old *Damaetas* lov'd to hear our song.
But O the heavy change, now thou art gone,
Now thou art gone, and never must return!
Thee Shepherd, thee the Woods, and desert Caves,
With wild Thyme and the gadding Vine o'ergrown,
And all their echoes mourn.
The Willows, and the Hazel Copses green,
Shall now no more be seen,
Fanning their joyous Leaves to thy soft layes.
As killing as the Canker to the Rose,
Or Taint-worm to the weanling Herds that graze,
Or Frost to Flowers, that their gay wardrop wear,
When first the White-thorn blows;
Such, *Lycidas,* thy loss to Shepherd's ear.
Where were ye Nymphs when the remorseless deep
Clos'd o'er the head of your lov'd *Lycidas?*
For neither were ye playing on the steep,
Where your old *Bards,* the famous *Druids* lie,
Nor on the shaggy top of *Mona* high,
Nor yet where *Deva* spreads her wizard stream:
Ay me, I fondly dream!
Had ye been there—for what could that have done?
What could the Muse herself that *Orpheus* bore,
The Muse herself, for her enchanting son
Whom Universal nature did lament,

29 feeding 36 *Damaetas:* like Lycidas, a pastoral name from Virgil's Eclogues. 40 straggling 46 newly weaned 47 wardrobe 48 blooms 54-55 *Mona* and *Deva:* the Roman names for Anglesey Island and the river Dee, near Chester. 58 *Muse:* Calliope.

When by the rout that made the hideous roar,
His gory visage down the stream was sent,
Down the swift *Hebrus* to the *Lesbian* shore.
   Alas! What boots it with uncessant care
To tend the homely slighted Shepherd's trade,
And strictly meditate the thankless Muse,
Were it not better done as others use,
To sport with *Amaryllis* in the shade,
Or with the tangles of *Neaera's* hair?
Fame is the spur that the clear spirit doth raise
(That last infirmity of Noble mind)
To scorn delights, and live laborious days;
But the fair Guerdon when we hope to find,
And think to burst out into sudden blaze,
Comes the blind *Fury* with th'abhorrèd shears,
And slits the thin-spun life. But not the praise,
Phoebus repli'd, and touch'd my trembling ears;
Fame is no plant that grows on mortal soil,
Nor in the glistering foil
Set off to th'world, nor in broad rumour lies,
But lives and spreads aloft by those pure eyes,
And perfet witness of all-judging *Jove*;
As he pronounces lastly on each deed,
Of so much fame in Heav'n expect thy meed.
   O Fountain *Arethuse,* and thou honour'd flood,
Smooth-sliding *Mincius,* crown'd with vocal reeds,
That strain I heard was of a higher mood:
But now my Oate proceeds,
And listens to the Herald of the Sea
That came in *Neptune's* plea,
He ask'd the Waves, and ask'd the Felon winds,
What hard mishap hath doom'd this gentle swain?

61 *the rout:* the Thracian women who tore Orpheus to pieces when he wouldn't sing for them. 64 profits 65 poet's craft 68-69 *Amaryllis, Neaera:* traditional names of unresisting shepherdesses. 73 reward 75 *blind Fury:* Atropos, the Fate who cuts the thread of man's life. 79 setting of a gem 82 perfect 85–86 *Arethuse:* The river Arethuse in Sicily is associated with Theocritus, while the river *Mincius* is near Virgil's birthplace in Italy. 89 Triton 90 on behalf of

And question'd every gust of rugged wings
That blows from off each beakèd Promontory;
They knew not of his story,
And sage *Hippotades* their answer brings,
That not a blast was from his dungeon stray'd,
The Air was calm, and on the level brine,
Sleek *Panope* with all her sisters play'd.
It was that fatal and perfidious Bark
Built in th'eclipse, and rigg'd with curses dark,
That sunk so low that sacred head of thine.
Next *Camus,* reverend Sire, went footing slow,
His Mantle hairy, and his Bonnet sedge,
Inwrought with figures dim, and on the edge
Like to that sanguine flower inscrib'd with woe.
Ah! Who hath reft (quoth he) my dearest pledge?
Last came, and last did go,
The Pilot of the *Galilean* lake,
Two massy Keyes he bore of metals twain,
(The Golden opes, the Iron shuts amain)
He shook his Miter'd locks, and stern bespake,
How well could I have spar'd for thee young swain,
Enow of such as for their bellies' sake,
Creep and intrude, and climb into the fold?
Of other care they little reck'ning make,
Than how to scramble at the shearers' feast,
And shove away the worthy bidden guest;
Blind mouths! that scarce themselves know how to hold
A Sheep-hook, or have learn'd ought else the least
That to the faithfull Herdman's art belongs!
What recks it them? What need they? They are sped;
And when they list, their lean and flashy songs
Grate on their scrannel Pipes of wretched straw,

96 *Hippotades:* Aeolus, the god of the winds. 99 sea nymph 103 *Camus:* a personification of the river Cam, from which Cambridge gets its name. 106 *sanguine flower:* the hyacinth; Apollo made it spring from the blood of the murdered boy Hyacinthus, its petals stained with the mark AI, "woe." 109 *the Pilot:* St. Peter, who holds the keys of salvation and damnation; *Miter'd* (l. 112) because he was the first Bishop of Rome. 122 matters (to) . . . prospering 124 thin

The hungry Sheep look up, and are not fed,
But swoln with wind, and the rank mist they draw,
Rot inwardly, and foul contagion spread:
Besides what the grim Wolf with privy paw
Daily devours apace, and nothing said,
But that two-handed engine at the door,
Stands ready to smite once, and smite no more.
Return *Alpheus*, the dread voice is past,
That shrunk thy streams; Return *Sicilian* Muse,
And call the Vales, and bid them hither cast
Their bells, and Flowrets of a thousand hues.
Ye valleys low where the mild whispers use,
Of shades and wanton winds, and gushing brooks,
On whose fresh lap the swart Star sparely looks,
Throw hither all your quaint enameld eyes,
That on the green turf suck the honied showres,
And purple all the ground with vernal flowres.
Bring the rathe Primrose that forsaken dies,
The tufted Crow-toe, and pale Jessamine,
The white Pink, and the Pansy freakt with jet,
The glowing Violet,
The Musk-rose, and the well-attir'd Woodbine,
With Cowslips wan that hang the pensive head,
And every flower that sad embroidery wears:
Bid *Amaranthus* all his beauty shed,
And Daffadillies fill their cups with tears,
To strew the Laureat Herse where *Lycid* lies.
For so to interpose a little ease,
Let our frail thoughts dally with false surmise.
Ay me! Whilst thee the shores, and sounding Seas
Wash far away, where ere thy bones are hurld,

130 *that two-handed engine:* engine means any "device." The image has never been satisfactorily explained. 132–133 *Alpheus:* the river Alpheus whose genius loved Arethuse; *Sicilian Muse* because Milton is returning to the pastoral mode after his jeremiad digression. 138 *swart Star:* blackening or scorching star; possibly Sirius because the sun is near it in the late summer "dog days." 139 exquisitely made 142 early 144 striped 149 *Amaranthus:* "the unfading flower." 151 bier

Whether beyond the stormy *Hebrides,*
Where thou perhaps under the whelming tide
Visit'st the bottom of the monstrous world;
Or whether thou to our moist vows deny'd,
Sleep'st by the fable of *Bellerus* old,
Where the great vision of the guarded Mount
Looks toward *Namancos* and *Bayona's* hold;
Look homeward Angel now, and melt with ruth,
And, O ye *Dolphins,* waft the hapless youth.
  Weep no more, woful Shepherds weep no more,
For *Lycidas* your sorrow is not dead,
Sunk though he be beneath the watry floor,
So sinks the day-star in the Ocean bed,
And yet anon repairs his drooping head,
And tricks his beams, and with new spangled Ore,
Flames in the forehead of the morning sky:
So *Lycidas* sunk low, but mounted high,
Through the dear might of him that walk'd the waves;
Where other groves, and other streams along,
With *Nectar* pure his oozy Locks he laves,
And hears the unexpressive nuptial Song,
In the blest Kingdoms meek of joy and love.
There entertain him all the Saints above,
In solemn troops, and sweet Societies
That sing, and singing in their glory move,
And wipe the tears for ever from his eyes.
Now *Lycidas* the Shepherds weep no more;
Henceforth thou art the Genius of the shore,
In thy large recompense, and shalt be good
To all that wander in that perilous flood.

156-163 *Hebrides:* Scottish islands far to the north of where King died. *Bellerus:* a legendary giant associated with Land's End in Cornwall, the southern tip of England. Milton imagines St. Michael, the patron of mariners, standing on St. Michael's *Mount,* an island off Land's End, looking southward toward Spain where *Bayona* and the mountains of *Namancos* are located. 163 pity 170 dresses in 176 inexpressible 176 *nuptial Song:* "the marriage supper of the Lamb"—Revelations 19:7. 183 guardian spirit

Thus sang the uncouth Swain to th'Oaks and rills,
While the still morn went out with Sandals gray,
He touch'd the tender stops of various Quills,
With eager thought warbling his *Dorick* lay:
And now the Sun had stretch'd out all the hills,
And now was dropt into the Western bay;
At last he rose, and twitch'd his Mantle blue:
To morrow to fresh Woods, and Pastures new.

188 pipes 189 rustic

Alexander Pope 1688–1744

THE LAMENTATION OF GLUMDALCLITCH, FOR THE LOSS OF GRILDRIG—A PASTORAL

Soon as *Glumdalclitch* mist her pleasing Care,
She wept, she blubber'd, and she tore her Hair.
No *British* Miss sincerer Grief has known,
Her Squirrel missing, or her Sparrow flown.
She furl'd her Sampler, and hawl'd in her Thread,
And stuck her Needle into *Grildrig's* Bed;
Then spread her Hands, and with a Bounce let fall
Her Baby, like the Giant in *Guild-hall.*
In Peals of Thunder now she roars, and now
She gently whimpers like a lowing Cow.
Yet lovely in her Sorrow still appears:
Her Locks dishevell'd, and her Flood of Tears
Seem like the lofty Barn of some rich Swain,
When from the Thatch drips fast a Show'r of Rain.

In vain she search'd each Cranny of the House,
Each gaping Chink impervious to a Mouse.
"Was it for this (she cry'd) with daily Care
Within thy Reach I set the Vinegar?
And fill'd the Cruet with the Acid Tide,
While Pepper-Water-Worms thy Bait supply'd;
Where twin'd the Silver Eel around thy Hook,
And all the little Monsters of the Brook.

From *Several Copies of Verses on Occasion of Mr. Gulliver's Travels* 1727.

The Lamentation . . . Grildrig: Based on Part II of *Gulliver's Travels,* "A Voyage to Brobdingnag," whose inhabitants are giants. Gulliver is befriended by Glumdalclitch, the nine-year-old princess of the country, and she calls him Grildrig, which Gulliver says means Mannikin in her language. While on a journey through Brobdingnag, a page leaves Gulliver by the seaside in the box which Glumdalclitch uses to carry him; the box is carried off by a seagull, and dropped into the ocean, where Gulliver is finally rescued by an English ship. 8 her doll

Sure in that Lake he dropt—My *Grilly's* drown'd"—
She dragg'd the Cruet, but no *Grildrig* found.
"Vain is thy Courage, *Grilly,* vain thy Boast;
But little Creatures enterprise the most.
Trembling, I've seen thee dare the Kitten's Paw;
Nay, mix with Children, as they play'd at Taw;
Nor fear the Marbles, as they bounding flew:
Marbles to them, but rolling Rocks to you.

"Why did I trust thee with that giddy Youth?
Who from a *Page* can ever learn the Truth?
Vers'd in Court Tricks, that Money-loving Boy
To some Lord's Daughter sold the living Toy;
Or rent him Limb from Limb in cruel Play,
As Children tear the Wings of Flies away;
From Place to Place o'er *Brobdingnag* I'll roam,
And never will return, or bring thee home.
But who hath Eyes to trace the passing Wind,
How then thy fairy Footsteps can I find?
Dost thou bewilder'd wander all alone,
In the green Thicket of a Mossy Stone,
Or tumbled from the Toadstool's slipp'ry Round,
Perhaps all maim'd, lie grov'ling on the Ground?
Dost thou, inbosom'd in the lovely Rose,
Or sunk within the Peach's Down, repose?
Within the King-Cup if thy Limbs are spread,
Or in the golden Cowslip's Velvet Head;
O show me, *Flora,* 'midst those Sweets, the Flow'r
Where sleeps my *Grildrig* in his fragrant Bow'r!
"But ah! I fear thy little Fancy roves;
On little Females, and on little Loves;
Thy Pigmy Children, and thy tiny Spouse,
The Baby Play-things that adorn thy House,
Doors, Windows, Chimnies, and the spacious Rooms,
Equal in Size to Cells of Honeycombs.
Hast thou for these now ventur'd from the Shore,
Thy Bark a Bean-shell, and a straw thy Oar?

28 at marbles

Or in thy Box, now bounding on the Main?
Shall I ne'er bear thy self and House again?
And shall I set thee on my Hand no more,
To see thee leap the Lines, and traverse o'er
My spacious Palm? Of Stature scarce a Span,
Mimick the Actions of a real Man?
No more behold thee turn my Watch's Key,
As Seamen at a Capstern Anchors weigh?
How wert thou wont to walk with cautious Tread,
A Dish of Tea like Milk-Pail on thy Head?
How chase the Mite that bore thy Cheese away,
And keep the rolling Maggot at a Bay?"

She said, but broken Accents stopt her Voice,
Soft as the Speaking Trumpet's mellow Noise:
She sobb'd a Storm, and wip'd her flowing Eyes,
Which seem'd like two broad Suns in misty Skies:
O squander not thy Grief, those Tears command
To weep upon our Cod in *Newfound-land*:
The plenteous Pickle shall preserve the Fish,
And *Europe* taste thy Sorrows in a Dish.

Walt Whitman 1819–1892

WHEN LILACS LAST IN THE DOORYARD BLOOM'D

1

When lilacs last in the dooryard bloom'd,
And the great star early droop'd in the western sky in the night,
I mourn'd, and yet shall mourn with ever-returning spring.

Ever-returning spring, trinity sure to me you bring,
Lilac blooming perennial and drooping star in the west,
And thought of him I love.

2

O powerful western fallen star!
O shades of night—O moody, tearful night!
O great star disappear'd—O the black murk that hides the star!
O cruel hands that hold me powerless—O helpless soul of me!
O harsh surrounding cloud that will not free my soul.

3

In the dooryard fronting an old farm-house near the white-wash'd palings,
Stands the lilac-bush tall-growing with heart-shaped leaves of rich green,
With many a pointed blossom rising delicate, with the perfume strong I love,

With every leaf a miracle—and from this bush in the dooryard,
With delicate-color'd blossoms and heart-shaped leaves of rich green,
A sprig with its flower I break.

From *Leaves of Grass,* eighth edition 1881.

4

In the swamp in secluded recesses,
A shy and hidden bird is warbling a song.

Solitary the thrush,
The hermit withdrawn to himself, avoiding the settlements,
Sings by himself a song.

Song of the bleeding throat,
Death's outlet song of life, (for well dear brother I know,
If thou wast not granted to sing thou would'st surely die.)

5

Over the breast of the spring, the land, amid cities,
Amid lanes and through old woods, where lately the violets peep'd from the ground, spotting the gray débris,
Amid the grass in the fields each side of the lanes, passing the endless grass,
Passing the yellow-spear'd wheat, every grain from its shroud in the dark-brown fields uprisen,
Passing the apple-tree blows of white and pink in the orchards,
Carrying a corpse to where it shall rest in the grave,
Night and day journeys a coffin.

6

Coffin that passes through lanes and streets,
Through day and night with the great cloud darkening the land,
With the pomp of the inloop'd flags with the cities draped in black,
With the show of the States themselves as of crape-veil'd women standing,
With processions long and winding and the flambeaus of the night,
With the countless torches lit, with the silent sea of faces and the unbared heads,
With the waiting depot, the arriving coffin, and the sombre faces,

With dirges through the night, with the thousand voices rising
strong and solemn,
With all the mournful voices of the dirges pour'd around the
coffin,
The dim-lit churches and the shuddering organs—where amid
these you journey,

With the tolling tolling bells' perpetual clang,
Here, coffin that slowly passes,
I give you my sprig of lilac.

7

(Nor for you, for one alone,
Blossoms and branches green to coffins all I bring,
For fresh as the morning, thus would I chant a song for you O
sane and sacred death.

All over bouquets of roses,
O death, I cover you over with roses and early lilies,
But mostly and now the lilac that blooms the first,
Copious I break, I break the sprigs from the bushes,
With loaded arms I come, pouring for you,
For you and the coffins all of you O death.)

8

O western orb sailing the heaven,
Now I know what you must have meant as a month since I
walk'd,
As I walk'd in silence the transparent shadowy night,
As I saw you had something to tell as you bent to me night
after night,
As you droop'd from the sky low down as if to my side, (while
the other stars all look'd on,)
As we wander'd together the solemn night, (for something
I know not what kept me from sleep,)
As the night advanced, and I saw on the rim of the west how
full you were of woe,
As I stood on the rising ground in the breeze in the cool trans-
parent night,

As I watch'd where you pass'd and was lost in the netherward
black of the night,
As my soul in its trouble dissatisfied sank, as where you sad orb,
Concluded, dropt in the night, and was gone.

9

Sing on there in the swamp,
O singer bashful and tender, I hear your notes, I hear your call,
I hear, I come presently, I understand you,
But a moment I linger, for the lustrous star has detain'd me,
The star my departing comrade holds and detains me.

10

O how shall I warble myself for the dead one there I loved?
And how shall I deck my song for the large sweet soul that has
gone?
And what shall my perfume be for the grave of him I love?

Sea-winds blown from east and west,
Blown from the Eastern sea and blown from the Western sea,
till there on the prairies meeting,
These and with these and the breath of my chant,
I'll perfume the grave of him I love.

11

O what shall I hang on the chamber walls?
And what shall the pictures be that I hang on the walls,
To adorn the burial-house of him I love?

Pictures of growing spring and farms and homes,
With the Fourth-month eve at sundown, and the gray smoke
lucid and bright,
With floods of the yellow gold of the gorgeous, indolent, sinking
sun, burning, expanding the air,
With the fresh sweet herbage under foot, and the pale green
leaves of the trees prolific,
In the distance the flowing glaze, the breast of the river, with
a wind-dapple here and there,

With ranging hills on the banks, with many a line against the sky, and shadows,
And the city at hand with dwellings so dense, and stacks of chimneys,
And all the scenes of life and the workshops, and the workmen homeward returning.

12

Lo, body and soul—this land,
My own Manhattan with spires, and the sparkling and hurrying tides, and the ships,
The varied and ample land, the South and the North in the light, Ohio's shores and flashing Missouri,
And ever the far-spreading prairies cover'd with grass and corn.

Lo, the most excellent sun so calm and haughty,
The violet and purple morn with just-felt breezes,
The gentle soft-born measureless light,
The miracle spreading bathing all, the fulfill'd noon,
The coming eve delicious, the welcome night and the stars,
Over my cities shining all, enveloping man and land.

13

Sing on, sing on you gray-brown bird,
Sing from the swamps, the recesses, pour your chant from the bushes,
Limitless out of the dusk, out of the cedars and pines.

Sing on dearest brother, warble your reedy song,
Loud human song, with voice of uttermost woe.

O liquid and free and tender!
O wild and loose to my soul—wondrous singer!
You only I hear—yet the star holds me, (but will soon depart,)
Yet the lilac with mastering odor holds me.

14

Now while I sat in the day and look'd forth,
In the close of the day with its light and the fields of spring, and the farmers preparing their crops,
In the large unconscious scenery of my land with its lakes and forests,
In the heavenly aerial beauty, (after the perturb'd winds and the storms,)
Under the arching heavens of the afternoon swift passing, and the voices of children and women,
The many-moving sea-tides, and I saw the ships how they sail'd,
And the summer approaching with richness, and the fields all busy with labor,
And the infinite separate houses, how they all went on, each with its meals and minutia of daily usages,
And the streets how their throbbings throbb'd, and the cities pent—lo, then and there,
Falling upon them all and among them all, enveloping me with the rest,
Appear'd the cloud, appear'd the long black trail,
And I knew death, its thought, and the sacred knowledge of death.

Then with the knowledge of death as walking one side of me,
And the thought of death close-walking the other side of me,
And I in the middle as with companions, and as holding the hands of companions,
I fled forth to the hiding receiving night that talks not,
Down to the shores of the water, the path by the swamp in the dimness,
To the solemn shadowy cedars and ghostly pines so still.

And the singer so shy to the rest receiv'd me,
The gray-brown bird I know receiv'd us comrades three,
And he sang the carol of death, and a verse for him I love.

From deep secluded recesses,
From the fragrant cedars and the ghostly pines so still,
Came the carol of the bird.

And the charm of the carol rapt me,
As I held as if by their hands my comrades in the night,
And the voice of my spirit tallied the song of the bird.

Come lovely and soothing death,
Undulate round the world, serenely arriving, arriving,
In the day, in the night, to all, to each,
Sooner or later delicate death.

Prais'd be the fathomless universe,
For life and joy, and for objects and knowledge curious,
And for love, sweet love—but praise! praise! praise!
For the sure-enwinding arms of cool-enfolding death.

Dark mother always gliding near with soft feet,
Have none chanted for thee a chant of fullest welcome?
Then I chant it for thee, I glorify thee above all,
I bring thee a song that when thou must indeed come, come unfalteringly.

Approach strong deliveress,
When it is so, when thou hast taken them I joyously sing the dead,
Lost in the loving floating ocean of thee,
Laved in the flood of thy bliss O death.

From me to thee glad serenades,
Dances for thee I propose saluting thee, adornments and feastings for thee,
And the sights of the open landscape and the high-spread sky are fitting,
And life and the fields, and the huge and thoughtful night.

The night in silence under many a star,
The ocean shore and the husky whispering wave whose voice I know,
And the soul turning to thee O vast and well-veil'd death,
And the body gratefully nestling close to thee.

Over the tree-tops I float thee a song,
Over the rising and sinking waves, over the myriad fields and the prairies wide,
Over the dense-pack'd cities all and the teeming wharves and ways,
I float this carol with joy, with joy to thee O death.

15

To the tally of my soul,
Loud and strong kept up the gray-brown bird,
With pure deliberate notes spreading filling the night.

Loud in the pines and cedars dim,
Clear in the freshness moist and the swamp-perfume,
And I with my comrades there in the night.

While my sight that was bound in my eyes unclosed,
As to long panoramas of visions.

And I saw askant the armies,
I saw as in noiseless dreams hundreds of battle-flags,
Borne through the smoke of the battles and pierc'd with missiles I saw them,
And carried hither and yon through the smoke, and torn and bloody,
And at last but a few shreds left on the staffs, (and all in silence,)
And the staffs all splinter'd and broken.

I saw battle-corpses, myriads of them,
And the white skeletons of young men, I saw them,
I saw the debris and debris of all the slain soldiers of the war,
But I saw they were not as was thought,

They themselves were fully at rest, they suffer'd not,
The living remain'd and suffer'd, the mother suffer'd,
And the wife and the child and the musing comrade suffer'd,
And the armies that remain'd suffer'd.

16

Passing the visions, passing the night,
Passing, unloosing the hold of my comrades' hands,
Passing the song of the hermit bird and the tallying song of my soul,
Victorious song, death's outlet song, yet varying ever-altering song,
As low and wailing, yet clear the notes, rising and falling, flooding the night,
Sadly sinking and fainting, as warning and warning, and yet again bursting with joy,
Covering the earth and filling the spread of the heaven,
As that powerful psalm in the night I heard from recesses,
Passing, I leave thee lilac with heart-shaped leaves,
I leave thee there in the door-yard, blooming, returning with spring.

I cease from my song for thee,
From my gaze on thee in the west, fronting the west, communing with thee,
O comrade lustrous with silver face in the night.

Yet each to keep and all, retrievements out of the night,
The song, the wondróus chant of the gray-brown bird,
And the tallying chant, the echo arous'd in my soul,
With the lustrous and drooping star with the countenance full of woe,
With the holders holding my hand nearing the call of the bird,
Comrades mine and I in the midst, and their memory ever to keep, for the dead I loved so well,
For the sweetest, wisest soul of all my days and lands—and this for his dear sake,
Lilac and star and bird twined with the chant of my soul,
There in the fragrant pines and the cedars dusk and dim.

Matthew Arnold 1822–1888

THYRSIS

A MONODY, *to commemorate the author's friend,* ARTHUR HUGH CLOUGH, *who died at Florence, 1861.*

How changed is here each spot man makes or fills!
In the two Hinkseys nothing keeps the same;
The village street its haunted mansion lacks,
And from the sign is gone Sibylla's name,
And from the roofs the twisted chimney-stacks—
Are ye too changed, ye hills?
See, 'tis no foot of unfamiliar men
To-night from Oxford up your pathway strays!
Here came I often, often, in old days—
Thyrsis and I; we still had Thyrsis then.

Runs it not here, the track by Childsworth Farm,
Past the high wood, to where the elm-tree crowns
The hill behind whose ridge the sunset flames?
The signal-elm, that looks on Ilsley Downs,
The Vale, the three lone weirs, the youthful Thames?—
This winter-eve is warm,
Humid the air! leafless, yet soft as spring,
The tender purple spray on copse and briers!
And that sweet city with her dreaming spires,
She needs not June for beauty's heightening,

Lovely all times she lies, lovely to-night!—
Only, methinks, some loss of habit's power
Befalls me wandering through this upland dim
Once pass'd I blindfold here, at any hour;
Now seldom come I, since I came with him.

From *Macmillan's Magazine* 1866.

2 *Hinkseys:* two villages near Oxford, where Arnold and Clough were students together. 4 *Sibylla:* Sibylla Kerr, an innkeeper at Oxford when Arnold was a student.

That single elm-tree bright
Against the west—I miss it! is it gone?
We prized it dearly; while it stood, we said,
Our friend, the Gipsy-Scholar, was not dead;
While the tree lived, he in these fields lived on.

Too rare, too rare, grow now my visits here,
But once I knew each field, each flower, each stick;
And with the country-folk acquaintance made
By barn in threshing-time, by new-built rick.
Here, too, our shepherd-pipes we first assay'd.
Ah me! this many a year
My pipe is lost, my shepherd's-holiday!
Needs must I lose them, needs with heavy heart
Into the world and wave of men depart;
But Thyrsis of his own will went away.

It irk'd him to be here, he could not rest.
He loved each simple joy the country yields,
He loved his mates; but yet he could not keep,
For that a shadow lour'd on the fields,
Here with the shepherds and the silly sheep.
Some life of men unblest
He knew, which made him droop, and fill'd his head.

29 *Gipsy-Scholar:* To his poem *The Scholar-Gipsy,* Arnold appended the following note: " 'There was very lately a lad in the University of Oxford, who was by his poverty forced to leave his studies there; and at last to join himself to a company of vagabond gypsies. Among these extravagant people . . . he quickly got so much of their love and esteem as that they discovered to him their mystery. After he had been a pretty while well exercised in the trade, there chanced to ride by a couple of scholars, who had formerly been of his acquaintance . . . . He recognized his old friends and told them that the people he went with were not such impostors as they were taken for, but that they had a traditional kind of learning among them, and could do wonders by the power of imagination, their fancy binding that of others: that himself had learned much of their art, and when he had compassed the whole secret, he intended, he said, to leave their company, and give the world an account of what he had learned.'—Glanvil's *Vanity of Dogmatizing,* 1661" 45 innocent

He went; his piping took a troubled sound
Of storms that rage outside our happy ground,
He could not wait their passing, he is dead.

So, some tempestuous morn in early June,
When the year's primal burst of bloom is o'er,
Before the roses and the longest day—
When garden-walks and all the grassy floor
With blossoms red and white of fallen May
And chestnut-flowers are strewn—
So have I heard the cuckoo's parting cry,
From the wet field, through the vext garden-trees,
Come with the volleying rain and tossing breeze:
The bloom is gone, and with the bloom go I!

Too quick despairer, wherefore wilt thou go?
Soon will the high Midsummer pomps come on,
Soon will the musk carnations break and swell,
Soon shall we have gold-dusted snapdragon,
Sweet-William with his homely cottage-smell,
And stocks in fragrant blow;
Roses that down the alleys shine afar,
And open, jasmine-muffled lattices,
And groups under the dreaming garden-trees,
And the full moon, and the white evening-star.

He hearkens not! light comer, he is flown!
What matters it? next year he will return,
And we shall have him in the sweet spring-days,
With whitening hedges, and uncrumpling fern,
And blue-bells trembling by the forest-ways,
And scent of hay new-mown.
But Thyrsis never more we swains shall see;
See him come back, and cut a smoother reed,
And blow a strain the world at last shall heed—
For Time, not Corydon, hath conquer'd thee!

Alack, for Corydon no rival now!—
But when Sicilian shepherds lost a mate,

Some good survivor with his flute would go,
Piping a ditty sad for Bion's fate;
And cross the unpermitted ferry's flow
And relax Pluto's brow,
And make leap up with joy the beauteous head
Of Proserpine, among whose crownèd hair
Are flowers first open'd on Sicilian air,
And flute his friend, like Orpheus, from the dead.

O easy access to the hearer's grace
When Dorian shepherds sang to Proserpine!
For she herself had trod Sicilian fields,
She knew the Dorian water's gush divine,
She knew each lily white which Enna yields,
Each rose with blushing face;
She loved the Dorian pipe, the Dorian strain.
But ah, of our poor Thames she never heard!
Her foot the Cumner cowslips never stirr'd;
And we should tease her with our plaint in vain!

Well! wind-dispersed and vain the words will be,
Yet, Thyrsis, let me give my grief its hour
In the old haunt, and find our tree-topp'd hill!
Who, if not I, for questing here hath power?
I know the wood which hides the daffodil,
I know the Fyfield tree,
I know what white, what purple fritillaries
The grassy harvest of the river-fields,
Above by Ensham, down by Sandford, yields,
And what sedged brooks are Thames's tributaries;

I know these slopes; who knows them if not I?—
But many a dingle on the loved hill-side,
With thorns once studded, old, white-blossom'd trees,

85 *ferry:* the boat which carried the souls of the dead across the river Styx into Hades. 95 *Enna:* place in Sicily near which Proserpine was gathering flowers when Pluto came and snatched her away to the underworld to be his queen. 107 flowers

Where thick the cowslips grew, and far descried
High tower'd the spikes of purple orchises,
Hath since our day put by
The coronals of that forgotten time;
Down each green bank hath gone the plough-boy's team,
And only in the hidden brookside gleam
Primroses, orphans of the flowery prime.

Where is the girl, who by the boatman's door,
Above the locks, above the boating throng,
Unmoor'd our skiff when through the Wytham flats,
Red loosestrife and blond meadow-sweet among
And darting swallows and light water-gnats,
We track'd the shy Thames shore?
Where are the mowers, who, as the tiny swell
Of our boat passing heaved the river-grass,
Stood with suspended scythe to see us pass?—
They all are gone, and thou art gone as well!

Yes, thou art gone! and round me too the night
In ever-nearing circle weaves her shade.
I see her veil draw soft across the day,
I feel her slowly chilling breath invade
The cheek grown thin, the brown hair sprent with grey;
I feel her finger light
Laid pausefully upon life's headlong train;—
The foot less prompt to meet the morning dew,
The heart less bounding at emotion new,
And hope, once crush'd, less quick to spring again.

And long the way appears, which seem'd so short
To the less practised eye of sanguine youth;
And high the mountain-tops, in cloudy air,
The mountain-tops where is the throne of Truth,
Tops in life's morning-sun so bright and bare!
Unbreachable the fort
Of the long-batter'd world uplifts its wall;

135 sprinkled

And strange and vain the earthly turmoil grows,
And near and real the charm of thy repose,
And night as welcome as a friend would fall.

But hush! the upland hath a sudden loss
Of quiet!—Look, adown the dusk hill-side,
A troop of Oxford hunters going home,
As in old days, jovial and talking, ride!
From hunting with the Berkshire hounds they come.
Quick! let me fly, and cross
Into yon farther field!—'Tis done; and see,
Back'd by the sunset, which doth glorify
The orange and pale violet evening-sky,
Bare on its lonely ridge, the Tree! the Tree!

I take the omen! Eve lets down her veil,
The white fog creeps from bush to bush about,
The west unflushes, the high stars grow bright,
And in the scatter'd farms the lights come out.
I cannot reach the signal-tree to-night,
Yet, happy omen, hail!
Hear it from thy broad lucent Arno-vale
(For there thine earth-forgetting eyelids keep
The morningless and unawakening sleep
Under the flowery oleanders pale),

Hear it, O Thyrsis, still our tree is there!—
Ah, vain! These English fields, this upland dim,
These brambles pale with mist engarlanded,
That lone, sky-pointing tree, are not for him;
To a boon southern country he is fled,
And now in happier air,
Wandering with the great Mother's train divine
(And purer or more subtle soul than thee,
I trow, the mighty Mother doth not see)
Within a folding of the Apennine,

167 *Arno-vale:* The river Arno flows through Florence, where Clough is buried in the Protestant Cemetery.

Thou hearest the immortal chants of old!—
Putting his sickle to the perilous grain
In the hot cornfield of the Phrygian king,
For thee the Lityerses-song again
Young Daphnis with his silver voice doth sing;
Sings his Sicilian fold,
His sheep, his hapless love, his blinded eyes—
And how a call celestial round him rang,
And heavenward from the fountain-brink he sprang,
And all the marvel of the golden skies.

There thou art gone, and me thou leavest here
Sole in these fields! yet will I not despair.
Despair I will not, while I yet descry
'Neath the mild canopy of English air
That lonely tree against the western sky.
Still, still these slopes, 'tis clear,
Our Gipsy-Scholar haunts, outliving thee!
Fields where soft sheep from cages pull the hay,
Woods with anemonies in flower till May,
Know him a wanderer still; then why not me?

A fugitive and gracious light he seeks,
Shy to illumine; and I seek it too.
This does not come with houses or with gold,
With place, with honour, and a flattering crew;
'Tis not in the world's market bought and sold—
But the smooth-slipping weeks

185 *Daphnis:* Arnold makes the following note: "Daphnis, the ideal Sicilian shepherd of Greek pastoral poetry, was said to have followed into Phrygia his mistress Piplea, who had been carried off by robbers, and to have found her in the power of the king of Phrygia, Lityerses. Lityerses used to make strangers try a contest with him in reaping corn, and to put them to death if he overcame them. Hercules arrived in time to save Daphnis, took upon himself the reaping-contest with Lityerses, overcame him, and slew him. The Lityerses-song connected with this tradition was . . . one of the early plaintive strains of Greek popular poetry, and used to be sung by corn-reapers. . . ."

Drop by, and leave its seeker still untired;
Out of the heed of mortals he is gone,
He wends unfollow'd, he must house alone;
Yet on he fares, by his own heart inspired.

Thou too, O Thyrsis, on like quest wast bound;
Thou wanderedst with me for a little hour!
Men gave thee nothing; but this happy quest,
If men esteem'd thee feeble, gave thee power,
If men procured thee trouble, gave thee rest.
And this rude Cumner ground,
Its fir-topped Hurst, its farms, its quiet fields,
Here cam'st thou in thy jocund youthful time,
Here was thine height of strength, thy golden prime!
And still the haunt beloved a virtue yields.

What though the music of thy rustic flute
Kept not for long its happy, country tone;
Lost it too soon, and learnt a stormy note
Of men contention-tost, of men who groan,
Which task'd thy pipe too sore, and tired thy throat—
It fail'd, and thou wast mute!
Yet hadst thou alway visions of our light,
And long with men of care thou couldst not stay,
And soon thy foot resumed its wandering way,
Left human haunt, and on alone till night.

Too rare, too rare, grow now my visits here!
'Mid city-noise, not, as with thee of yore,
Thyrsis! in reach of sheep-bells is my home.
—Then through the great town's harsh, heart-wearying roar,
Let in thy voice a whisper often come,
To chase fatigue and fear:
Why faintest thou? I wander'd till I died.
Roam on! The light we sought is shining still.
Dost thou ask proof? Our tree yet crowns the hill,
Our Scholar travels yet the loved hill-side.

William Carlos Williams 1883–1963

AN ELEGY FOR D. H. LAWRENCE

Green points on the shrub
and poor Lawrence dead.
The night damp and misty
and Lawrence no more in the world
to answer April's promise
with a fury of labor
against waste, waste and life's
coldness.

Once he received a letter—
he never answered it—
praising him: so English
he had thereby raised himself
to an unenglish greatness.
Dead now and it grows clearer
what bitterness drove him.

This is the time.
The serpent in the grotto
water dripping from the stone
into a pool.
Mediterranean evenings. Ashes
of Cretan fires. And to the north
forsythia hung with
yellow bells in the cold.

Poor Lawrence
worn with a fury of sad labor
to create summer from
spring's decay. English
women. Men driven not to love
but to the ends of the earth.

From *Selected Poems* 1949.

The serpent turning his
stone-like head,
the fixed agate eyes turn also.

And unopened jonquils
hang their folded heads. No
summer. But for Lawrence
full praise in this
half cold half season—
before trees are in leaf and
tufted grass stars
unevenly the bare ground.

Slowly the serpent leans
to drink by the tinkling water
the forked tongue alert.
Then fold after fold,
glassy strength, passing
a given point,
as by desire drawn
forward bodily, he glides
smoothly in.

To stand by the sea or walk
again along a river's bank and talk
with a companion, to halt
watching where the edge of water
meets and lies upon
the unmoving shore—
Flood waters rise, and will rise,
rip the quiet valley
trap the gypsy and the girl.
She clings drowning to
a bush in flower.

Remember, now, Lawrence dead.
Blue squills in bloom—to
the scorched aridity of
the Mexican plateau. Or baked

public squares in the cities of
Mediterranean islands
where one waits for busses and
boats come slowly along the water
arriving.

But the sweep of spring over
temperate lands, meadows and woods
where the young walk and talk
incompletely,
straining to no summer,
hearing the frogs, speaking of
birds and insects—

Febrile spring moves not to heat
but always more slowly,
burdened by a weight of leaves.
Nothing now
to burst the bounds—
remains confined by them. Heat,
heat! Unknown. Poor Lawrence,
dead and only the drowned
fallen dancing from the deck
of a pleasure boat
unfading desire.

Rabbits, imaginings, the
drama, literature, satire.
The serpent cannot move
his stony eyes, scarcely sees
but touching the air
with his forked tongue surmises
and his body which dipped
into the cold water
is gone.

Violently the satiric sun
that leads April not to
the panting dance but to stillness

in, into the brain, dips
and is gone also,
And sisters return
through the dusk
to the measured rancor
of their unbending elders.

Greep, greep, greep the cricket
chants where the snake
with agate eyes leaned to the water.
Sorrow to the young
that Lawrence has passed
unwanted from England.
And in the gardens forsythia
and in the woods
now the crinkled spice-bush
in flower.

W. H. Auden 1907—

IN MEMORY OF W. B. YEATS

(died January 1939)

I

He disappeared in the dead of winter:
The brooks were frozen, the airports almost deserted,
And snow disfigured the public statues;
The mercury sank in the mouth of the dying day.
What instruments we have agree
The day of his death was a dark cold day.

Far from his illness
The wolves ran on through the evergreen forests,
The peasant river was untempted by the fashionable quays;
By mourning tongues
The death of the poet was kept from his poems.

But for him it was his last afternoon as himself,
An afternoon of nurses and rumours;
The provinces of his body revolted,
The squares of his mind were empty,
Silence invaded the suburbs,
The current of his feeling failed; he became his admirers.

Now he is scattered among a hundred cities
And wholly given over to unfamiliar affections;
To find his happiness in another kind of wood
And be punished under a foreign code of conscience.
The words of a dead man
Are modified in the guts of the living.

But in the importance and noise of to-morrow
When the brokers are roaring like beasts on the floor of the
Bourse,

From *Another Time* 1940.
25 *Bourse:* the Parisian Stock Exchange.

And the poor have the sufferings to which they are fairly
accustomed,
And each in the cell of himself is almost convinced of his
freedom,
A few thousand will think of this day
As one thinks of a day when one did something slightly
unusual.
What instruments we have agree
The day of his death was a dark cold day.

II

You were silly like us; your gift survived it all;
The parish of rich women, physical decay,
Yourself: mad Ireland hurt you into poetry.
Now Ireland has her madness and her weather still,
For poetry makes nothing happen: it survives
In the valley of its saying where executives
Would never want to tamper; it flows south
From ranches of isolation and the busy griefs,
Raw towns that we believe and die in; it survives,
A way of happening, a mouth.

III

Earth, receive an honoured guest:
William Yeats is laid to rest.
Let the Irish vessel lie
Emptied of its poetry.

In the nightmare of the dark
All the dogs of Europe bark,
And the living nations wait,
Each sequestered in its hate;

Intellectual disgrace
Stares from every human face,
And the seas of pity lie
Locked and frozen in each eye.

Follow, poet, follow right
To the bottom of the night,
With your unconstraining voice
Still persuade us to rejoice;

With the farming of a verse
Make a vineyard of the curse,
Sing of human unsuccess
In a rapture of distress;

In the deserts of the heart
Let the healing fountain start,
In the prison of his days
Teach the free man how to praise.

W. R. Rodgers 1909–1969

A LAST WORD

(*For Louis MacNeice, died September 1963*)

Only a green hill
And a man with a spade
Opening the old accounts-book of earth
And writing *paid*.

Under the highly improbable sky,
Needlessly blue,
He piles the cold clay. It is all,
You might say, so dead true

To life, the meek clay
Turning the other cheek
To the clap of the spade
Waits to inherit the earth of the man
Whom it has made.

But he made it
That made him; he put
The word on it that gave
Life and limb.
Now to speak of an end
Is to begin.

From *Essex Roundabout* 1963.

The Ballad

When Coleridge and Wordsworth set about to reject a poetic tradition they regarded as effete and to write a new kind of poetry using "a selection of the real language of men in a state of vivid sensation," they were both aware of another tradition, native, ancient, and still strong, among the illiterate people of England and Scotland: that of the popular ballad. Whether popular by origin or by adaptation, these ballads had been scoured down by oral transmission to the stylistic wonders they are: the rapid, elliptic narrative; the trenchant speech; the glimpses of nature and of natural magic that are relics, perhaps, of ancient religion preserved because of the power of their appeal to the imagination; the heroic strong unsentimental passions.

Sidney had confessed his barbarousness in responding to the trumpet-like heart-stirring power of "the old song of Percy and Douglas," but had found the style "rude," "evil appareled in the dust and cobwebs of that uncivil age"; Addison, not without apologies, had compared its narrative technique to Homer's; but about the time Coleridge was born the great age of ballad collecting had begun, as the spread of literacy caused a flowering (as we think now) and (as was always thought) the rapid and irreversible decline of the oral tradition. Meanwhile there had been, among the ignorant literate, a parallel and mingling tradition of ballads which we distinguish by another name, the broadside ballads, like the ones Falstaff threatened to have made about Prince Hal and sung to "filthy tunes," a kind of poetry for the most part justly scorned. So that in 1798 the popular ballads were liked by the best and the least educated while the great middle multitude looked down upon them from their own smug well-trodden heights. *Lyrical Ballads* was a book whose publication was perfectly timed.

It is one thing to appreciate popular art, even to make successful copies or forgeries (the last stanza of Scott's "Twa Corbies" seems to be one, a good one though obvious now); it's something else to make the true imitation that goes to the quick, is neither servile nor patronizing with its models, speaks with its own voice, and so remains single. The Chinese, whose canon of popular poetry the *Shih Ching* happens to have just 305 poems, the same number as Child's *English and Scottish Popular Ballads*, have been doing it for twenty-five centuries. In Spain too the popular and ancient *romance* style has been used all along by poets whose learning didn't make them stupid. The accomplishment is rarer in English. To appreciate the *Rime of the Ancient Mariner* study its defects.

For a while after they had become museum pieces in England, the ballads lived on among illiterate folk in the Appalachians,—"where the pure products of America go crazy." Some of the best tunes were collected there. *The Black Jack Gipsy* became *My Gypsum Davy, Lord Randall Billy Boy, The Three Ravens Billy McGee McGaw*. Imaginations which have no peasant traditions to give them character "flutter and flaunt sheer rags." But with what life, still today. I was teaching the course that inspired this book so long ago that I used to compare Coleridge with Robert Zimmerman, a college graduate from Minnesota who liked the songs Woody Guthrie wrote going down the road feeling bad. Sir Walter Scott with W. C. Handy for their adaptations; Captain Beefheart. The beat goes on. I have limited this chapter to the Child ballads and their literary heirs somewhat regretfully, with only so much space, hoping to do the one thing well. Other popular traditions that are flourishing among us now and making their way into "sophisticated" literature are mainly oral and electronic and better represented by records than by a book anyway. As you already know yourself.

Anonymous Spanish Romances

COUNT ARNALDOS

Who ever will find such fortune
On the waters of the sea
As befell Count Arnoldos
On St. John's Day morning?
As he was going hunting
With his hawk on his hand
He saw a galley
Making in for the land.
Its sails were of silk,
Of fine silk its rigging,
The sailor at the helm
Came singing a song
At which the sea grew smooth
And the winds became gentle,
And the fish that go in the deep
Came swimming to the top,
And the birds that go flying
Came to perch on the mast.
Then spoke Count Arnaldos,
You will hear what he said:
  "I beg you in God's name, sailor,
Repeat that song to me."
The sailor made him answer,
This was his reply:
  "I repeat that song to no one
But to him who comes with me."

From *Spanish Ballads* (five poems), translated by W. S. Merwin 1927—. *Romance:* This word is Spanish. It denotes, principally, verse narrative in assonant couplets.

LANZAROTE

The King had three little sons,
Three little sons and no more,
And out of anger at them
He cursed them every one.
One turned into a stag,
Into a dog, another,
And the other turned into a Moor
And crossed the ocean waters.
  Lanzarote was walking
At leisure among the ladies;
One of them cried out to him:
  "Stay, knight, oh stay!
If such might be my fortune
My fate would be fulfilled
If I were to be married to you,
If it pleased you to wed me,
And if, for my bride-gift, you gave me
That stag with the white foot."
  "With all my heart, my lady,
I would give it to you
If I knew the country
Where that stag was reared."
  Now Lanzarote has taken horse,
Now he has mounted, and now he departs.
With him, ranging before him,
Are his two hounds on the leash.
He has come to a hermitage
Where a hermit is living:
  "God watch over you, good man."
  "And a good welcome to you;
To judge from the hounds you have
    with you
It seems that you are a hunter."
  "You that live in sanctity,
Hermit, tell me:

Lanzarote: Lancelot.

That stag with the white feet,
Where does he stay?"
  "My son, do not go from this place
Before it is day;
I will tell you what I have seen
And all that is known to me.
This last night he went past here
Two hours before dawn;
Seven lions were with him
And a mother lioness.
Seven counts are lying dead,
And of knights a great number.
God preserve you forever, my son,
Wherever you go,
For whoever sent you to this place
Hoped never again to see you.
Ah, Lady Quintañones,
May a bad fire burn you,
Since so many excellent knights
Have lost their lives for you!"

THE MOORESS MORAYMA

I was the Mooress Morayma,
A Moorish girl, and pretty;
A Christian came to my door,
Alas for me, to deceive me.
In Moorish speech he addressed me,
And he knew it well:
"Open the door to me, Moorish girl,
Allah keep you from evil."
"Open to you, oh wretch that I am,
Not knowing who you may be?"
"I am the Moor Mazote,
Your own mother's brother;
I have killed a Christian,
The constable is close behind me;
Unless you let me in, my life,
You will see them kill me here."
Alas for me, when I heard this
I rose up from my bed,
I threw a little cloak around me,
Not finding my silk shift;
I went over to the door
And I opened it all the way.

THE MOORISH KING WHO LOST GRANADA

The Moorish King was riding
Through the city of Granada,
From the Gate of Elvira
To the Gate of Vivarrambla,
Alas for my Alhama!

Letters had come to him to say
That Alhama had been taken;
He threw the letters into the fire
And killed the messenger.
Alas for my Alhama!
He got down from the mule he was riding
And he mounted a horse;
Up through the Zacatín
He rode to the Alhambra.
Alas for my Alhama!
When he came into the Alhambra
He commanded them
To blow upon their trumpets,
Their long horns of silver.
Alas for my Alhama!
And to beat upon the war drums
A quick call-to-arms
So that his Moors should hear it
In Vega and Granada.
Alas for my Alhama!
All the Moors who heard the sound
Which summons to bloody Mars
One by one and two by two
Formed up in a great array.
Alas for my Alhama!
Then spoke a venerable Moor,
He spoke in this manner:
"King, why have you sent for us?
What is this summons for?"
Alas for my Alhama!
"You must be acquainted, my friends,
With a new calamity:
Christians of great bravery
Have taken from us Alhama."
Alas for my Alhama!

There spoke an elder
With a long beard and gray hair:
  "That's just as you deserve, good King,
Good King, that's what you deserve!
      Alas for my Alhama!
  "You killed the Abencerrajes,
The flower of Granada;
You laid hands on the renegades
From renowned Córdoba.
      Alas for my Alhama!
  "For what you have done, King, you deserve
The heaviest penalty:
You deserve to lose your life and kingdom
And here to lose Granada!"
      Alas for my Alhama!

DEATH AND THE LOVER

Last night I dreamed a dream,
A little dream, from my soul,
I dreamed about my love,
That I held her in my arms;
I saw a white lady enter,
White, whiter than the cold snow.
  "Where did you come in, love?
How did you come in, my life?
The doors are closed, the windows,
The shutters."
  "I am not love, young lover,
But Death, whom God has sent you."
  "Ah Death, severe though you are,
One day of life grant me!"
  "One day it cannot be,
One hour only."
  In haste he put on his shoes,

In more haste his clothes,
And now he is in the street
Where his love lives.
  "Open the door to me, white love,
Open the door to me, girl!"
  "How should I open to you
When it is not time?
My father has not gone to the palace
Nor is my mother sleeping."
  "Open to me this night
Or never, beloved;
Death is close behind me,
I would have life beside you."
  "Go under the window
Where I stitched and embroidered,
I will throw you a silken cord
For you to climb;
If it does not reach to you
I will add my braided hair."
  The fine silk has broken
And on the instant Death was there:
  "Let us depart, young lover,
For the hour is over."

English and Scottish Popular Ballads

JUDAS [23]

Hit wes upon a Scere-thorsday that ure loverd aros;
Ful milde were the wordes he spec to Judas.

"Judas, thou most to Jurselem, oure mete for to bugge;
Thritti platen of selver thou bere up o'thi rugge.

"Thou comest fer i' the brode strete, fer i' the brode strete;
Summe of thine cunesmen ther thou meist i-mete."

Imette wid is soster, the swikele wimon:
"Judas, thou were worthe me stende the wid ston;

"Judas, thou were worthe me stende the wid ston,
For the false prophete that thou bilevest upon."

"Be stille, leve soster, thin herte the tobreke!
Wiste min loverd Crist, ful well he wolde be wreke."

"Judas, go thou on the roc, heie up-on the ston;
Lei thin heved i' my barm, slep thou the anon."

Sone so Judas of slepe was awake,
Thritti platen of selver from hym weren itake.

Judas [23]. The numbers of these ballads are those in *The English and Scottish Popular Ballads,* ed. Francis James Child, 1882-1898. Reference has also been made to *English and Scottish Popular Ballads,* ed. H. C. Sargent and G. L. Kittredge, 1932. Some of the music and text is drawn from B. H. Bronson, ed., *The Traditional Tunes of the Child Ballads,* 1962.

1 It was on a Maundy Thursday that Our Lord arose 2 spoke 3 meat (= food) . . . buy 4 pieces . . . back 6 kinsmen . . . meet; *cunesmen* emended from "tunesmen" by Kenneth Sisam 7 treacherous 8 Judas, you deserve to be stoned by me 10 on account of 11 Be still, dear sister, your heart will burst 12 If Christ my Lord knew . . . avenged 13 high 14 head . . . bosom

He drov hym selve bi the top, that al it lavede ablode;
The Jewes out of Jurselem awenden he were wode.

Foret hym com the riche Jew that heiste Pilatus:
"Wolte sulle thi loverd, that hette Jesus?"

"I nul sulle my loverd for nones cunnes eiste,
Bote hit be for the thritti platen that he me bi-taiste."

"Wolte sulle thi lord Crist for enes cunnes golde?"
"Nay, bote hit be for the platen that he habben wolde."

In him com ur lord gon, as is postles seten at mete:
"Wou sitte ye, postles, ant wi nule ye ete?

"Wou sitte ye, postles, ant wi nule ye ete?
Ic am iboust ant isold to day for our mete."

Up stod him Judas: "Lord, am I that . . . ?
I nas never o'the stude ther me the evel spec."

Up him stod Peter, ant spec wid al is miste,
Thau Pilatus him come wid ten hundred cnistes,

Thau Pilatus him come wid ten hundred cnistes,
"Yet ic wolde, loverd, for thi love fiste."

"Still thou be, Peter, wel I the i-cnowe;
Thou wolt fur-sake me thrien ar the coc him crowe."

17 He tore his hair until it was entirely bathed in blood. "The MS. has 'top' not 'cop' (head)."—Kenneth Sisam. 18 imagined . . . mad 19 forth to him . . . was called 20 sell . . . is called 21 I will not sell my Lord for any sort of goods 22 unless . . . he gave me 23 any 24 wants to have 25 In to them came Our Lord, as his apostles were sitting at their meal 26 Why are you sitting, apostles, and why will you not eat? 28 bought and sold 29 is it I . . . ? 30 I was never in the place where [they] spoke evil of you to me 31 might 32 though . . . knights 34 fight 36 Thou wilt forsake me three times before the cock crows

THE THREE RAVENS [26]

There were three ravens sat on a tree,
Downe a downe, hay down, hay downe
There were three ravens sat on a tree,
With a downe
There were three ravens sat on a tree,
They were as blacke as they might be.
With a downe derrie, derrie, derrie, downe, downe

The one of them said to his mate,
"Where shall we our breakefast take?"

"Downe in yonder greene field,
There lies a knight slain under his shield.

"His hounds they lie downe at his feete,
So well they can their master keepe.

"His haukes they flie so eagerly,
There's no fowle dare him come nie."

Downe there comes a fallow doe,
As great with yong as she might goe.

Collected by Thomas Ravenscroft, *Melismata,* 1611.
15 near

She lift up his bloudy hed,
And kist his wounds that were so red.

She got him upon her backe,
And carried him to earthen lake.

She buried him before the prime,
She was dead herselfe ere even-song time.

God send every gentleman,
Such haukes, such hounds, and such a leman.

21 pit 25 mistress

THE TWA CORBIES [26]

As I was walking all alane
I heard twa corbies making mane,
The tane unto the tither say,
"Whare sall we gang and dine the day?"

"In behint yon auld fail dyke
I wot there lies a new-slain knight;
Naebody kens that he lies there
But his hawk, his hound, and his lady fair.

"His hound is to the hunting gane,
His hawk to fetch the muirfowl hame,
His lady's tane anither mate,
Sae we may mak' our dinner sweet.

"Ye'll sit on his white hause-bane,
And I'll pyke out his bonnie blue e'en;
Wi' ae lock o' his gowden hair
We'll theek our nest when it grows bare.

Tune collected by George Eyre-Todd, *Ancient Scottish Ballads,* n.d. From "tradition." Text from Scott's *Minstrelsy,* with insignificant alteration.

2 moan 4 The tune calls for a refrain, which Sir Walter Scott, who collected the words, did not record. "Fal the lal the lal the lay, / Fal the lal the lal the lay" will do. 5 turf wall 7 knows 10 moorfowl 11 taken 13 neckbone 16 thatch

"Mony a ane for him mak's mane,
But nane shall ken whare he is gane;
O'er his white banes, when they are bare,
The wind sall blaw for evermair."

TAM LIN [39]

O I forbid you, maidens a'
That wear gowd on your hair,
To come or gae by Carterhaugh,
For young Tam Lin is there.

There's nane that gaes by Carterhaugh
But they leave him a wad;
Either their rings, or green mantles,
Or else their maidenhead.

Janet has belted her green kirtle,
A little aboon her knee,
And she has broded her yellow hair
A little aboon her bree;
And she's awa to Carterhaugh
As fast as she can hie.

When she came to Carterhaugh,
Tam-Lin was at the well,
And there she fand his steed standing
But away was himsel.

She had na pu'd a double rose
A rose but only twa,
Till up then started young Tam-Lin,
Says, Lady, thou's pu' nae mae.

Collected by James Johnson, *The Scots Musical Museum*, vol. V.
2 gold 6 forfeit 9 skirt 12 brow 14 hurry 22 thou shalt pull no more

Why pu's thou the rose, Janet,
And why breaks thou the wand!
Or why comes thou to Carterhaugh
Withoutten my command?

Carterhaugh it is my ain,
My daddie gave it me;
I'll come and gang by Carterhaugh
And ask nae leave at thee.

Janet has kilted her green kirtle,
A little aboon her knee,
And she has snooded her yellow hair,
A little aboon her bree,
And she is to her father's ha,
As fast as she can hie.

Four and twenty ladies fair,
Were playing at the ba,
And out then cam the fair Janet,
Ance the flower amang them a',

Four and twenty ladies fair,
Were playing at the chess,
And out then cam the fair Janet,
As green as onie glass.

Out then spak an auld grey knight,
Lay o'er the castle wa',
And says, Alas, fair Janet for thee,
But we'll be blamed a'.

Haud your tongue, ye auld fac'd knight,
Some ill death may 'e die,
Father my bairn on whom I will,
I'll father nane on thee.

30 from thee 33 tied with a ribbon 35 house 38 ball 40 once 46 leaning over 49 hold 51 child

Out then spak her father dear,
And he spak meek and mild,
And ever alas, sweet Janet, he says,
I think thou gaes wi' child.

If that I gae wi' child, father,
Mysel maun bear the blame;
There's ne'er a laird about your ha,
Shall get the bairn's name.

If my Love were an earthly knight,
As he's an elfin grey;
I wad na gie my ain true-love
For nae lord that ye hae.

The steed that my true-love rides on,
Is lighter than the wind;
Wi' siller he is shod before,
Wi' burning gowd behind.

Janet has kilted her green kirtle
A little aboon her knee;
And she has snooded her yellow hair
A little aboon her brie;
And she's awa to Carterhaugh
As fast as she can hie.

When she cam to Carterhaugh,
Tam-Lin was at the well;
And there she fand his steed standing,
But away was himsel.

She had na pu'd a double rose,
A rose but only twa,
Till up then started young Tam-Lin,
Says, Lady thou pu's nae mae.

58 must 67 silver

Why pu's thou the rose Janet,
    Amang the groves sae green,
And a' to kill the bonie babe
    That we gat us between.

O tell me, tell me, Tam-Lin she says,
    For's sake that died on tree,
If e'er ye was in holy chapel,
    Or Christendom did see.

Roxbrugh he was my grandfather,
    Took me with him to bide
And ance it fell upon a day
    That wae did me betide.

And ance it fell upon a day,
    A cauld day and a snell.
When we were frae the hunting come
    That frae my horse I fell.
The queen o' Fairies she caught me,
    In yon green hill to dwell.

And pleasant is the fairy-land;
    But, an eerie tale to tell!
Ay at the end of seven years
    We pay a tiend to hell.
I am sae fair and fu' o' flesh
    I'm fear'd it be mysel.

But the night is Halloween, lady,
    The morn is Hallowday;
Then win me, win me, an ye will,
    For weel I wat ye may.

Just at the mirk and midnight hour
    The fairy folk will ride;

94 woe   96 biting   103 always   104 tithe   110 well I know

And they that wad their truelove win,
At Milescross they maun bide.

But how shall I thee ken Tam-Lin,
Or how my true love know,
Amang sae mony unco knights,
The like I never saw?

O first let pass the black Lady,
And syne let pass the brown;
But quickly run to the milk white steed,
Pu ye his rider down.

For I'll ride on the milk-white steed,
And ay nearest the town.
Because I was an earthly knight
They gie me that renown.

My right hand will be glov'd lady,
My left hand will be bare.
Cockt up shall my bonnet be,
And kaim'd down shall my hair,
And thae's the takens I gie thee,
Nae doubt I will be there.

They'll turn me in your arms lady,
Into an esk and adder,
But hald me fast and fear me not,
I am your bairn's father.

They'll turn me to a bear sae grim,
And then a lion bold.
But hold me fast and fear me not,
As ye shall love your child.

113 would 115 know 117 strange 120 afterwards 122 pull 131 these are the signs 134 newt

Again they'll turn me in your arms,
    To a red het gaud of airn.
But hold me fast and fear me not,
    I'll do to you nae harm.

And last they'll turn me in your arms,
    Into the burning lead;
Then throw me into well water,
    O throw me in wi' speed.

And then I'll be your ain true love,
    I'll turn a naked knight.
Then cover me wi' your green mantle,
    And cover me out o' sight.

Gloomy, gloomy was the night,
    And eerie was the way,
As fair Jenny in her green mantle
    To Milescross she did gae.

About the middle o' the night,
    She heard the bridles ring;
This lady was as glad at that
    As any earthly thing.

First she let the black pass by,
    And syne she let the brown;
But quickly she ran to the milk white steed,
    And pu'd the rider down.

Sae weel she minded what he did say
    And young Tam Lin did win;
Syne cover'd him wi' her green mantle
    As blythe's a bird in spring.

142 bar of iron

Out then spak the queen o' fairies,
    Out of a bush o broom;
Them that has gotten young Tam Lin,
    Has gotten a stately groom.

Out then spak the queen o' fairies,
    And an angry queen was she;
Shame betide her ill-far'd face,
    And an ill death may she die,
For she's ta'en awa the boniest knight
    In a' my companie.

But had I kend Tam Lin, she says,
    What now this night I see,
I wad hae taen out thy twa grey een,
    And put in twa een o' tree.

175 befall . . . ill-favored 177 handsomest 179 known 181 eyes 182 wood

CLARK COLVEN [42]

Clark Colven and his gay lady,
As they walk'd to yon garden green,
A belt about her middle gimp,
Which cost Clark Colven crowns fifteen.
"O hearken well now, my good lord,
O hearken well to what i say;
When ye gae to the walls o' Stream,
Be sure ye touch nae well far'd may."
"O had your tongue, my gay lady,
An' dinna deave me wi' your din;
For i saw never a fair woman
But wi' her body i cou'd sin."
He mounted on his berry-brown steed,
An' merry merry rade he on,
Till he came til the walls o' Stream,
An' there he saw the mermaiden.
"Ye wash, ye wash, ye bonny may,
And ay's ye wash your sark o' silk."
"It's a' for you, ye gentle knight,
My skin is whiter than the milk."
He's taen her by the milk-white hand,
And likewise by the grass-green sleeve,
An' laid her down upon the green,
Nor of his lady speer'd he leave.

Sung by Mrs. Brown, Falkland, Aberdeenshire, who was the source of some of the best ballad versions. Her nephew's manuscript, now lost, was copied by Joseph Ritson about 1792.

1 cleric 3 slender 8 well-formed maiden 9 hold 10 deafen 14 road 18 shift 24 asked

Ohon! alas! says Clark Colven,
An' ay sae sair's i mean my head.
And merrily leugh the mermaiden:
"O, even on, till ye be dead.
But out ye tak' your little pen-knife,
An' frae my sark ye shear a gare,
Row that about your lovely head,
And the pain you'll never feel nae mair."
Out has he taen his little pen-knife,
An' frae her sark he's shorn a gare,
Row'd that about his lovely head;
But the pain increased mair and mair.
Ohon! alas! says Clark Colven,
An' ay sae sair's i mean my head.
An' merrily leugh the mermaiden:
" 'Twill ay be war 'till ye be dead."
Then out he drew his trusty blade,
An' thought wi' it to be her dead;
But she became a fish again,
And merrily sprang into the fleed.
He's mounted on his berry-brown steed,
An' dowy, dowy rade he hame,
'Till he came to his lady's bow'r door,
An' heavily he lighted down.
"O mither, mither, mak' my bed,
An', gentle lady, lay me down;
O brither, brither, unbend my bow,
'Twill never be bent by me again."
His mither she has made his bed,
His gentle lady laid him down,
His brother he has unbent his bow,
'Twas never bent by him again.

26 sore . . . lament 27 laughed 29 unless 30 triangular piece of cloth; gore 31 roll 40 worse 42 death 44 flood 46 doleful 49 mother 51 brother

SIR PATRICK SPENS [58]

The king sits in Dunfermline toon,
A drinkin' at the wine,
And he has ca'd for the finest skipper
In Fife and a' the land.

Then oot it spak an auld carle,
Stuid by the king's ain knee;
Said, "Patrick Spens is the strangest sailor
That ever sailed the sea."

The king has screivit a breid letter
And signed it wi's ain hand;
And sent it to young Patrick Spens,
Was walking on Leith sands.

"To Norrowa', to Norrowa',
To Norrowa' ower the faem;
The King's dochter o' Norrowa',
'Tis ye maun bring her hame."

When he leukit the letter on,
A muckle laugh gaed he,
But ere he done the readin' o't,
The tears blinded his e'e.

Sung by Ewan MacColl, Riverside LP record RLP 624 (Bl), K. S. Goldstein, ed. From the singing of MacColl's father.

3 called 5 fellow 6 stood . . . own 7 strongest 9 written . . . broad 13 Norway 14 foam 16 must 17 looked 18 great . . . gave

"O, wha' is it's done this fell deed
I pray ye tell to me;
Although it were my ain faither,
An ill death may he dee."

They hadna been in Norrowa'
A week but barely three,
When a' the lords o' Norrowa'
Did up and spak' so free.

"These ootland Scots waste our King's gowd
And swallow oor Queen's fee."
"Weary fa' the tongue that spak
Sic a muckle lee."

"How can this be?" said Patrick Spens,
"I pray ye tell to me.
The bows o' my ship are wrocht wi' gowd
And there's twal kists o' white money.

"Tak tent, tak tent, my gweed men a',
And mind ye be weel forn,
For come it wind or come it hail,
Oor gweed ship sails the morn."

Then oot it spak the weatherman,
"I fear we'll a' be drooned,
For I saw the new mune late yestreen
Wi' the auld mune in her airms."

They hadna sailed abune an hour,
An hour but and a half,
When the lift grew laich and the wind blew haich,
And the ship it was a wrack.

29 foreign 30 wealth 32 lie 36 twelve chests 37 take care . . . good 38 well to the fore 40 our 45 above 47 sky grew low . . . high

"O, where will I get a bonnie lad
To tak' my steer in hand?
While I climb up the high topmast
To see if I can spy land."

He hadna gane a step, a step,
A step but barely ane,
When the bows o' our gweedly ship did brak'
And the saut-sea it cam in.

O, laith, laith, were our gweed Scots lords
To wat their cork-heeled shoon,
But lang ere a' the play was done,
They wat their hats abune.

O, lang, lang, will our ladies sit
Wi' their fans intil their hands,
Before they see Sir Patrick Spens
Come sailing to the land.

Half ower, half ower to Aberdour,
Where the sea's sae wide and deep,
It's there it lies Sir Patrick Spens
Wi' the Scots lords at his feet.

50 tiller   56 salt   57 loath   58 wet . . . shoes

LADY MAISERY [65]

The young lords o' the north country
  Have all a wooing gane,
To win the love o' lady Maisery,
  But of them she would ha' nane.
O they have courted lady Maisery
  Wi' broaches and wi' rings,
An' they ha' courted her lady Maisery
  Wi' a' kin' kind o' things.
An' they ha' sought her lady Maisery
  Frae father and frae mother,
An' they have sought her lady Maisery
  Frae sister and frae brother.
And they ha' follow'd her lady Maisery
  Through cha'mer and through ha'
But a' that they could say to her,
  Her answer still was na'.
"O had your tongues, young men, she says,
  An' think nae mair o' me,
For i've gi'n my love to an English lord,
  An' i have nae mair to gi."
Her fathers kitchy boy hard that,
  Ane ill deid may he dee!
An' he has on to her brother
  As fast as gang could he.

Sung by Mrs. Brown, Falkland, Aberdeenshire, and copied by Joseph Ritson about 1792; see the earlier note about *Clark Colven*.

6 brooches   8 *a' kin' kind:* a redundant construction   14 chamber . . . hall   19 given   21 kitchen boy   22 death . . . die   23 gone

"O is my father and mother well,
  But and my brothers three?
Gin my sister lady Mais'ry be well,
  There's naething can ail me."
"Your father and your mother is well,
  Likewise your brothers three;
Your sister lady Maisery is well,
  So big wi' bairn gangs she."
"Gin this be true you tell to me,
  My malison light on thee!
But gin it be a lie you tell,
  You shall be hanged hi'."
He's done him to his sisters bow'r
  Wi' meikle deil and care,
An' there he saw her lady Maisery
  Keming her yallow hair.
"O wha is aught that bairn, he says,
  That ye sae big are wi'?
An' gin you winna own the truth,
  This moment you shall die."
She turn'd her right and round about,
  An' the kem fell frae her hand,
A trembling seiz'd her fair body,
  An' her rosy cheek grew wan.
"O, pardon me, my brother dear,
  An' the truth i'll own to thee;
My bairn it is to lord William,
  And now he is betrothed to me."
"O, could na ye gotten dukes or lords
  Into your own country,
That ye drew up wi' an English dog,
  To bring this shame on me?
But ye man gie up the English blood,
  The moment your babe is born,
For gin you keep by'm an hour longer
  Your life shall be forborn."

32 child 34 curse 38 much dole 41 who owns 43 will not 57 must

"I will gie up this English blood
  Till my young babe be born,
But the never a day nor hour langer,
  Though my life should be forborn."
"O, whare is a' my merry young men,
  Whom i gie meat and fee,
To pu' the thistle and the thorn,
  To burn this vile whore wi'?"
"O, whare will i get a bonny boy,
  To help me in my need?
To run with haste to lord William,
  An' bid him come wi' speed?"
O, out it spake a bonny boy,
  Stood by her brothers side,
"O, i would run your errand, lady,
  O'er all the world wide.
Aft have i run your errands, lady,
  Wi' sa't tears on my cheek;
Aft have i run your errands, lady,
  Whan blawn baith win' and weet."
O, whan he came to broken brigs,
  He bent his bow and swam,
An' whan he came to green grass growing,
  He took off his sheen and ran.
And (whan) he came to lord Williams yates,
  He bade na to chap or ca',
But set his bent bow till his breast,
  An' lightly lap the wa';
And or the porter was at the gate,
  The boy was in the ha'.
"O is my biggins broken, boy?
  Or is my towers won?
Or is my lady lighter yet,
  Of a dear daughter or son?"
"Your biggins is no brunt, my lord,

66 property 67 pull 80 When the wind and rain are blowing 81 bridges 84 shoes 85 gates 86 He did not wait to knock or call 88 leaped . . . wall 89 ere 91 buildings 95 burned

Nor is your towers won,
But the fairest lady in a' the land
For you this day man burn."
"O, saddle to me the black, the black,
Or saddle to me the brown,
O, saddle to me the swiftest steed
That e'er rode frae a town."
Or he was near a mile awa'
She hear'd his wild horse sneeze:
"Mend up the fire, my false brother,
It's nae come to my knees."
And whan he lighted at the yate,
She hard his bridle ring:
"Mend up the fire, my false brother,
It's far yet frae my chin.
Mend up the fire to me, she says,
Mend up the fire to me,
For i see him coming hard and fast
Will soon men' 't up to thee.
O, gin my hands had been loose, Willie,
So hard as they are bound,
I would have turn'd me frae the gleed,
An' casten out your young son."
"O i'll gar burn for thee, Mais'ry,
Your sister and your brother;
An' i'll gar burn for thee, Mais'ry,
Your father and your mother;
And i'll gar burn for thee, Mais'ry,
The chief of all your kin;
An' the last bonfire that i come to,
Mysel' i will cast in."

108 heard   117 fire   119 cause (to)

THE UNQUIET GRAVE [78]

I'll do so much for my sweetheart
As any young man may;
I'll sit and mourn all on her grave
A twelve month and a day.

The twelve months and the day was past
The ghost began to speak:
What makes you sit all on my grave
And will not let me sleep?

There is one thing more I want sweetheart
There is one thing more I crave,
And that is a kiss from your lily-white lips
And then I'll go from your grave.

My lips are cold as clay sweetheart,
My breath smell heavy and strong
And if you kiss my lily-white lips
Your time will not be long.

From Cecil Sharp, *One Hundred English Folk Songs,* 1916. Sung by Mrs. William Rea, Somerset, 1904.

THE WIFE OF USHER'S WELL [79]

There lived a wife at Usher's Well,
And a wealthy wife was she,
She had three stout and stalwart sons,
And sent them o'er the sea.

They hadna been a week from her,
A week but barely ane,
When word came to the carline wife,
That her three sons were gane.

They hadna been a week from her,
A week but barely three,
When word came to the carline wife,
That her sons she'd never see.

"I wish the wind may never cease,
Nor fashes in the flood,
Till my three sons come hame to me,
In earthly flesh and blood!"

It fell about the Martinmas,
When nights are lang and mirk,
The carline wife's three sons came hame,
And their hats were o' the birk.

It neither grew in syke nor ditch,
Nor yet in ony sheugh;

From Sir Walter Scott, *Poetical Works* 1833-1834.
19 old 20 birch 21 trench 22 furrow

But at the gates o' Paradise,
    That birk grew fair eneugh.

"Blow up the fire, my maidens!
    Bring water from the well!
For a' my house shall feast this night,
    Since my three sons are well."

And she has made to them a bed,
    She's made it large and wide;
And she's ta'en her mantle her about,
    Sat down at the bed-side.

Up then crew the red red cock,
    And up and crew the gray;
The eldest to the youngest said,
    " 'Tis time we were away."

The cock he hadna craw'd but once,
    And clapp'd his wings at a',
Whan the youngest to the eldest said,
    "Brother, we must awa.

"The cock doth craw, the day doth daw,
    The channerin' worm doth chide;
Gin we be mist out o' our place,
    A sair pain we maun bide.

"Fare ye weel, my mother dear!
    Fareweel to barn and byre!
And fare ye weel, the bonny lass,
    That kindles my mother's fire."

42 fretful 43 if . . . missed 44 sore . . . must 46 stable

GLENLOGIE [238]

There were six and six nobles
        Rode round Banchory fair
But bonny Glenlogie
        Was flower that was there

There were nine & nine nobles
        Sat in the king's hall
        But bonny Glenlogie
Was flower o'er them a'

Down came Jeanie Gordon
        She came tripping downstairs
And she has faun sick wi' Glenlogie
        Above all that was there

She called on his footman
        As he passed by her side
Says oh what's he that young man
        And where does he bide

His title is Glenlogie
        When he is from home
But he of the grand Gordons
        And his name is Lord John

Collected by Gavin Grieg from the singing of John McAllan in the north of Scotland, about 1910.

11 fallen

Glenlogie, Glenlogie
    You'll be constant and kind
    I've laid my love on you
And I'll tell you my mind

He turned him round quickly
    As the Gordons do a'
Says I thank you Jeanie Gordon
    But your tocher's owre sma.

She called on her maiden
    To make her a bed
    Wi' ribbons and napkins
    To tie up her head

And down came her father
He came tripping down stairs
Says oh what ails you Jeanie
That you're lying there.

He's a nice little fellow
    With a dark rolling eye
If I get not Glenlogie
    For him I will die

O hold your tongue Jeanie
    And give up your folly
I'll lead you to Drumwhindle
    He has more gold than he

Oh hold your tongue father
    And let Jeannie be
If I get not Glenlogie
    For him I will dee.

Her father had a chaplain
    A man o' great skill

28 dowry's too small 48 die

He wrote a broad letter
And he penned it weel

When Glenlogie got the letter
He was among men
He gave a loud laugh
Says oh what does she mean.

But ere Glenlogie read the letter
The tears came down large
What a pity a leal virgin
Should die for my cause

You'll go saddle the black steed
Go saddle the brown
For bonny Jeanie Gordon
She'll be deid or I win.

Or they got them saddled
And down by yon green
Bonny Glenlogie
He was three miles him leen

When they came to Bethelnie
There was nobody there
But ae bonny lassie
She was combing her hair

He said "Bonny lassie
You'll take me by the hand
And lead me to the chamber
Jeannie Gordon lies in."

Oh pale and wan was she
When Glenlogie came in
But red and rosy grew she
Or Glenlogie got ben

59 true 64 unless I get there 68 alone 80 in

Oh where's your pain Jeannie,
    Does it lie in your head
The pain that ye be under
    Does it lie in your side

Oh no no Glenlogie
    You're far from the part
The pain that I lie under
    It lies in my heart.

You'll turn you round Jeanie
    Turn to your right side
And I'll be the bridegroom
    And you'll be the bride

Now Jeannie she's got married
And her tocher down told
    Bonny Jean o' Bethelnie
Scarcely sixteen years old

Oh Bethelnie, oh Bethelnie,
    It shines where it stands
And the heather bells round it
    Shines o'er Fyvie's land.

Alexander Pope 1688–1744

DUKE UPON DUKE

To Lordings proud I tune my Lay,
  Who feast in Bower or Hall:
Though Dukes they be, to Dukes I say,
  That Pride will have a Fall.

Now, that this same it is right sooth,
  Full plainly doth appear,
From what befel *John* Duke of *Guise,*
  And *Nic.* of *Lancastere.*

When *Richard Coeur de Lyon* reign'd,
  (Which means a Lion's Heart)
Like him his Barons rag'd and roar'd,
  Each play'd a Lion's Part.

A Word and Blow was then enough,
  (Such Honour did them prick)
If you but turn'd your Cheek, a Cuff,
  And if your A—se, a Kick.

Look in their Face, they tweak'd your Nose,
  At ev'ry Turn fell to 't;
Come near, they trod upon your Toes;
  They fought from Head to Foot.

Of these, the Duke of *Lancastere*
  Stood Paramount in Pride;
He kick'd, and cuff'd, and tweak'd, and trod
  His Foes, and Friends beside.

Duke upon Duke. "An Excellent New Ballad. To the Tune of Chevy Chase." 1720.

7–8 Sir John Guise was M.P. from Gloucestershire 1705-1710, and from Marlowe 1722-1727. His enemy, Lechmere, was Chancellor of the Duchy of Lancaster.

Firm on his Front his Beaver sate,
So broad, it hid his Chin;
For why? he deem'd no Man his Mate,
And fear'd to tan his Skin.

With *Spanish* Wool he dy'd his Cheek,
With Essence oil'd his Hair;
No Vixen Civet-Cat so sweet,
Nor could so scratch and tear.

Right tall he made himself to show,
Though made full short by G—d:
And when all other Dukes did bow,
This Duke did only nod.

Yet courteous, blithe, and debonair,
To *Guise*'s Duke was he;
Was never such a loving Pair,
How could they disagree?

Oh, thus it was. He lov'd him dear,
And cast how to requite him:
And having no Friend left but this,
He deem'd it meet to fight him.

Forthwith he drench'd his desp'rate Quill;
And thus he did indite:
"This Eve at Whisk ourself will play,
Sir Duke! be here to Night."

Ah no, ah no, the guileless *Guise*
Demurely did reply,
I cannot go, nor yet can stand,
So sore the Gout have I.

The Duke in Wrath call'd for his Steeds,
And fiercely drove them on;

25 *Beaver:* visor of the helmet

Lord! Lord! how rattl'd then thy Stones,
  Oh Kingly *Kensington*!

All in a Trice he rush'd on *Guise,*
  Thrust out his Lady dear,
He tweak'd his Nose, trod on his Toes,
  And smote him on the Ear.

But mark, how 'midst of Victory,
  Fate plays her old Dog Trick!
Up leap'd Duke *John,* and knock'd him down,
  And so down fell Duke *Nic.*

Alas, oh *Nic*! Oh *Nic.* alas!
  Right did thy Gossip call thee:
As who should say, alas the Day,
  When *John* of *Guise* shall maul thee.

For on thee did he clap his Chair,
  And on that Chair did sit;
And look'd, as if he meant therein
  To do—what was not fit.

Up didst thou look, oh woeful Duke!
  Thy Mouth yet durst not ope,
Certes for fear, of finding there
  A T—d instead of Trope.

"Lye there, thou Caitiff vile! quoth *Guise,*
  No *Sheet* is here to save thee:
The Casement it is shut likewise;
  Beneath my Feet I have thee.

"If thou hast ought to speak, speak out."
  Then *Lancastere* did cry,
"Know'st thou not me, nor yet thy self?
  Who thou, and whom am I?

66 godmother   75 truly   76 figure of speech

"Know'st thou not me, who (God be prais'd)
Have brawl'd, and quarrel'd more,
Than all the Line of *Lancastere*
That battl'd heretofore?

"In Senates fam'd for many a Speech,
And (what some awe must give ye,
Tho' laid thus low beneath thy breech,)
Still of the Council Privy.

"Still of the *Dutchy* Chancellor,
Durante Life I have it;
And turn, as now thou dost on me,
Mine A—e on them that gave it."

But now the Servants they rush'd in;
And Duke *Nic.* up leap'd he:
I will not cope against such odds,
But, *Guise*! I'll fight with thee:

To-morrow with thee will I fight
Under the Greenwood Tree;
"No, not to-morrow, but to night
(Quoth *Guise*) I'll fight with thee."

And now the Sun declining low
Bestreak'd with Blood the Skies;
When, with his Sword at Saddle Bow,
Rode forth the vailant *Guise*!

Full gently praunch'd he o'er the Lawn;
Oft' roll'd his Eyes around,
And from the Stirrup stretch'd, to find
Who was not to be found.

94 while life lasts

Long brandish'd he the Blade in Air,
　　Long look'd the Field all o'er:
At length he spy'd the Merry-men brown,
　　And eke the Coach and four.

From out the Boot bold *Nicholas*
　　Did wave his Wand so white,
As pointing out the gloomy Glade
　　Wherein he meant to fight.

All in that dreadful Hour, so calm
　　Was *Lancastere* to see,
As if he meant to take the Air,
　　Or only take a Fee.

And so he did—for to *New Court*
　　His rowling Wheels did run:
Not that he shunn'd the doubtful Strife,
　　But *Bus'ness* must be done.

Back in the Dark, by *Brompton* Park,
　　He turn'd up through the Gore;
So slunk to *Cambden* House so high,
　　All in his Coach and four.

Mean while Duke *Guise* did fret and fume,
　　A Sight it was to see;
Benumm'd beneath the Evening Dew,
　　Under the Greenwood Tree.

Then, wet and weary, home he far'd,
　　Sore mutt'ring all the way,
"The Day I meet him, *Nic.* shall rue
　　The Cudgel of that Day.

115

120

125

130

135

140

116 also

"Mean Time on every Pissing-Post
   Paste we this Recreant's Name,
So that each Pisser-by shall read,
   And piss against the same."

Now God preserve our gracious King!
   And grant, his Nobles all
May learn this Lesson from Duke *Nic.*
   That *Pride will have a Fall.*

Robert Burns 1759–1796

JOHN BARLEYCORN. A BALLAD.

There was three kings into the east,
  Three kings both great and high,
An' they hae sworn a solemn oath
  John Barleycorn should die.

They took a plough an' plough'd him down,
  Put clods upon his head,
An' they hae sworn a solemn oath
  John Barleycorn was dead.

But the cheerful spring came kindly on,
  And showers began to fall;
John Barleycorn got up again,
  And sore surpris'd them all.

The sultry suns of summer came,
  And he grew thick and strong,
His head weel arm'd wi' pointed spears,
  That no one should him wrong.

The sober autumn enter'd mild,
  When he grew wan and pale:
His bending joints and drooping head
  Show'd he began to fail.

His colour sicken'd more and more,
  He faded into age;
And then his enemies began
  To show their deadly rage.

From *Poems, Chiefly in the Scottish Dialect* 1787.
15 well

They've taen a weapon, long and sharp,
  And cut him by the knee;
Then ty'd him fast upon a cart,
  Like a rogue for forgerie.

They laid him down upon his back,
  And cudgell'd him full sore;
They hung him up before the storm,
  And turn'd him o'er and o'er.

They fillèd up a darksome pit,
  With water to the brim,
They heavèd in John Barleycorn,
  There let him sink or swim.

They laid him out upon the floor,
  To work him farther woe,
And still, as signs of life appear'd,
  They toss'd him to and fro.

They wasted, o'er a scorching flame,
  The marrow of his bones;
But a miller us'd him worst of all,
  For he crush'd him 'tween two stones.

And they hae taen his very heart's blood,
  And drank it round and round!
And still the more and more they drank,
  Their joy did more abound.

John Barleycorn was a hero bold,
  Of noble enterprize,
For if you do but taste his blood,
  'Twill make your courage rise.

'Twill make a man forget his woe;
   'Twill heighten all his joy:
'Twill make the widow's heart to sing,
   Though the tear were in her eye.

Then let us toast John Barleycorn,
   Each man a glass in hand:
And may his great posterity
   Ne'er fail in old Scotland!

William Blake 1757–1827

THE CRYSTAL CABINET

The Maiden caught me in the Wild,
Where I was dancing merrily;
She put me into her Cabinet
And Lock'd me up with a golden Key.

This Cabinet is form'd of Gold
And Pearl & Crystal shining bright,
And within it opens into a World
And a little lovely Moony Night.

Another England there I saw,
Another London with its Tower,
Another Thames & other Hills,
And another pleasant Surrey Bower,

Another Maiden like herself,
Translucent, lovely, shining clear,
Threefold each in the other clos'd
O, what a pleasant trembling fear!

O, what a smile! a threefold Smile
Fill'd me, that like a flame I burn'd;
I bent to Kiss the lovely Maid,
And found a Threefold Kiss return'd.

I strove to seize the inmost Form
With ardor fierce & hands of flame,
But burst the Crystal Cabinet,
And like a Weeping Babe became—

These three poems from manuscript were first published by Geoffrey Keynes in *The Complete Writings of William Blake* 1925.

A weeping Babe upon the wild,
And Weeping Woman pale reclin'd,
And in the outward air again
I fill'd with woes the passing Wind.

THE MENTAL TRAVELLER

I travel'd thro' a Land of Men,
A Land of Men & Women too,
And heard & saw such dreadful things
As cold Earth wanderers never knew.

For there the Babe is born in joy
That was begotten in dire woe;
Just as we Reap in joy the fruit
Which we in bitter tears did sow.

And if the Babe is born a Boy
He's given to a Woman Old,
Who nails him down upon a rock,
Catches his shrieks in cups of gold.

She binds iron thorns around his head,
She pierces both his hands & feet,
She cuts his heart out at his side
To make it feel both cold & heat.

Her fingers number every Nerve,
Just as a Miser counts his gold;
She lives upon his shrieks & cries,
And she grows young as he grows old.

Till he becomes a bleeding youth,
And she becomes a Virgin bright;
Then he rends up his Manacles
And binds her down for his delight.

He plants himself in all her Nerves,
Just as a Husbandman his mould;
And she becomes his dwelling place
And Garden fruitful seventy fold.

An agèd Shadow, soon he fades,
Wand'ring round an Earthly Cot,
Full fillèd all with gems & gold
Which he by industry had got.

And these are the gems of the Human Soul,
The rubies & pearls of a lovesick eye,
The countless gold of the akeing heart,
The martyr's groan & the lover's sigh.

They are his meat, they are his drink;
He feeds the Beggar & the Poor
And the wayfaring Traveller:
For ever open is his door.

His grief is their eternal joy;
They make the roofs & walls to ring;
Till from the fire on the hearth
A little Female Babe does spring.

And she is all of solid fire
And gems & gold, that none his hand
Dares stretch to touch her Baby form,
Or wrap her in his swaddling-band.

But She comes to the Man she loves,
If young or old, or rich or poor;
They soon drive out the agèd Host,
A Beggar at another's door.

He wanders weeping far away,
Until some other take him in;
Oft blind & age-bent, sore distrest,
Until he can a Maiden win.

And to allay his freezing Age
The Poor Man takes her in his arms;
The Cottage fades before his sight,
The Garden & its lovely Charms.

The Guests are scatter'd thro' the land,
For the Eye altering alters all;
The Senses roll themselves in fear,
And the flat Earth becomes a Ball;

The stars, sun, Moon, all shrink away,
A desart vast without a bound,
And nothing left to eat or drink,
And a dark desart all around.

The honey of her Infant lips,
The bread & wine of her sweet smile,
The wild game of her roving Eye,
Does him to Infancy beguile;

For as he eats & drinks he grows
Younger & younger every day;
And on the desart wild they both
Wander in terror & dismay.

Like the wild Stag she flees away,
Her fear plants many a thicket wild;
While he pursues her night & day,
By various arts of Love beguil'd,

By various arts of Love & Hate,
Till the wide desart planted o'er
With Labyrinths of wayward Love,
Where roam the Lion, Wolf & Boar,

Till he becomes a wayward Babe,
And she a weeping Woman Old.
Then many a Lover wanders here;
The Sun & Stars are nearer roll'd.

The trees bring forth sweet Extacy
To all who in the desart roam;
Till many a City there is Built,
And many a pleasant Shepherd's home.

But when they find the frowning Babe,
Terror strikes thro' the region wide:
They cry "The Babe! the Babe is Born!"
And flee away on Every side.

For who dare touch the frowning form,
His arm is wither'd to its root;
Lions, Boars, Wolves, all howling flee,
And every Tree does shed its fruit.

And none can touch that frowning form,
Except it be a Woman Old;
She nails him down upon the Rock,
And all is done as I have told.

LET THE BROTHELS OF PARIS BE OPENED

"Let the Brothels of Paris be opened
With many an alluring dance
To awake the Pestilence thro' the city,"
Said the beautiful Queen of France.

The King awoke on his couch of gold,
As soon as he heard these tidings told:
"Arise & come, both fife & drum,
And the Famine shall eat both crust & crumb."

Then he swore a great & solemn Oath:
"To kill the people I am loth,
But If they rebel, they must go to hell:
They shall have a Priest & a passing bell."

Then old Nobodaddy aloft
Farted & belch'd & cough'd,
And said, "I love hanging & drawing & quartering
Every bit as well as war & slaughtering.
Damn praying & singing,
Unless they will bring in
The blood of ten thousand by fighting or swinging."

The Queen of France just touched this Globe,
And the Pestilence darted from her robe;
But our good Queen quite grows to the ground,
And a great many suckers grow all around.

Fayette beside King Lewis stood;
He saw him sign his hand;
And soon he saw the famine rage
About the fruitful land.

Fayette beheld the Queen to smile
And wink her lovely eye;
And soon he saw the pestilence
From street to street to fly.

Fayette beheld the King & Queen
In tears & iron bound;
But mute Fayette wept tear for tear,
And guarded them around.

Fayette, Fayette, thou'rt bought & sold,
And sold is thy happy morrow;
Thou gavest the tears of Pity away
In exchange for the tears of sorrow.

Who will exchange his own fire side
For the steps of another's door?
Who will exchange his wheaten loaf
For the links of a dungeon floor?

O, who would smile on the wintry seas,
& Pity the stormy roar?
Or who will exchange his new born child
For the dog at the wintry door?

Samuel Taylor Coleridge 1772–1834

THE RIME OF THE ANCIENT MARINER

Facile credo, plures esse Naturas invisibiles quam visibiles in rerum universitate. Sed horum omnium familiam quis nobis enarrabit? et gradus et cognationes et discrimina et singulorum munera? Quid agunt? quae loca habitant? Harum rerum notitiam semper ambivit ingenium humanum, nunquam attigit. Juvat, interea, non diffiiteor, quandoque in animo, tanquam in tabula, majoris et melioris mundi imaginem contemplari: ne mens assuefacta hodiernae vitae minutiis se contrahat nimis, et tota subsidat in pusillas cogitationes. Sed veritati interea invigilandum est, modusque servandus, ut certa ab incertis, diem a nocte, distinguamus.—T. BURNET, *Archaeol. Phil.* p. 68.

[*I easily believe that there are more invisible than visible beings in the universe. But who will tell us the family, the ranks, the relationships, the differences, the respective functions of all these? What do they do? What places do they inhabit? The human mind has always circled around knowledge of these questions, but has never attained it. Yet, I have no doubt that it is pleasant to contemplate in one's mind sometimes, as in a picture, the image of a bigger and better world: lest the mind, accustomed to the details of everyday life, be too much narrowed, and entirely settle itself in trifling thoughts. But meanwhile we must be watching for truth, while practicing restraint, so that we may distinguish the certain from the uncertain, day from night.*]

ARGUMENT

How a Ship having passed the Line was driven by storms to the cold Country towards the South Pole; and how from thence she made her course to the tropical Latitude of the Great Pacific Ocean; and of the strange things that befell; and in what manner the Ancyent Marinere came back to his own Country.

PART I

An ancient Mariner meeteth three Gallants bidden to a wedding-feast, and detaineth one.

It is an ancient Mariner,
And he stoppeth one of three.
"By thy long grey beard and glittering eye,
Now wherefore stopp'st thou me?

From *Lyrical Ballads* 1798. This version incorporates the marginal notes and revisions from the edition of 1817.

The Bridegroom's doors are opened wide,
And I am next of kin;
The guests are met, the feast is set:
May'st hear the merry din."

He holds him with his skinny hand,
"There was a ship," quoth he.
"Hold off! unhand me, grey-beard loon!"
Eftsoons his hand dropt he.

The Wedding-Guest is spell-bound by the eye of the old seafaring man, and constrained to hear his tale.

He holds him with his glittering eye—
The Wedding-Guest stood still,
And listens like a three years' child:
The Mariner hath his will.

The Wedding-Guest sat on a stone:
He cannot choose but hear;
And thus spake on that ancient man,
The bright-eyed Mariner.

"The ship was cheered, the harbour cleared,
Merrily did we drop
Below the kirk, below the hill,
Below the lighthouse top.

The Mariner tells how the ship sailed southward with a good wind and fair weather, till it reached the line.

The Sun came up upon the left,
Out of the sea came he!
And he shone bright, and on the right
Went down into the sea.

Higher and higher every day,
Till over the mast at noon—"
The Wedding-Guest here beat his breast,
For he heard the loud bassoon.

The Wedding-Guest heareth the bridal music; but the Mariner continueth his tale.

The bride hath paced into the hall,
Red as a rose is she;
Nodding their heads before her goes
The merry minstrelsy.

23 church

The Wedding-Guest he beat his breast,
Yet he cannot choose but hear;
And thus spake on that ancient man,
The bright-eyed Mariner.

The ship driven by a storm toward the south pole.

"And now the STORM-BLAST came, and he
Was tyrannous and strong:
He struck with his o'ertaking wings,
And chased us south along.

With sloping masts and dipping prow,
As who pursued with yell and blow
Still treads the shadow of his foe,
And forward bends his head,
The ship drove fast, loud roared the blast,
And southward aye we fled.

And now there came both mist and snow,
And it grew wondrous cold:
And ice, mast-high, came floating by.
As green as emerald.

The land of ice, and of fearful sounds where no living thing was to be seen.

And through the drifts the snowy clifts
Did send a dismal sheen:
Nor shapes of men nor beasts we ken—
The ice was all between.

The ice was here, the ice was there,
The ice was all around:
It cracked and growled, and roared and howled,
Like noises in a swound!

Till a great sea-bird, called the Albatross, came through the snow-fog, and was received with great joy and hospitality.

At length did cross an Albatross,
Thorough the fog it came;
As if it had been a Christian soul,
We hailed it in God's name.

It ate the food it ne'er had eat,
And round and round it flew.
The ice did split with a thunder-fit;
The helmsman steered us through!

57 perceive 62 swoon

And lo! the Albatross proveth a bird of good omen, and followeth the ship as it returned northward through fog and floating ice.

And a good south wind sprung up behind;
The Albatross did follow,
And every day, for food or play,
Came to the mariner's hollo!

In mist or cloud, on mast or shroud,
It perched for vespers nine;
Whiles all the night, through fog-smoke white,
Glimmered the white Moon-shine."

The ancient Mariner inhospitably killeth the pious bird of good omen.

"God save thee, ancient Mariner!
From the fiends, that plague thee thus!—
Why look'st thou so?"—With my cross-bow
I shot the ALBATROSS.

PART II

The Sun now rose upon the right:
Out of the sea came he,
Still hid in mist, and on the left
Went down into the sea.

And the good south wind still blew behind,
But no sweet bird did follow,
Nor any day for food or play
Came to the mariners' hollo!

His shipmates cry out against the ancient Mariner, for killing the bird of good luck.

And I had done a hellish thing,
And it would work 'em woe:
For all averred, I had killed the bird
That made the breeze to blow.
Ah wretch! said they, the bird to slay,
That made the breeze to blow!

But when the fog cleared off, they justify the same, and thus make themselves accomplices in the crime.

Nor dim nor red, like God's own head,
The glorious Sun uprist:
Then all averred, I had killed the bird
That brought the fog and mist.
'Twas right, said they, such birds to slay,
That bring the fog and mist.

The fair breeze continues; the ship enters the Pacific Ocean, and sails northward, even till it reaches the Line.

The fair breeze blew, the white foam flew,
The furrow followed free;
We were the first that ever burst
Into that silent sea.

Down dropt the breeze, the sails dropt down,
'Twas sad as sad could be;
And we did speak only to break
The silence of the sea!

The ship hath been suddenly becalmed.

All in a hot and copper sky,
The bloody Sun, at noon,
Right up above the mast did stand,
No bigger than the Moon.

Day after day, day after day,
We stuck, nor breath nor motion;
As idle as a painted ship
Upon a painted ocean.

And the Albatross begins to be avenged.

Water, water, every where,
And all the boards did shrink;
Water, water, every where,
Nor any drop to drink.

The very deep did rot: O Christ!
That ever this should be!
Yea, slimy things did crawl with legs
Upon the slimy sea.

About, about, in reel and rout
The death-fires danced at night;
The water, like a witch's oils,
Burnt green, and blue and white.

127 dance and uproar 128 *death-fires:* phosphorescent gleams on the ship's riggings which sailors believed to forecast disaster.

A Spirit had followed them; one of the invisible inhabitants of this planet, neither departed souls nor angels; concerning whom the learned Jew, Josephus, and the Platonic Constantinopolitan, Michael Psellus, may be consulted. They are very numerous, and there is no climate or element without one or more.

And some in dreams assurèd were
Of the Spirit that plagued us so;
Nine fathom deep he had followed us
From the land of mist and snow.

And every tongue, through utter drought,
Was withered at the root;
We could not speak, no more than if
We had been choked with soot.

The shipmates, in their sore distress, would fain throw the whole guilt on the ancient Mariner: in sign whereof they hang the dead sea-bird round his neck.

Ah! well a-day! what evil looks
Had I from old and young!
Instead of the cross, the Albatross
About my neck was hung.

PART III

There passed a weary time. Each throat
Was parched, and glazed each eye.
A weary time! a weary time!
How glazed each weary eye,
When looking westward, I beheld
A something in the sky.

The ancient Mariner beholdeth a sign in the element afar off.

At first it seemed a little speck,
And then it seemed a mist;
It moved and moved, and took at last
A certain shape, I wist.

A speck, a mist, a shape, I wist!
And still it neared and neared:
As if it dodged a water-sprite,
It plunged and tacked and veered.

152 perceived

At its nearer approach, it seemeth him to be a ship; and at a dear ransom he freeth his speech from the bonds of thirst.

With throats unslaked, with black lips baked,
We could nor laugh nor wail;
Through utter drought all dumb we stood!
I bit my arm, I sucked the blood,
And cried, A sail! a sail!

With throats unslaked, with black lips baked,
Agape they heard me call:

A flash of joy;

Gramercy! they for joy did grin,
And all at once their breath drew in,
As they were drinking all.

And horror follows. For can it be a ship that comes onward without wind or tide?

See! see! (I cried) she tacks no more!
Hither to work us weal;
Without a breeze, without a tide,
She steadies with upright keel!

The western wave was all a-flame.
The day was well nigh done!
Almost upon the western wave
Rested the broad bright Sun;
When that strange shape drove suddenly
Betwixt us and the Sun.

It seemeth him but the skeleton of a ship.

And straight the Sun was flecked with bars,
(Heaven's Mother send us grace!)
As if through a dungeon-grate he peered
With broad and burning face.

And its ribs are seen as bars on the face of the setting Sun.

Alas! (thought I, and my heart beat loud)
How fast she nears and nears!
Are those *her* sails that glance in the Sun,
Like restless gossameres?

The Spectre-Woman and her Death-mate, and no other on board the skeleton ship.

Are those *her* ribs through which the Sun
Did peer, as through a grate?
And is that Woman all her crew?
Is that a DEATH? and are there two?
Is DEATH that woman's mate?

168 good fortune

Like vessel, like crew!

Her lips were red, *her* looks were free,
Her locks were yellow as gold:
Her skin was as white as leprosy,
The Night-mare LIFE-IN-DEATH was she,
Who thicks man's blood with cold.

Death and Life-in-Death have diced for the ship's crew, and she (the latter) winneth the ancient Mariner.

The naked hulk alongside came,
And the twain were casting dice;
'The game is done! I've won! I've won!'
Quoth she, and whistles thrice.

No twilight within the courts of the Sun.

The Sun's rim dips; the stars rush out:
At one stride comes the dark;
With far-heard whisper, o'er the sea,
Off shot the spectre-bark.

At the rising of the Moon,

We listened and looked sideways up!
Fear at my heart, as at a cup,
My life-blood seemed to sip!
The stars were dim, and thick the night,
The steersman's face by his lamp gleamed white;
From the sails the dew did drip—
Till clomb above the eastern bar
The hornèd Moon, with one bright star
Within the nether tip.

One after another,

One after one, by the star-dogged Moon,
Too quick for groan or sigh,
Each turned his face with a ghastly pang,
And cursed me with his eye.

His shipmates drop down dead.

Four times fifty living men,
(And I heard nor sigh nor groan)
With heavy thump, a lifeless lump,
They dropped down one by one.

But Life-in-Death begins her work on the ancient Mariner.

The souls did from their bodies fly,—
They fled to bliss or woe!
And every soul, it passed me by,
Like the whizz of my cross-bow!

209 climbed

PART IV

The Wedding-Guest feareth that a Spirit is talking to him;

"I fear thee, ancient Mariner!
I fear thy skinny hand!
And thou art long, and lank, and brown,
As is the ribbed sea-sand.

I fear thee and thy glittering eye,
And thy skinny hand, so brown."—
Fear not, fear not, thou Wedding-Guest!
This body dropt not down.

But the ancient Mariner assureth him of his bodily life, and proceedeth to relate his horrible penance.

Alone, alone, all, all alone,
Alone on a wide wide sea!
And never a saint took pity on
My soul in agony.

He despiseth the creatures of the calm,

The many men, so beautiful!
And they all dead did lie:
And a thousand thousand slimy things
Lived on; and so did I.

And envieth that *they* should live, and so many lie dead.

I looked upon the rotting sea,
And drew my eyes away;
I looked upon the rotting deck,
And there the dead men lay.

I looked to heaven, and tried to pray;
But or ever a prayer had gusht,
A wicked whisper came, and made
My heart as dry as dust.

I closed my lids, and kept them close,
And the balls like pulses beat;
For the sky and the sea, and the sea and the sky
Lay like a load on my weary eye,
And the dead were at my feet.

But the curse liveth for him in the eye of the dead men.

The cold sweat melted from their limbs,
Nor rot nor reek did they:
The look with which they looked on me
Had never passed away.

An orphan's curse would drag to hell
A spirit from on high;
But oh! more horrible than that
Is the curse in a dead man's eye!
Seven days, seven nights, I saw that curse,
And yet I could not die.

In his loneliness and fixedness he yearneth towards the journeying Moon, and the stars that still sojourn, yet still move onward; and every where the blue sky belongs to them, and is their appointed rest, and their native country and their own natural homes, which they enter unannounced, as lords that are certainly expected and yet there is a silent joy at their arrival.

The moving Moon went up the sky,
And no where did abide:
Softly she was going up,
And a star or two beside—

Her beams bemocked the sultry main,
Like April hoar-frost spread;
But where the ship's huge shadow lay,
The charmèd water burnt alway
A still and awful red.

By the light of the Moon he beholdeth God's creatures of the great calm.

Beyond the shadow of the ship,
I watched the water-snakes:
They moved in tracks of shining white,
And when they reared, the elfish light
Fell off in hoary flakes.

Within the shadow of the ship
I watched their rich attire:
Blue, glossy green, and velvet black,
They coiled and swam; and every track
Was a flash of golden fire.

Their beauty and their happiness.

He blesseth them in his heart.

O happy living things! no tongue
Their beauty might declare:
A spring of love gushed from my heart,
And I blessed them unaware:
Sure my kind saint took pity on me,
And I blessed them unaware.

The spell begins to break.

The self-same moment I could pray;
And from my neck so free
The Albatross fell off, and sank
Like lead into the sea.

PART V

Oh sleep! it is a gentle thing,
Beloved from pole to pole!
To Mary Queen the praise be given!
She sent the gentle sleep from Heaven,
That slid into my soul.

By grace of the holy Mother, the ancient Mariner is refreshed with rain.

The silly buckets on the deck,
That had so long remained,
I dreamt that they were filled with dew;
And when I awoke, it rained.

My lips were wet, my throat was cold,
My garments all were dank;
Sure I had drunken in my dreams,
And still my body drank.

I moved, and could not feel my limbs:
I was so light—almost
I thought that I had died in sleep,
And was a blessèd ghost.

He heareth sounds and seeth strange sights and commotions in the sky and the element.

And soon I heard a roaring wind:
It did not come anear;
But with its sound it shook the sails,
That were so thin and sere.

The upper air burst into life!
And a hundred fire-flags sheen,
To and fro they were hurried about!
And to and fro, and in and out,
The wan stars danced between.

297 simple

And the coming wind did roar more loud,
And the sails did sigh like sedge;
And the rain poured down from one black cloud;
The Moon was at its edge.

The thick black cloud was cleft, and still
The Moon was at its side:
Like waters shot from some high crag,
The lightning fell with never a jag,
A river steep and wide.

The bodies of the ship's crew are inspired [inspirited, *S. L.*] and the ship moves on;

The loud wind never reached the ship,
Yet now the ship moved on!
Beneath the lightning and the Moon
The dead men gave a groan.

They groaned, they stirred, they all uprose,
Nor spake, nor moved their eyes;
It had been strange, even in a dream,
To have seen those dead men rise.

The helmsman steered, the ship moved on;
Yet never a breeze up-blew;
The mariners all 'gan work the ropes,
Where they were wont to do;
They raised their limbs like lifeless tools—
We were a ghastly crew.

The body of my brother's son
Stood by me, knee to knee:
The body and I pulled at one rope,
But he said nought to me.

But not by the souls of the men, nor by daemons of earth or middle air, but by a blessed troop of angelic spirits, sent down by the invocation of the guardian saint.

"I fear thee, ancient Mariner!"
Be calm, thou Wedding-Guest!
'Twas not those souls that fled in pain,
Which to their corses came again,
But a troop of spirits blest:

For when it dawned—they dropped their arms,
And clustered round the mast;
Sweet sounds rose slowly through their mouths,
And from their bodies passed.

Around, around, flew each sweet sound,
Then darted to the Sun;
Slowly the sounds came back again,
Now mixed, now one by one.

Sometimes a-dropping from the sky
I heard the sky-lark sing;
Sometimes all little birds that are,
How they seemed to fill the sea and air
With their sweet jargoning!

And now 'twas like all instruments,
Now like a lonely flute;
And now it is an angel's song,
That makes the heavens be mute.

It ceased; yet still the sails made on
A pleasant noise till noon,
A noise like of a hidden brook
In the leafy month of June,
That to the sleeping woods all night
Singeth a quiet tune.

Till noon we quietly sailed on,
Yet never a breeze did breathe:
Slowly and smoothly went the ship,
Moved onward from beneath.

The lonesome Spirit from the south-pole carries on the ship as far as the Line, in obedience to the angelic troop, but still requireth vengeance.

Under the keel nine fathom deep,
From the land of mist and snow,
The spirit slid: and it was he
That made the ship to go.
The sails at noon left off their tune,
And the ship stood still also.

The Sun, right up above the mast,
Had fixed her to the ocean:
But in a minute she 'gan stir,
With a short uneasy motion—
Backwards and forwards half her length
With a short uneasy motion.

Then like a pawing horse let go,
She made a sudden bound:
It flung the blood into my head,
And I fell down in a swound.

The Polar Spirit's fellow-daemons, the invisible inhabitants of the element, take part in his wrong; and two of them relate, one to the other, that penance long and heavy for the ancient Mariner hath been accorded to the Polar Spirit, who returneth southward.

How long in that same fit I lay,
I have not to declare;
But ere my living life returned,
I heard and in my soul discerned
Two voices in the air.

"Is it he?" quoth one, "Is this the man?
By him who died on cross,
With his cruel bow he laid full low
The harmless Albatross.

The spirit who bideth by himself
In the land of mist and snow,
He loved the bird that loved the man
Who shot him with his bow."

The other was a softer voice,
As soft as honey-dew:
Quoth he, "The man hath penance done,
And penance more will do."

PART VI

FIRST VOICE

"But tell me, tell me! speak again,
Thy soft response renewing—
What makes that ship drive on so fast?
What is the ocean doing?"

SECOND VOICE

"Still as a slave before his lord,
The ocean hath no blast;
His great bright eye most silently
Up to the Moon is cast—

If he may know which way to go;
For she guides him smooth or grim.
See, brother, see! how graciously
She looketh down on him."

FIRST VOICE

The Mariner hath been cast into a trance; for the angelic power causeth the vessel to drive northward faster than human life could endure.

"But why drives on that ship so fast,
Without or wave or wind?"

SECOND VOICE

"The air is cut away before,
And closes from behind.

Fly, brother, fly! more high, more high!
Or we shall be belated:
For slow and slow that ship will go,
When the Mariner's trance is abated."

The super-natural motion is retarded; the Mariner awakes, and his penance begins anew.

I woke, and we were sailing on
As in a gentle weather:
'Twas night, calm night, the moon was high;
The dead men stood together.

All stood together on the deck,
For a charnel-dungeon fitter:
All fixed on me their stony eyes,
That in the Moon did glitter.

The pang, the curse, with which they died,
Had never passed away:
I could not draw my eyes from theirs,
Nor turn them up to pray.

The curse is finally expiated.

And now this spell was snapt: once more
I viewed the ocean green,
And looked far forth, yet little saw
Of what had else been seen—

Like one, that on a lonesome road
Doth walk in fear and dread,
And having once turned round walks on,
And turns no more his head;

Because he knows, a frightful fiend
Doth close behind him tread.

But soon there breathed a wind on me,
Nor sound nor motion made:
Its path was not upon the sea,
In ripple or in shade.

It raised my hair, it fanned my cheek
Like a meadow-gale of spring—
It mingled strangely with my fears,
Yet it felt like a welcoming.

Swiftly, swiftly flew the ship,
Yet she sailed softly too:
Sweetly, sweetly blew the breeze—
On me alone it blew.

And the ancient Mariner beholdeth his native country.

Oh! dream of joy! is this indeed
The light-house top I see?
Is this the hill? is this the kirk?
Is this mine own countree?

We drifted o'er the harbour-bar,
And I with sobs did pray—
O let me be awake, my God!
Or let me sleep alway.

The harbour-bay was clear as glass,
So smoothly it was strewn!
And on the bay the moonlight lay,
And the shadow of the Moon.

The rock shone bright, the kirk no less,
That stands above the rock:
The moonlight steeped in silentness
The steady weathercock.

And the bay was white with silent light,
Till rising from the same,
Full many shapes, that shadows were,
In crimson colours came.

The angelic spirits leave the dead bodies,

And appear in their own forms of light.

A little distance from the prow
Those crimson shadows were:
I turned my eyes upon the deck—
Oh, Christ! what saw I there!

Each corse lay flat, lifeless and flat,
And, by the holy rood!
A man all light, a seraph-man,
On every corse there stood.

This seraph-band, each waved his hand:
It was a heavenly sight!
They stood as signals to the land,
Each one a lovely light;

This seraph-band, each waved his hand,
No voice did they impart—
No voice; but oh! the silence sank
Like music on my heart.

But soon I heard the dash of oars,
I heard the Pilot's cheer;
My head was turned perforce away
And I saw a boat appear.

The Pilot and the Pilot's boy,
I heard them coming fast:
Dear Lord in Heaven! it was a joy
The dead men could not blast.

I saw a third—I heard his voice:
It is the Hermit good!
He singeth loud his godly hymns
That he makes in the wood.
He'll shrieve my soul, he'll wash away
The Albatross's blood.

PART VII

The Hermit of the Wood,

This Hermit good lives in that wood
Which slopes down to the sea.
How loudly his sweet voice he rears!

He loves to talk with marineres
That come from a far countree.

He kneels at morn, and noon, and eve—
He hath a cushion plump:
It is the moss that wholly hides
The rotted old oak-stump.

The skiff-boat neared: I heard them talk,
"Why, this is strange, I trow!
Where are those lights so many and fair,
That signal made but now?"

Approacheth the ship with wonder.

"Strange, by my faith!" the Hermit said—
"And they answered not our cheer!
The planks looked warped! and see those sails,
How thin they are and sere!
I never saw aught like to them,
Unless perchance it were

Brown skeletons of leaves that lag
My forest-brook along;
When the ivy-tod is heavy with snow,
And the owlet whoops to the wolf below,
That eats the she-wolf's young."

"Dear Lord! it hath a fiendish look—
(The Pilot made reply)
I am a-feared"—"Push on, push on!"
Said the Hermit cheerily.

The boat came closer to the ship,
But I nor spake nor stirred;
The boat came close beneath the ship,
And straight a sound was heard.

The ship suddenly sinketh.

Under the water it rumbled on,
Still louder and more dread:
It reached the ship, it split the bay;
The ship went down like lead.

535 ivy bush

The ancient Mariner is saved in the Pilot's boat.

Stunned by that loud and dreadful sound,
Which sky and ocean smote,
Like one that hath been seven days drowned
My body lay afloat;
But swift as dreams, myself I found
Within the Pilot's boat.

Upon the whirl, where sank the ship,
The boat spun round and round;
And all was still, save that the hill
Was telling of the sound.

I moved my lips—the Pilot shrieked
And fell down in a fit;
The holy Hermit raised his eyes,
And prayed where he did sit.

I took the oars: the Pilot's boy,
Who now doth crazy go,
Laughed loud and long, and all the while
His eyes went to and fro.
"Ha! ha!" quoth he, "full plain I see,
The Devil knows how to row."

And now, all in my own countree,
I stood on the firm land!
The Hermit stepped forth from the boat,
And scarcely he could stand.

The ancient Mariner earnestly entreateth the Hermit to shrieve him; and the penance of life falls on him.

"O shrieve me, shrieve me, holy man!"
The Hermit crossed his brow.
"Say quick," quoth he, "I bid thee say—
What manner of man art thou?"

Forthwith this frame of mine was wrenched
With a woful agony,
Which forced me to begin my tale;
And then it left me free.

And ever and anon through out his future life an agony constraineth him to travel from land to land;

Since then, at an uncertain hour,
That agony returns:
And till my ghastly tale is told,
This heart within me burns.

I pass, like night, from land to land;
I have strange power of speech;
That moment that his face I see,
I know the man that must hear me:
To him my tale I teach.

What loud uproar bursts from that door!
The wedding-guests are there:
But in the garden-bower the bride
And bride-maids singing are:
And hark the little vesper bell,
Which biddeth me to prayer!

O Wedding-Guest! this soul hath been
Alone on a wide wide sea:
So lonely 'twas, that God himself
Scarce seemèd there to be.

O sweeter than the marriage-feast,
'Tis sweeter far to me,
To walk together to the kirk
With a goodly company!—

To walk together to the kirk,
And all together pray,
While each to his great Father bends,
Old men, and babes, and loving friends
And youths and maidens gay!

And to teach, by his own example, love and reverence to all things that God made and loveth.

Farewell, farewell! but this I tell
To thee, thou Wedding-Guest!
He prayeth well, who loveth well
Both man and bird and beast.

He prayeth best, who loveth best
All things both great and small;
For the dear God who loveth us,
He made and loveth all.

The Mariner, whose eye is bright,
Whose beard with age is hoar,
Is gone: and now the Wedding-Guest
Turned from the bridegroom's door.

He went like one that hath been stunned,
And is of sense forlorn:
A sadder and a wiser man,
He rose the morrow morn.

William Wordsworth 1770–1850

"STRANGE FITS OF PASSION HAVE I KNOWN"

Strange fits of passion have I known:
And I will dare to tell,
But in the Lover's ear alone,
What once to me befel.

When she I loved looked every day
Fresh as a rose in June,
I to her cottage bent my way,
Beneath an evening moon.

Upon the moon I fixed my eye,
All over the wide lea;
With quickening pace my horse drew nigh
Those paths so dear to me.

And now we reached the orchard-plot;
And, as we climbed the hill,
The sinking moon to Lucy's cot
Came near, and nearer still.

In one of those sweet dreams I slept,
Kind Nature's gentlest boon!
And all the while my eyes I kept
On the descending moon.

My horse moved on; hoof after hoof
He raised, and never stopped:
When down behind the cottage roof,
At once, the bright moon dropped.

From *Lyrical Ballads,* second edition 1800 (two poems).

What fond and wayward thoughts will slide
Into a Lover's head!
"O mercy!" to myself I cried,
"If Lucy should be dead!"

LUCY GRAY; OR, SOLITUDE

Oft I had heard of Lucy Gray:
And, when I crossed the wild,
I chanced to see at break of day
The solitary child.

No mate, no comrade Lucy knew;
She dwelt on a wide moor,
—The sweetest thing that ever grew
Beside a human door!

You yet may spy the fawn at play,
The hare upon the green;
But the sweet face of Lucy Gray
Will never more be seen.

"To-night will be a stormy night—
You to the town must go;
And take a lantern, Child, to light
Your mother through the snow."

"That, Father! will I gladly do:
'Tis scarcely afternoon—
The minster-clock has just struck two,
And yonder is the moon!"

At this the Father raised his hook,
And snapped a faggot-band;
He plied his work;—and Lucy took
The lantern in her hand.

Not blither is the mountain roe:
With many a wanton stroke
Her feet disperse the powdery snow,
That rises up like smoke.

The storm came on before its time:
She wandered up and down;
And many a hill did Lucy climb:
But never reached the town.

The wretched parents all that night
Went shouting far and wide;
But there was neither sound nor sight
To serve them for a guide.

At day-break on a hill they stood
That overlooked the moor;
And thence they saw the bridge of wood,
A furlong from their door.

They wept—and, turning homeward, cried,
"In heaven we all shall meet;"
—When in the snow the mother spied
The print of Lucy's feet.

Then downwards from the steep hill's edge
They tracked the footmarks small;
And through the broken hawthorn hedge,
And by the long stone-wall;

And then an open field they crossed:
The marks were still the same;
They tracked them on, nor ever lost;
And to the bridge they came.

They followed from the snowy bank
Those footmarks, one by one,
Into the middle of the plank;
And further there were none!

—Yet some maintain that to this day
She is a living child;
That you may see sweet Lucy Gray
Upon the lonesome wild.

O'er rough and smooth she trips along,
And never looks behind;
And sings a solitary song
That whistles in the wind.

Sir Walter Scott 1771–1832

PROUD MAISIE

Proud Maisie is in the wood,
  Walking so early;
Sweet Robin sits on the bush,
  Singing so rarely.

"Tell me, thou bonny bird,
  When shall I marry me?"—
"When six braw gentlemen
  Kirkward shall carry ye."

"Who makes the bridal bed,
  Birdie, say truly?"—
"The gray-headed sexton
  That delves the grave duly.

"The glow-worm o'er grave and stone
  Shall light thee steady.
The owl from the steeple sing,
  'Welcome, proud lady.' "

From *The Heart of Midlothian* 1818.
8 churchward

John Keats 1795–1821

LA BELLE DAME SANS MERCI

O what can ail thee Knight at arms
Alone and palely loitering?
The sedge has withered from the Lake
And no birds sing!

O what can ail thee Knight at arms
So haggard, and so woe begone?
The Squirrel's granary is full
And the harvest's done.

I see a lilly on thy brow
With anguish moist and fever dew,
And on thy cheeks a fading rose
Fast withereth too—

I met a Lady in the Meads
Full beautiful, a faery's child
Her hair was long, her foot was light
And her eyes were wild—

I made a Garland for her head,
And bracelets too, and fragrant Zone
She look'd at me as she did love
And made sweet moan—

I set her on my pacing steed
And nothing else saw all day long
For sidelong would she bend and sing
A faery's song—

From *Macmillan's Magazine,* August 1888—the first version, from an 1819 letter.
18 belt

She found me roots of relish sweet
And honey wild and manna dew
And sure in language strange she said
I love thee true—

She took me to her elfin grot
And there she wept and sigh'd full sore,
And there I shut her wild wild eyes
With kisses four.

And there she lullèd me asleep
And there I dream'd Ah Woe betide!
The latest dream I ever dreamt
On the cold hill side

I saw pale Kings, and Princes too
Pale warriors death pale were they all
They cried La belle dame sans merci
Thee hath in thrall.

I saw their starv'd lips in the gloam
With horrid warning gapèd wide,
And I awoke, and found me here
On the cold hill's side

And this is why I sojourn here
Alone and palely loitering;
Though the sedge is withered from the Lake
And no birds sing— . . .

Rudyard Kipling 1865–1936

DANNY DEEVER

"What are the bugles blowin' for?" said Files-on-Parade.
"To turn you out, to turn you out," the Colour-Sergeant said.
"What makes you look so white, so white?" said Files-on-Parade.
"I'm dreadin' what I've got to watch," the Colour-Sergeant said.
For they're hangin' Danny Deever, you can hear the Dead March play,
The regiment's in 'ollow square—they're hangin' him to-day;
They've taken of his buttons off an' cut his stripes away,
An' they're hangin' Danny Deever in the mornin'.

"What makes the rear-rank breathe so 'ard?" said Files-on-Parade.
"It's bitter cold, it's bitter cold," the Colour-Sergeant said.
"What makes that front-rank man fall down?" said Files-on-Parade.
"A touch o' sun, a touch o' sun," the Colour-Sergeant said.
They are hangin' Danny Deever, they are marchin' of 'im round,
They 'ave 'alted Danny Deever by 'is coffin on the ground;
An' 'e'll swing in 'arf a minute for a sneakin' shootin' hound—
O they're hangin' Danny Deever in the mornin'!

" 'Is cot was right-'and cot to mine," said Files-on-Parade.
" 'E's sleepin' out an' far to-night," the Colour-Sergeant said.
"I've drunk 'is beer a score o' times," said Files-on-Parade.
" 'E's drinkin' bitter beer alone," the Colour-Sergeant said.

From *Barrack Room Ballads* 1889-1891.

They are hangin' Danny Deever, you must mark 'im to 'is place,
For 'e shot a comrade sleepin'—you must look 'im in the face;
Nine 'undred of 'is county an' the regiment's disgrace,
While they're hangin' Danny Deever in the mornin'.

"What's that so black agin' the sun?" said Files-on-Parade.
"It's Danny fightin' 'ard for life," the Colour-Sergeant said.
"What's that that whimpers over'ead?" said Files-on-Parade.
"It's Danny's soul that's passin' now," the Colour-Sergeant said.
For they're done with Danny Deever, you can 'ear the quickstep play,
The regiment's in column, an' they're marchin' us away;
Ho! the young recruits are shakin', an' they'll want their beer to-day,
After hangin' Danny Deever in the mornin'.

William Butler Yeats 1865–1939

COLONEL MARTIN

I

THE Colonel went out sailing,
He spoke with Turk and Jew,
With Christian and with Infidel,
For all tongues he knew.
"O what's a wifeless man?" said he,
And he came sailing home.
He rose the latch and went upstairs
And found an empty room.
The Colonel went out sailing.

II

"I kept her much in the country
And she was much alone,
And though she may be there," he said,
"She may be in the town.
She may be all alone there,
For who can say?" he said.
"I think that I shall find her
In a young man's bed."
The Colonel went out sailing.

III

The Colonel met a pedlar,
Agreed their clothes to swop,
And bought the grandest jewelry
In a Galway shop,
Instead of thread and needle
Put jewelry in the pack,
Bound a thong about his hand,
Hitched it on his back.
The Colonel went out sailing.

From *Last Poems* 1936-1939.

IV

The Colonel knocked on the rich man's door,
"I am sorry," said the maid,
"My mistress cannot see these things,
But she is still abed,
And never have I looked upon
Jewelry so grand."
"Take all to your mistress,"
And he laid them on her hand.
The Colonel went out sailing.

V

And he went in and she went on
And both climbed up the stair,
And O he was a clever man,
For he his slippers wore.
And when they came to the top stair
He ran on ahead,
His wife he found and the rich man
In the comfort of a bed.
The Colonel went out sailing.

VI

The Judge at the Assize Court,
When he heard that story told,
Awarded him for damages
Three kegs of gold.
The Colonel said to Tom his man,
"Harness an ass and cart,
Carry the gold about the town,
Throw it in every part."
The Colonel went out sailing.

If they think they ha' snared our Goodly Fere
They are fools to the last degree.
"I'll go to the feast," quo' our Goodly Fere,
"Though I go to the gallows tree."

"Ye ha' seen me heal the lame and blind,
And wake the dead," says he,
"Ye shall see one thing to master all:
'Tis how a brave man dies on the tree."

A son of God was the Goodly Fere
That bade us his brothers be.
I ha' seen him cow a thousand men.
I have seen him upon the tree.

He cried no cry when they drave the nails
And the blood gushed hot and free,
The hounds of the crimson sky gave tongue
But never a cry cried he.

I ha' seen him cow a thousand men
On the hills o' Galilee,
They whined as he walked out calm between,
Wi' his eyes like the grey o' the sea,

Like the sea that brooks no voyaging
With the winds unleashed and free,
Like the sea that he cowed at Genseret
Wi' twey words spoke' suddently.

A master of men was the Goodly Fere,
A mate of the wind and sea,
If they think they ha' slain our Goodly Fere
They are fools eternally.

I ha' seen him eat o' the honey-comb
Sin' they nailed him to the tree.

John Crowe Ransom 1888—

CAPTAIN CARPENTER

Captain Carpenter rose up in his prime
Put on his pistols and went riding out
But had got wellnigh nowhere at that time
Till he fell in with ladies in a rout.

It was a pretty lady and all her train
That played with him so sweetly but before
An hour she'd taken a sword with all her main
And twined him of his nose for evermore.

Captain Carpenter mounted up one day
And rode straightway into a stranger rogue
That looked unchristian but be that as may
The Captain did not wait upon prologue.

But drew upon him out of his great heart
The other swung against him with a club
And cracked his two legs at the shinny part
And let him roll and stick like any tub.

Captain Carpenter rode many a time
From male and female took he sundry harms
He met the wife of Satan crying "I'm
The she-wolf bids you shall bear no more arms."

Their strokes and counters whistled in the wind
I wish he had delivered half his blows
But where she should have made off like a hind
The bitch bit off his arms at the elbows.

From *Chills and Fever* 1924.
4 crowd

And Captain Carpenter parted with his ears
To a black devil that used him in this wise
O Jesus ere his threescore and ten years
Another had plucked out his sweet blue eyes.

Captain Carpenter got up on his roan
And sallied from the gate in hell's despite
I heard him asking in the grimmest tone
If any enemy yet there was to fight?

"To any adversary it is fame
If he risk to be wounded by my tongue
Or burnt in two beneath my red heart's flame
Such are the perils he is cast among.

"But if he can he has a pretty choice
From an anatomy with little to lose
Whether he cut my tongue and take my voice
Or whether it be my round red heart he choose."

It was the neatest knave that ever was seen
Stepping in perfume from his lady's bower
Who at this word put in his merry mien
And fell on Captain Carpenter like a tower.

I would not knock old fellows in the dust
But there lay Captain Carpenter on his back
His weapons were the old heart in his bust
And a blade shook between rotten teeth alack.

The rogue in scarlet and grey soon knew his mind
He wished to get his trophy and depart
With gentle apology and touch refined
He pierced him and produced the Captain's heart.

God's mercy rest on Captain Carpenter now
I thought him Sirs an honest gentleman
Citizen husband soldier and scholar enow
Let jangling kites eat of him if they can.

But God's deep curses follow after those
That shore him of his goodly nose and ears
His legs and strong arms at the two elbows
And eyes that had not watered seventy years.

The curse of hell upon the sleek upstart
That got the Captain finally on his back
And took the red red vitals of his heart
And made the kites to whet their beaks clack clack.

Federico García Lorca 1899–1936

BALLAD OF THE MOON, MOON

The moon came to the forge
with her bustle of spikenards.
The child looks, looks.
The child is looking.
In the trembling air
the moon moves her arms
showing breasts hard as tin,
erotic and pure.

Fly, moon, moon, moon,
for if the gypsies come
they'll make rings
and white necklaces
out of your heart.

Child, let me dance!
When the gypsies come
they'll find you on the anvil
with your little eyes closed.

Fly, moon, moon, moon,
because I hear their horses.

Child, leave me alone, and don't
touch my starchy whiteness.

The horseman draws near
beating the drum of the plain.
Within the forge the child
has its eyes closed.

From *Romancero Gitano* 1928 (two poems). Translated by Langston Hughes 1902-1967.

Through the olive groves
come gypsies bronzed and dreamy,
their heads held high
and their eyes half-closed.

How the owl hoots!
How it hoots in the tree-tops!
Through the sky the moon goes
with a child by the hand.

Within the forge
gypsies weep, crying loudly.
The air veils her, veils her.
The air is veiling her.

THE BALLAD OF THE SLEEPWALKER

Green as I would have you green.
Green wind. Green branches.
The boat on the sea
and the horse in the mountains.
With a shadow around her waist
she dreams on her railing,
green flesh, green hair,
with eyes of cold silver.
Green as I would have you green.
Under the gypsy moon
things are looking at her
but she can't look back at them.

Green as I would have you green.
Big frosty stars
accompany the fish of darkness
opening the road to dawn.
The fig-tree polishes the wind.
with the sandpaper of its branches,
and like a wild cat the mountain
bristles with acid fibres.

But who's coming? And whence?
She lingers on her railing,
green flesh, green hair,
dreaming of the bitter sea.

Friend, let me change
my horse for your house,
my saddle for your looking-glass,
my knife for your blanket.
Friend, I've come bleeding
from the mountain passes of Cabra.

If I could, youngster,
we'd close the deal.
But I am no longer I,
and this house is not my house.

Friend, I would like to die
decently in my bed
by steel, if I could
on sheets of Holland linen.
Don't you see this cut I have
from my chest to my throat?

Three hundred dark roses
stain your white shirt front.
Your blood oozes pungent
around the edge of your waistband.
But I am no longer I,
and this house is not my house.

Let me go up at least
as high as the highest railings.
Let me go up!
Up to the green railings!
Banisters of the moon
where the falling water sounds.

The two friends go up,
up toward the highest railing,

leaving a trail of blood,
leaving a trail of tears,
Little tin-plate lanterns
tremble on the roof-tops.
A thousand tambourines of crystal
wound the early dawn.

Green as I would have you green.
Green wind. Green branches.
The two friends went up.
A steady wind left in the mouth
a strange taste of gall,
mint, and sweet basil.

> Friend, where is she, tell me?
> Where is your bitter maiden?
> How often she waited for you!
> How often she would wait,
> Cool face, black hair,
> at this green railing.

On the face of the cistern
a gypsy girl sways.
Green flesh, green hair,
with eyes of cold silver.
An icicle of moonlight
supports her on the water.
The night becomes intimate
as a little plaza.
Drunken Civil Guards
pound on the door.
Green as I would have you green.
Green wind. Green branches.
The boat on the sea
and the horse in the mountains.

Dylan Thomas 1914–1953

BALLAD OF THE LONG-LEGGED BAIT

The bows glided down, and the coast
Blackened with birds took a last look
At his thrashing hair and whale-blue eye;
The trodden town rang its cobbles for luck.

Then good-bye to the fishermanned
Boat with its anchor free and fast
As a bird hooking over the sea,
High and dry by the top of the mast,

Whispered the affectionate sand
And the bulwarks of the dazzled quay.
For my sake sail, and never look back,
Said the looking land.

Sails drank the wind, and white as milk
He sped into the drinking dark;
The sun shipwrecked west on a pearl
And the moon swam out of its hulk.

Funnels and masts went by in a whirl.
Good-bye to the man on the sea-legged deck
To the gold gut that sings on his reel
To the bait that stalked out of the sack,

For we saw him throw to the swift flood
A girl alive with his hooks through her lips;
All the fishes were rayed in blood,
Said the dwindling ships.

Good-bye to chimneys and funnels,
Old wives that spin in the smoke,

From *Collected Poems* 1943.

He was blind to the eyes of candles
In the praying windows of waves

But heard his bait buck in the wake
And tussle in a shoal of loves.
Now cast down your rod, for the whole
Of the sea is hilly with whales,

She longs among horses and angels,
The rainbow-fish bend in her joys,
Floated the lost cathedral
Chimes of the rocked buoys.

Where the anchor rode like a gull
Miles over the moonstruck boat
A squall of birds bellowed and fell,
A cloud blew the rain from its throat;

He saw the storm smoke out to kill
With fuming bows and ram of ice,
Fire on starlight, rake Jesu's stream;
And nothing shone on the water's face

But the oil and bubble of the moon,
Plunging and piercing in his course
The lured fish under the foam
Witnessed with a kiss.

Whales in the wake like capes and Alps
Quaked the sick sea and snouted deep,
Deep the great bushed bait with raining lips
Slipped the fins of those humpbacked tons

And fled their love in a weaving dip.
Oh, Jericho was falling in their lungs!
She nipped and dived in the nick of love,
Spun on a spout like a long-legged ball

Till every beast blared down in a swerve
Till every turtle crushed from his shell
Till every bone in the rushing grave
Rose and crowed and fell!

Good luck to the hand on the rod,
There is thunder under its thumbs;
Gold gut is a lightning thread,
His fiery reel sings off its flames,

The whirled boat in the burn of his blood
Is crying from nets to knives,
Oh the shearwater birds and their boatsized brood
Oh the bulls of Biscay and their calves

Are making under the green, laid veil
The long-legged beautiful bait their wives.
Break the black news and paint on a sail
Huge weddings in the waves,

Over the wakeward-flashing spray
Over the gardens of the floor
Clash out the mounting dolphin's day,
My mast is a bell-spire,

Strike and smoothe, for my decks are drums,
Sing through the water-spoken prow
The octopus walking into her limbs
The polar eagle with his tread of snow.

From salt-lipped beak to the kick of the stern
Sing how the seal has kissed her dead!
The long, laid minute's bride drifts on
Old in her cruel bed.

Over the graveyard in the water
Mountains and galleries beneath
Nightingale and hyena
Rejoicing for that drifting death

Sing and howl through sand and anemone
Valley and sahara in a shell,
Oh all the wanting flesh his enemy
Thrown to the sea in the shell of a girl

Is old as water and plain as an eel;
Always good-bye to the long-legged bread
Scattered in the paths of his heels
For the salty birds fluttered and fed

And the tall grains foamed in their bills;
Always good-bye to the fires of the face,
For the crab-backed dead on the sea-bed rose
And scuttled over her eyes,

The blind, clawed stare is cold as sleet.
The tempter under the eyelid
Who shows to the selves asleep
Mast-high moon-white women naked

Walking in wishes and lovely for shame
Is dumb and gone with his flame of brides.
Sussanah's drowned in the bearded stream
And no-one stirs at Sheba's side

But the hungry kings of the tides;
Sin who had a woman's shape
Sleeps till Silence blows on a cloud
And all the lifted waters walk and leap.

Lucifer that bird's dropping
Out of the sides of the north
Has melted away and is lost
Is always lost in her vaulted breath,

107 *Sussanah:* see the Apocrypha. Susanna was bathing and inspired lust in two elders who were spying on her. One attacked her and blamed her for enticing him, but her good name was cleared by Daniel. 113 *Lucifer:* the name given to Venus when it appears as the morning star.

Venus lies star-struck in her wound
And the sensual ruins make
Seasons over the liquid world,
White springs in the dark.

Always good-bye, cried the voices through the shell,
Good-bye always for the flesh is cast
And the fisherman winds his reel
With no more desire than a ghost.

Always good luck, praised the finned in the feather
Bird after dark and the laughing fish
As the sails drank up the hail of thunder
And the long-tailed lightning lit his catch.

The boat swims into the six-year weather,
A wind throws a shadow and it freezes fast.
See what the gold gut drags from under
Mountains and galleries to the crest!

See what clings to hair and skull
As the boat skims on with drinking wings!
The statues of great rain stand still,
And the flakes fall like hills.

Sing and strike his heavy haul
Toppling up the boatside in a snow of light!
His decks are drenched with miracles.
Oh miracle of fishes! The long dead bite!

Out of the urn the size of a man
Out of the room the weight of his trouble
Out of the house that holds a town
In the continent of a fossil

One by one in dust and shawl,
Dry as echoes and insect-faced,
His fathers cling to the hand of the girl
And the dead hand leads the past,

Leads them as children and as air
On to the blindly tossing tops;
The centuries throw back their hair
And the old men sing from newborn lips:

Time is bearing another son.
Kill Time! She turns in her pain!
The oak is felled in the acorn
And the hawk in the egg kills the wren.

He who blew the great fire in
And died on a hiss of flames
Or walked on the earth in the evening
Counting the denials of the grains

Clings to her drifting hair, and climbs;
And he who taught their lips to sing
Weeps like the risen sun among
The liquid choirs of his tribes.

The rod bends low, divining land,
And through the sundered water crawls
A garden holding to her hand
With birds and animals

With men and women and waterfalls
Trees cool and dry in the whirlpool of ships
And stunned and still on the green, laid veil
Sand with legends in its virgin laps

And prophets loud on the burned dunes;
Insects and valleys hold her thighs hard,
Time and places grip her breast bone,
She is breaking with seasons and clouds;

Round her trailed wrist fresh water weaves,
With moving fish and rounded stones
Up and down the greater waves
A separate river breathes and runs;

Strike and sing his catch of fields
For the surge is sown with barley,
The cattle graze on the covered foam,
The hills have footed the waves away,

With wild sea fillies and soaking bridles
With salty colts and gales in their limbs
All the horses of his haul of miracles
Gallop through the arched, green farms,

Trot and gallop with gulls upon them
And thunderbolts in their manes.
O Rome and Sodom To-morrow and London
The country tide is cobbled with towns,

And steeples pierce the cloud on her shoulder
And the streets that the fisherman combed
When his long-legged flesh was a wind on fire
And his loin was a hunting flame

Coil from the thoroughfares of her hair
And terribly lead him home alive
Lead her prodigal home to his terror,
The furious ox-killing house of love.

Down, down, down, under the ground,
Under the floating villages,
Turns the moon-chained and water-wound
Metropolis of fishes,

There is nothing left of the sea but its sound,
Under the earth the loud sea walks,
In deathbeds of orchards the boat dies down
And the bait is drowned among hayricks,

Land, land, land, nothing remains
Of the pacing, famous sea but its speech,
And into its talkative seven tombs
The anchor dives through the floors of a church.

Good-bye, good luck, struck the sun and the moon,
To the fisherman lost on the land.
He stands alone at the door of his home,
With his long-legged heart in his hand.

Miguel Hernández 1910–1942

WAR

All the mothers in the world
hide their wombs, tremble,
and wish they could turn back
into blind virginities,
into that solitary beginning,
the past, leaving nothing behind.
Virginity is left
pale, frightened.
The sea howls thirst and the earth
howls to be water.
Hatred flames out
and the screaming slams doors.
Voices shake like lances,
voices like bayonets.
Mouths step forward like fists,
fists arrive like hooves.
Breasts like hoarse walls,
legs like sinewy paws.
The heart quickens,
storms, blows up.
It throws sudden black spume
into the eye.
Blood thrashes about in the body,
flings the head off,
and searches for another body, a wound
to leap through, outside.
Blood parades through the world,
caged, baffled.
Flowers wither
devoured by the grass.
A lust for murder possesses
the secret places of the lily.

From *Cancionero de Ausencias.* Translated by James Wright 1927—.

Every living body longs to be joined
to a piece of cold metal:
to be married and possessed
horribly.
To disappear: a vast anxiety,
spreading, rules everything.
A ghostly procession of banners,
a fantastic flag,
a myth of nations: a
grave fiction of frontiers.
Outraged musics,
tough as boots, scar
the face of every hope
and the tender core.
The soul rages, fury.
Tears burst like lightning.
What do I want with light
if I stumble into darkness?
Passions like horns,
songs, trumpets that urge
the living to eat the living,
to raze themselves stone by stone.
Whinnies. Reverberations. Thunder.
Slaverings. Kisses. Wheels.
Spurs. Crazy swords
tear open a huge wound.

Then silence, mute
as cotton, white as bandages,
scarlet as surgery,
mutilated as sadness.
Silence. And laurel
in a corner among bones.
And a hysterical drum,
a tense womb, beats
behind the innumerable
dead man who never gets past.

The Ode

TO CALL A POEM an ode is to promise a certain elevation of style and feeling and to claim for it some connection with the ancients. To the ancients it meant a poem fit for music, as it did to Michael Drayton who was among the first to write odes in English:

> And why not I, as he
> That's greatest, if as free,
> (In sundry strains that strive
> Since there so many be)
>   Th'old *Lyric* kind revive?

He meant "lyric" quite literally: to be sung accompanied by a lyre or harp. He goes on to name his precursors: not only Pindar and Horace (and, of course, Orpheus, Hermes, Amphion) but also King David, whose Psalms were lately thought to be "fully written in metre, as all learned Hebraists agree, although the rules be not yet fully found"; classical, biblical harpers, and also ancients in Britain:

> And diversly though strung,
> So anciently We sung
>   To it, that Now scarce known,
> If first it did belong
> To *Greece*, or if our Own,

And why not I . . . : from "To Himself, and the Harp" in *Odes, with Other Lyric Poesies* 1619.

fully written in metre . . . : Sir Philip Sidney's *Defense of Poesy,* 1595

ancient druids "imbrew'd With Gore, on Altars rude," Irish and Welsh harpers:

> Th'old British Bards, upon their Harps,
> For falling Flats, and rising Sharps,
>   That curiously were strung;
> To stir their Youth to Warlike Rage,
> Or their wild Fury to assuage,
>   In these loose Numbers sung.

A "curious" musical scale different from the diatonic? My guess is that it was what you hear now only from the bagpipes; perhaps it was the way John Hewes was still tuning his harp in Warwickshire (Hewes, the Welsh poet Ralegh sent over the Atlantic with Amadas and Barlowe, whose first marvelous description of Virginia Drayton still echoes in his Ode to the Virginian Voyage twenty years later). Hewes was part of Sir Henry Goodyear's household when Drayton, a little page "like to a pigmy, scarce ten years old," asked him what he must read to become a poet; dedicating "these *Lyric* pieces short and few" to Sir Henry in 1619, Drayton, in his fifties as he writes, hopes

> They may become John Hewes his lyre
> Which oft at *Polesworth* by the fire
>   Hath made us gravely merry.

If the ode really is to be sung, its art is partly being ready for the melody: "a Song, moduled to the ancient Harp, and neither too short-breathed, as hasting to the end, nor composed of the longest Verses, as unfit for the sudden Turns and lofty Tricks which Apollo used to manage it." And even if it's not to be set to music, the rhythms of the proper ode are different from those of ordinary speech. Departures from the ostensible meter are

Th'old British Bards . . . : from the dedicatory poem to *Odes, with Other Lyric Poesies.*

a Song, moduled to the ancient Harp . . . : from Drayton's dedication To The Reader.

not in the accents of speech but in some other melody counter-pointed: not

> Call us what you will, we'are made such by love

but

> Darkling I listen; and, for many a time

where the metrical norm is the same; even in relatively regular verses the one tends towards plain speech, the other, music—Donne's

> For Godsake hold your tongue, and let me love

against Keats's

> My heart aches, and a drowsy numbness pains
> My sense.

I believe that it's the rhythm at least as much as the diction that is at the heart of the lofty quality associated with the ode; the diction too is rather lofty or serious because it deals fitly with thoughts or occasions that are, in the old sense, *solempne,* deeply and naturally ceremonious. It is this expectation that makes the ode apt for playful uses in the hands of a Gray or a Neruda.

Drayton distinguished between the kinds according to their use: the inimitable Pindaric ode of triumphs, the amorous Anacreontic, and the Horation or mixed. Now we usually distinguish them according to the metrical form, the full Pindaric with its turn, counterturn, and stand; the homostrophic or Horatian; and the Irregular, named after Sextus Irregulus, the last great poet of the Roman decadence whose imitations of

Petronius Arbiter, while greatly admired for their ingenuity, have yet to be fully explained.

In any case the ode has always been a kind of poetry that is enthusiastic but consciously and unashamedly civilized, even in the hands of rural, Romantic or American poets: Herrick and Clare, Coleridge and Keats, Duncan and Frank O'Hara. The poems in this chapter show that it is sometimes possible to be civilized without being a stick. Honor to old wild gods.

Pindar 522?–443 B.C.

SEVENTH OLYMPIC HYMN

for Diagoras of Rhodes, winner in boxing, 464 B.C.

STROPHE

Take in prospering hand   a shining cup
which holds the vine-flow
and proffer it, flecked with foam,
to the young man, who will be bridegroom:
      "Our houses meet!"   True
gold, this pride of fortune,
this feast   to celebrate
a new friendship,   to raise him out of
the guests' envy of
                  the bride's love:

ANTISTROPHE

so, I pour no lesser libation,   this nectar,
this Muses' gift   .   it is my mind's gift pours,
delighting,
propitiation for the victories at Olympia and Pytho.
a man is possessed by the good turning to name him:
another time, the Beauty of the Gift   (of freshness)
looks over another man,   and his initiation.
the phorminx' sweetness and the many-toned oboe

EPODE

accompany us   on shipboard   .   now Diagoras and I
come to land where
                  I sing of
the sea's child   by Aphrodite,   Rhodes, bride of

Inscribed in gold letters in the temple at Lindos.

Translated by Robin Blaser 1925—. From *Caterpillar Magazine* 12, July, 1970.

18 lyre's

Helios . this poem repays him who, out of the boxing-match,
unflinching, fit to be crowned at Alpheos' River with laurel
and at Kastalia, is mythically larger and his father
Damagetos, whom Dike gathered,
who both live on the three-citied island,
among Argive spearmen,
near by the headland of far-spreading Asia.

STROPHE

I bear the news I put the events
straight for the thought of their beginnings,
from Herakles,
from Tlepolemos first, wide ruling,
from their father's source, they spring up joyous
from Zeus' desguise . they are Amyntorids
from Astydameia's mother-right . numberless
errors hang around men's minds no way to invent

ANTISTROPHE

now or at the finish, not-knowing, a man's best of the gods' gifts.
and so, Alkmene's bastard brother, Lykymnios,
came from his mother's rooms at Tiryns, Midea's,
to die struck down by the hard wild-olive staff,
embittered, the raised hand of Tlepolemos, who founded
this island so mania enters the mind's skill
and drives the knower to wander off . he went to ask the god's voice.

EPODE

in the adytum fragrance, the Golden-Haired One
spoke of his ships' sailing straight out of wave-breaking Lerna
to that sea-girt grassland where
the king of the gods, once let fall a gold-storm,

35 fame 45 sanctuary

gold snowing   .   the high brightness drenched the city,
the smooth-bronze axe cut   .   Hephaistos' handwork.
Athena,   out of the crown of her father's head, sprang
joyous   shouting   called out.
Awe wakened Ouranos and the mother Gaia.

STROPHE

and the daimonion,   the light-bringing,   Hyperion's
son, commanded his loved children to guard
over the event,   mindful of the debt,
first founders of the goddess' altar   in clear view
and the holy offering set in place,
kindling the heart of the father,
stirring the maiden of the whistling spear   .   Prometheus
and Aidos,   who measure with awe,   caught men up
with prowess   and the joy acts inward and outward
from the first thought.

ANTISTROPHE

unexpected,   a cloud intercepts us   nearby Lethe
the virtu is lost   out of place
in us   into the air
they did not carry the sperm-fire   when they climbed the
high hill
no glowing ash at hand   .   without fire, they prepared
her grove.
above the Akropolis,   Zeus gathered the clouds,
pale-yellow, and sent a gold rain upon them,   and the
Owl-Faced,

EPODE

glaring, silvery,   sent along companion-gifts,
every art,   and they surpassed all the men of the earth
with the skill of their hands   .   shaped as if life caught
them

53 *Ouranos* and *Gaia:* the sky and the earth. 54-55 *Hyperion's son:* Helios, the sun.

and motion,   their works lined the streets   .   word
spread far and wide   .   art's language
discloses powers without trickery   sophia   when
men tell old legends.   when Zeus and the deathless gods
chose shares of the earth, Rhodes was not yet
seen in the sea's open water,   the sea-land hidden in the
salt-deep.

STROPHE

Helios was gone   and no one pointed to his share of it,
no place was apportioned   .   so the sacred Sun
was left out   he questioned   and Zeus settled
to recast the lots   .   but Helios stopped that
when he looked down into the gray-clear sea.
he said   I see the mantle swelling   out of the sea-floor,
I see my lot rising   abundance for men
from gaia and hillsides for good flocks.

ANTISTROPHE

quickly, he called Lachesis of the gold-bound hair
to raise her hands   to swear   by the high oath of the
gods,
without double-talk,
bending her head along with the son of Kronos: the
island
would be his share,   left to him alone   after she shot up
into the bright air   .   the talk over   .   from where
he looked down, his desire fell to meet her   budding against
the sea-spray,

EPODE

the sea-land is held by the dazzle of the sun-flow,   father
who reins the hard-breathing horses' fire   .   they mixed,
and Rhodes bore seven sons,   who take up
his gift of thought,   most knowing among the first men,

87 *Lachesis:* one of the Fates.

as their father gave pieces of land from gaia   to Kamiros
and the first-born
Ialysos, and to Lindos,   divided three ways,   wide apart
with cities named for them   and three rock-seats.

STROPHE

it let loose   the outcome of bloodshed   (the other face)
turns the
hardship to sweetness   :   set for Tlepolemos, the first
from Tiryns,
god-like,
burnt offering of sheep there,   the procession   and
Diagoras
twice in the games' judgment stood crowned with flowers,
and four times at famous Ismos   the good fortune   again
and again at Nemea   and rock-strewn Athens;

ANTISTROPHE

marked by the bronze shield at Argos, by his skill at Arcadia
and Thebes,   by the crowds at the old games of the
Boeotians,
at Pelana,   and at Aigina, six times the winner   .   at
Megara
the stone tablet tells no other tale   O Zeus   father,
guardian of wide-backed Mt. Atabyrios,   take
this hymn   (the marriage-cry)   set for the winner at
Olympia,

EPODE

this fighter   who, among the powers,   met skill's
beauty,
matched his own clenched fists   let his gift be in the eyes
of townsmen and strangers   over him,   the Graces
turning against hybris   he travels   straight on the way
his fathers left   aware of the good turn of events

surely do not hide this share of the gift
of the seed of Kallianax : the Eratidai
are touched by
gods' love, the city holds the beauty of the
flower-bringer
Thalia . but in a moment, the winds hit and turn

bound for

121 *Kallianax:* ancestor of Diagoras; *Eratidai:* Diagoras' family name.

Sophocles 496–406 B.C.

COLONUS' PRAISE

Come praise Colonus' horses, and come praise
The wine-dark of the wood's intricacies,
The nightingale that deafens daylight there,
If daylight ever visit where,
Unvisited by tempest or by sun,
Immortal ladies tread the ground
Dizzy with harmonious sound,
Semele's lad a gay companion.

And yonder in the gymnasts' garden thrives
The self-sown, self-begotten shape that gives
Athenian intellect its mastery,
Even the grey-leaved olive-tree
Miracle-bred out of the living stone;
Nor accident of peace nor war
Shall wither that old marvel, for
The great grey-eyed Athene stares thereon.

Who comes into this country, and has come
Where golden crocus and narcissus bloom,
Where the Great Mother, mourning for her daughter
And beauty-drunken by the water
Glittering among grey-leaved olive-trees,
Has plucked a flower and sung her loss;
Who finds abounding Cephisus
Has found the loveliest spectacle there is.

Because this country has a pious mind
And so remembers that when all mankind
But trod the road, or splashed about the shore,

From *Oedipus at Colonus*. Translated by William Butler Yeats 1865-1939; from *The Tower* 1928.
8 *Semele's lad:* Dionysus

Poseidon gave it bit and oar,
Every Colonus lad or lass discourses
Of that oar and of that bit;
Summer and winter, day and night,
Of horses and horses of the sea, white horses.

Horace 65–8 B.C.

THE PRAISE OF PINDAR

Pindar is imitable by none;
The Phoenix Pindar is a vast species alone.
Who e'er but Daedalus with waxen wings could fly,
And neither sink too low nor soar too high?
What could he who follow'd claim,
But of vain boldness the unhappy fame,
And by his fall a sea to name?
Pindar's unnavigable song
Like a swoln flood from some steep mountain pours along;
The ocean meets with such a voice,
From his enlargèd mouth, as drowns the ocean's noise.

So Pindar does new words and figures roll
Down his impetuous dithyrambick tide,
Which in no channel deigns t' abide,
Which neither banks nor dykes control:
Whether th' immortal Gods he sings,
In a no less immortal strain,
Or the great acts of God-descended kings,
Who in his numbers still survive and reign;
Each rich-embroider'd line,
Which their triumphant brows around
By his sacred hand is bound,
Does all their starry diadems outshine.

Whether at Pisa's race he please
To carve in polish'd verse the conqueror's images;
Whether the swift, the skilful, or the strong,
Be crownèd in his nimble, artful, vigorous song;
Whether some brave young man's untimely fate,
In words worth dying for, he celebrate—

Odes IV.2: "Pindarum quiquis studet aemulari." A version by Abraham Cowley 1618-1667; from *Pindaric Odes* 1656.

13 *dithyramb:* a Greek lyric form which Pindar used and refined in his poetry. 24 *Pisa:* after the 6th century B.C. called Olympia.

Such mournful, and such pleasing words,
As joy to his mother's and his mistress' grief affords—
He bids him live and grow in fame;
Among the stars he sticks his name;
The grave can but the dross of him devour,
So small is Death's, so great the Poet's, power!

Lo, how th' obsequious wind, and swelling air,
The Theban swan does upwards bear
Into the walks of clouds, where he does play,
And with extended wings opens his liquid way!
Whilst, alas! my timorous Muse
Unambitious tracks pursues;
Does with weak, unballast wings,
About the mossy brooks and springs,
About the trees' new-blossom'd heads,
About the gardens' painted beds,
About the fields and flowery meads,
And all inferior beauteous things,
Like the laborious bee,
For little drops of honey flee,
And there with humble sweets contents her industry.

37 *The Theban swan:* Pindar was born in Boeotia, near Thebes.

SOLVITUR ACRIS HIEMS

Winter to Spring: the west wind melts the frozen rancour,
The windlass drags to sea the thirsty hull;
Byre is no longer welcome to beast or fire to ploughman,
The field removes the frost-cap from his skull.

Venus of Cythera leads the dances under the hanging
Moon and the linked line of Nymphs and Graces
Beat the ground with measured feet while the busy Fire-God
Stokes his red-hot mills in volcanic places.

Now is the time to twine the spruce and shining head with myrtle,
Now with flowers escaped the earthy fetter,
And sacrifice to the woodland god in shady copses
A lamb or a kid, whichever he likes better.

Equally heavy is the heel of white-faced Death on the pauper's
Shack and the towers of kings, and O my dear
The little sum of life forbids the ravelling of lengthy
Hopes. Night and the fabled dead are near

And the narrow house of nothing past whose lintel
You will meet no wine like this, no boy to admire
Like Lycidas who today makes all young men a furnace
And whom tomorrow girls will find a fire.

Odes I.4. Translated by Louis MacNeice 1907-1963; from *The Earth Compels* 1936-1938.

Solvitur Acris Hiems: Harsh winter melts.

5 *Cythera:* one of the Ionian islands in the south of Greece, near where some traditions say Venus sprang from the sea-foam.

"THIS MONUMENT WILL OUTLAST"

This monument will outlast metal and I made it
More durable than the king's seat, higher than pyramids.
Gnaw of the wind and rain?
Impotent
The flow of the years to break it, however many.

Bits of me, many bits, will dodge all funeral,
O Libitina-Persephone and, after that,
Sprout new praise. As long as
Pontifex and the quiet girl pace the Capitol
I shall be spoken where the wild flood Aufidus
Lashes, and Daunus ruled the parched farmland:

Power from lowliness: "First brought Aeolic song to Italian fashion"—
Wear pride, work's gain! O Muse Melpomene,
By your will bind the laurel.
My hair, Delphic laurel.

Odes III.30: "Monumentum aere perennius." Translated by Ezra Pound 1885—; from *Confucius to Cummings* 1926.

1 *This monument* . . . : the third book, of which this ode is the last. 7 *Libitina-Persephone:* meaning death. 10-11 *Aufidus* . . . *Daunus:* a river and a legendary king, respectively, of Apulia, Horace's homeland. 13 *Melpomene:* the tragic Muse.

Edmund Spenser 1552?–1599

EPITHALAMION

Ye learnèd sisters, which have oftentimes
Been to me aiding, others to adorn,
Whom ye thought worthy of your graceful rimes,
That even the greatest did not greatly scorn
To hear their names sung in your simple lays,
But joyèd in their praise;
And when ye list your own mishaps to mourn,
Which death, or love, or fortune's wreck did raise,
Your string could soon to sadder tenor turn,
And teach the woods and waters to lament
Your doleful dreariment.
Now lay those sorrowful complaints aside;
And having all your heads with girland crowned,
Help me mine own love's praises to resound;
Ne let the same of any be envide:
So Orpheus did for his own bride;
So I unto myself alone will sing;
The woods shall to me answer and my echo ring.

Early, before the world's light-giving lamp
His golden beam upon the hills doth spread,
Having dispersed the night's uncheerful damp,
Do ye awake; and with fresh lustihead
Go to the bower of my belovèd love,
My truest turtle-dove,
Bid her awake; for Hymen is awake,
And long since ready forth his masque to move,
With his bright tead that flames with many a flake,
And many a bachelor to wait on him,
In their fresh garments trim.
Bid her awake therefore, and soon her dight,
For lo! the wished day is come at last,

From *Amoretti and Epithalamion* 1595.
1 the Muses 15 envied 27 torch . . . spark 30 make ready

That shall, for all the pains and sorrows past,
Pay to her usury of long delight:
And whilst she doth her dight,
Do ye to her of joy and solace sing,
That all the woods may answer and your echo ring.

Bring with you all the nymphs that you can hear
Both of the rivers and the forests green,
And of the sea that neighbours to her near:
All with gay girlands goodly well beseen.
And let them also with them bring in hand
Another gay girland
For my fair love, of lilies and of roses,
Bound true-love wise with a blue silk riband.
And let them make great store of bridal posies,
And let them eke bring store of other flowers,
To deck the bridal bowers.
And let the ground whereas her foot shall tread,
For fear the stones her tender foot should wrong,
Be strewed with fragrant flowers all along,
And diap'red like the discoloured mead.
Which done, do at her chamber door await,
For she will waken straight;
The whiles do ye this song unto her sing,
The woods shall to you answer, and your echo ring.

Ye nymphs of Mulla, which with careful heed
The silver scaly trouts do tend full well,
And greedy pikes which use therein to feed
(Those trouts and pikes all others do excel);
And ye likewise, which keep the rushy lake,
Where none do fishes take:
Bind up the locks the which hang scattered light,
And in his waters, which your mirror make,
Behold your faces as the crystal bright,

56 *Mulla:* poetic name for the Irish Awbeg River, near Spenser's home.

That when you come whereas my love doth lie,
No blemish she may spy.
And eke, ye lightfoot maids, which keep the deer,
That on the hoary mountain use to tower;
And the wild wolves, which seek them to devour,
With your steel darts do chase from coming near;
Be also present here,
To help to deck her, and to help to sing,
That all the woods may answer and your echo ring.

Wake now, my love, awake! for it is time;
The rosy morn long since left Tithone's bed,
All ready to her silver coach to climb;
And Phoebus gins to shew his glorious head.
Hark! how the cheerful birds do chant their lays
And carol of Love's praise.
The merry lark her matins sings aloft;
The thrush replies, the mavis descant plays,
The ouzel shrills, the ruddock warbles soft;
So goodly all agree, with sweet consent,
To this day's merriment.
Ah! my dear love, why do ye sleep thus long,
When meeter were that ye should now awake,
T'await the coming of your joyous make,
And hearken to the birds' love-learnèd song,
The dewy leaves among!
For they of joy and pleasance to you sing,
That all the woods them answer and their echo ring.

My love is now awake out of her dreams,
And her fair eyes, like stars that dimmèd were
With darksome cloud, now shew their goodly beams
More bright than Hesperus his head doth rear.
Come now ye damsels, daughters of delight,
Help quickly her to dight:

68 *tower:* climb to a height, a term from falconry. 75 *Tithone:* Tithonus, husband of Eos, or Aurora, the dawn. 87 mate 95 evening star

But first come, ye fair hours, which were begot
In Jove's sweet paradise, of Day and Night;
Which do the seasons of the year allot,
And all, that ever in this world is fair,
Do make and still repair:
And ye three handmaids of the Cyprian Queen,
The which do still adorn her beauty's pride,
Help to adorn my beautifullest bride:
And, as ye her array, still throw between
Some graces to be seen;
And, as ye use to Venus, to her sing,
The whiles the woods shall answer and your echo ring.

Now is my love all ready forth to come:
Let all the virgins therefore well await:
And ye fresh boys, that tend upon her groom,
Prepare yourselves, for he is coming straight.
Set all your things in seemly good array,
Fit for so joyful day:
The joyfull'st day that ever sun did see.
Fair sun! shew forth thy favourable ray,
And let thy lifeful heat not fervent be,
For fear of burning her sunshiny face,
Her beauty to disgrace.
O fairest Phoebus, father of the Muse,
If ever I did honour thee aright,
Or sing the thing that mote thy mind delight,
Do not thy servant's simple boon refuse;
But let this day, let this one day, be mine;
Let all the rest be thine.
Then I thy sovereign praises loud will sing,
That all the woods shall answer, and their echo ring.

Hark, how the minstrels gin to shrill aloud
Their merry music that resounds from far,
The pipe, the tabor, and the trembling croud,

103 *Cyprian Queen:* Venus. Her handmaidens are the Three Graces.
131 small drum . . . fiddle

That well agree withouten breach or jar.
But most of all the damsels do delight
When they their timbrels smite,
And thereunto do dance and carol sweet,
That all the senses they do ravish quite;
The whiles the boys run up and down the street,
Crying aloud with strong confusèd noise,
As if it were one voice,
Hymen, iö Hymen, Hymen, they do shout;
That even to the heavens their shouting shrill
Doth reach, and all the firmament doth fill;
To which the people standing all about,
As in approvance, do thereto applaud,
And loud advance her laud;
And evermore they Hymen, Hymen sing,
That all the woods them answer and their echo ring.

Lo! where she comes along with portly pace,
Like Phoebe from her chamber of the east,
Arising forth to run her mighty race,
Clad all in white, that seems a virgin best.
So well it her beseems, that ye would ween
Some angel she had been.
Her long loose yellow locks like golden wire,
Sprinkled with pearl, and perling flowers atween,
Do like a golden mantle her attire;
And, being crownèd with a girland green,
Seem like some maiden queen.
Her modest eyes, abashèd to behold
So many gazers as on her do stare,
Upon the lowly ground affixèd are;
Ne dare lift up her countenance too bold,
But blush to hear her praises sung so loud,
So far from being proud.
Nathless do ye still loud her praises sing,
That all the woods may answer and your echo ring.

148 proud   155 mingling

Tell me, ye merchants' daughters, did ye see
So fair a creature in your town before?
So sweet, so lovely, and so mild as she,
Adorned with beauty's grace and virtue's store;
Her goodly eyes like sapphires shining bright,
Her forehead ivory white,
Her cheeks like apples which the sun hath ruddied,
Her lips like cherries charming men to bite,
Her breast like to a bowl of cream uncrudded,
Her paps like lilies budded,
Her snowy neck like to a marble tower;
And all her body like a palace fair,
Ascending up, with many a stately stair,
To honour's seat and chastity's sweet bower.
Why stand ye still, ye virgins, in amaze,
Upon her so to gaze,
Whiles ye forget your former lay to sing,
To which the woods did answer and your echo ring?

But if ye saw that which no eyes can see,
The inward beauty of her lively sprite,
Garnished with heavenly gifts of high degree,
Much more then would ye wonder at that sight,
And stand astonished like to those which read
Medusa's mazeful head.
There dwells sweet love, and constant chastity,
Unspotted faith, and comely womanhead,
Regard of honour, and mild modesty;
There virtue reigns as queen in royal throne,
And giveth laws alone,
The which the base affections do obey,
And yield their services unto her will;
Ne thought of thing uncomely ever may
Thereto approach to tempt her mind to ill.
Had ye once seen these her celestial treasures,
And unrevealèd pleasures,

175 uncurdled 186 spirit 189 saw

Then would ye wonder, and her praises sing,
That all the woods should answer and your echo ring.

Open the temple gates unto my love,
Open them wide that she may enter in,
And all the posts adorn as doth behove,
And all the pillars deck with girlands trim,
For to receive this saint with honour due,
That cometh in to you.
With trembling steps, and humble reverence,
She cometh in, before th'Almighty's view;
Of her ye virgins learn obedience,
Whenso ye come into those holy places,
To humble your proud faces;
Bring her up to th'high altar, that she may
The sacred ceremonies there partake,
The which do endless matrimony make;
And let the roaring organs loudly play
The praises of the Lord in lively notes;
The whiles, with hollow throats,
The choristers the joyous anthem sing,
That all the woods may answer and their echo ring.

Behold, whiles she before the altar stands,
Hearing the holy priest that to her speaks,
And blesseth her with his two happy hands,
How the red roses flush up in her cheeks,
And the pure snow with goodly vermeil stain,
Like crimson dyed in grain:
That even th'angels, which continually
About the sacred altar do remain,
Forget their service and about her fly,
Oft peeping in her face, that seems more fair
The more they on it stare.
But her sad eyes, still fastened on the ground,
Are governèd with goodly modesty,

228 colorfast

That suffers not one look to glance awry,
Which may let in a little thought unsound.
Why blush ye, love, to give to me your hand,
The pledge of all our band?
Sing, ye sweet angels, Alleluia sing,
That all the woods may answer and your echo ring.

Now all is done: bring home the bride again;
Bring home the triumph of our victory:
Bring home with you the glory of her gain,
With joyance bring her and with jollity.
Never had man more joyful day than this,
Whom heaven would heap with bliss.
Make feast therefore now all this livelong day;
This day for ever to me holy is.
Pour out the wine without restraint or stay,
Pour not by cups, but by the bellyful,
Pour out to all that wull,
And sprinkle all the posts and walls with wine,
That they may sweat, and drunken be withal.
Crown ye God Bacchus with a coronal,
And Hymen also crown with wreaths of vine;
And let the Graces dance unto the rest,
For they can do it best:
The whiles the maidens do their carol sing,
To which the woods shall answer and their echo ring.

Ring ye the bells, ye young men of the town,
And leave your wonted labours for this day:
This day is holy; do ye write it down,
That ye for ever it remember may.
This day the sun is in his chiefest height,
With Barnaby the bright,
From whence declining daily by degrees,
He somewhat loseth of his heat and light,
When once the Crab behind his back he sees.

252 will 266 *Barnaby:* St. Barnabas' Day, 11 July, was the summer solstice in the calendar of Spenser's time.

But for this time it ill ordainèd was,
To choose the longest day in all the year,
And shortest night, when longest fitter were:
Yet never day so long, but late would pass.
Ring ye the bells, to make it wear away,
And bonfires make all day;
And dance about them, and about them sing,
That all the woods may answer and your echo ring.

Ah, when will this long weary day have end,
And lend me leave to come unto my love?
How slowly do the hours their numbers spend!
How slowly does sad Time his feathers move!
Haste thee, O fairest planet, to thy home,
Within the western foam:
Thy tired steeds long since have need of rest.
Long though it be, at last I see it gloom,
And the bright evening star with golden crest
Appear out of the east.
Fair child of beauty! glorious lamp of love!
That all the host of heaven in ranks dost lead,
And guidest lovers through the nightès dread,
How cheerfully thou lookest from above,
And seem'st to laugh atween thy twinkling light,
As joying in the sight
Of these glad many, which for joy do sing,
That all the woods them answer, and their echo ring!

Now cease, ye damsels, your delights forepast;
Enough is it that all the day was yours:
Now day is done, and night is nighing fast,
Now bring the bride into the bridal bowers.
The night is come, now soon her disarray,
And in her bed her lay;
Lay her in lilies and in violets,
And silken curtains over her display,
And odoured sheets, and arras coverlets.

282 the sun 304 tapestry

Behold how goodly my fair love does lie,
In proud humility!
Like unto Maia, whenas Jove her took
In Tempe, lying on the flow'ry grass,
Twixt sleep and wake, after she weary was,
With bathing in the Acidalian brook.
Now it is night, ye damsels may be gone,
And leave my love alone,
And leave likewise your former lay to sing:
The woods no more shall answer, nor your echo ring.

Now welcome, night! thou night so long expected,
That long day's labour dost at last defray,
And all my cares, which cruel Love collected,
Hast summed in one, and cancellèd for aye:
Spread thy broad wing over my love and me,
That no man may us see;
And in thy sable mantle us enwrap,
From fear of peril and foul horror free.
Let no false treason seek us to entrap,
Nor any dread disquiet once annoy
The safety of our joy;
But let the night be calm and quietsome,
Without tempestuous storms or sad affray:
Like as when Jove with fair Alcmena lay,
When he begot the great Tirynthian groom:
Or like as when he with thyself did lie
And begot Majesty.
And let the maids and young men cease to sing,
Ne let the woods them answer nor their echo ring.

307 *Maia:* the eldest of the Pleiades and mother of Hermes (Mercury) by Zeus. In Roman mythology Maia became associated with growth and fertility. 316 repay 327 fright 328 *Alcmena:* the last mortal woman visited by Zeus. She gave birth to Hercules, who performed twelve immense labors for the king of Tiryns. The union of Jove and Night which produced Majesty (ll. 330-331) is probably Spenser's own invention.

Let no lamenting cries, nor doleful tears,
Be heard all night within, nor yet without:
Ne let false whispers, breeding hidden fears,
Break gentle sleep with misconceivèd doubt.
Let no deluding dreams, nor dreadful sights,
Make sudden sad affrights;
Ne let house-fires, nor lightning's helpless harms,
Ne let the Pouke, nor other evil sprites,
Ne let mischievous witches with their charms,
Ne let hobgoblins, names whose sense we see not,
Fray us with things that be not:
Let not the screech-owl nor the stork be heard,
Nor the night-raven, that still deadly yells;
Nor damnèd ghosts, called up with mighty spells,
Nor grisly vultures, make us once afeard:
Ne let th'unpleasant quire of frogs still croaking
Make us to wish their choking.
Let none of these their dreary accents sing;
Ne let the woods them answer, nor their echo ring.

But let still silence true night-watches keep,
That sacred peace may in assurance reign,
And timely sleep, when it is time to sleep,
May pour his limbs forth on your pleasant plain;
The whiles an hundred little wingèd loves,
Like divers feathered doves,
Shall fly and flutter round about your bed,
And in the secret dark, that none reproves,
Their pretty stealths shall work, and snares shall spread
To filch away sweet snatches of delight,
Concealed through covert night.
Ye sons of Venus, play your sports at will!
For greedy pleasure, careless of your toys,
Thinks more upon her paradise of joys,
Than what ye do, albeit good or ill.
All night therefore attend your merry play,

341 *Pouke:* Hobgoblin, identified in medieval tradition with Satan.
344 frighten 357 cupids

For it will soon be day:
Now none doth hinder you, that say or sing;
Ne will the woods now answer nor your echo ring.

Who is the same, which at my window peeps?
Or whose is that fair face that shines so bright?
Is it not Cynthia, she that never sleeps,
But walks about high heaven all the night?
O fairest goddess, do thou not envy
My love with me to spy:
For thou likewise didst love, though now unthought,
And for a fleece of wool, which privily
The Latmian shepherd once unto thee brought,
His pleasures with thee wrought.
Therefore to us be favourable now;
And sith of women's labours thou hast charge,
And generation goodly dost enlarge,
Incline thy will t'effect our wishful vow,
And the chaste womb inform with timely seed,
That may our comfort breed:
Till which we cease our hopeful hap to sing;
Ne let the woods us answer nor our echo ring.

And thou, great Juno! which with awful might
The laws of wedlock still dost patronize;
And the religion of the faith first plight
With sacred rites hast taught to solemnize;
And eke for comfort often callèd art
Of women in their smart;
Eternally bind thou this lovely band,
And all thy blessings unto us impart.
And thou, glad Genius! in whose gentle hand

374 the moon 378-387 *The Latmian shepherd:* Endymion, who was visited nightly by the moon goddess. Spenser seems to be combining this story with that of Pan, who, in the fleece of a ram, lured Cynthia into the woods and seduced her. Although more traditionally the goddess was associated with chastity, she is sometimes also concerned with childbirth. 396 loving 398 *Genius:* the god or spirit of procreation.

The bridal bower and genial bed remain,
Without blemish or stain:
And the sweet pleasures of their love's delight
With secret aid dost succour and supply,
Till they bring forth the fruitful progeny;
Send us the timely fruit of this same night.
And thou, fair Hebe! and thou, Hymen free!
Grant that it may so be.
Till which we cease your further praise to sing;
Ne any woods shall answer nor your echo ring.

And ye high heavens, the temple of the gods,
In which a thousand torches flaming bright
Do burn, that to us wretched earthly clods
In dreadful darkness lend desirèd light;
And all ye powers which in the same remain,
More than we men can feign,
Pour out your blessing on us plenteously,
And happy influence upon us rain,
That we may raise a large posterity,
Which from the earth, which they may long possess,
With lasting happiness,
Up to your haughty palaces may mount;
And, for the guerdon of their glorious merit,
May heavenly tabernacles there inherit,
Of blessèd saints for to increase the count.
So let us rest, sweet love, in hope of this,
And cease till then our timely joys to sing;
The woods no more us answer, nor our echo ring.

Song, made in lieu of many ornaments,
With which my love should duly have been decked,
Which cutting off through hasty accidents,
Ye would not stay your due time to expect,
But promised both to recompense;
Be unto her a goodly ornament,
And for short time an endless monument.

399 marriage 405 *Hebe:* goddess of youth. 414 imagine 421 reward

Michael Drayton 1563–1631

TO THE VIRGINIAN VOYAGE

You brave heroic minds
Worthy your country's name,
    That honour still pursue
    Go, and subdue
Whilst loitering hinds
Lurk here at home, with shame.

Britons, you stay too long;
Quickly aboard bestow you,
    And with a merry gale
    Swell your stretch'd sail,
With vows as strong
As the winds that blow you.

Your course securely steer,
West and by south forth keep;
    Rocks, lee-shores, nor shoals,
    When Aeolus scowls,
You need not fear,
So absolute the deep.

And cheerfully at sea
Success you still entice
    To get the pearl and gold,
    And ours to hold
Virginia,
Earth's only paradise,

Where nature hath in store
Fowl, venison and fish,
    And the fruitfullest soil
    Without your toil,

From *Odes, with Other Lyric Poesies* 1619.

Three harvests more,
All greater than your wish.

And the ambitious vine
Crowns with his purple mass
    The cedar reaching high
    To kiss the sky,
The cypress, pine
And useful sassafras.

To whose the golden age
Still nature's laws doth give;
    Nor other cares attend
    But them to defend
From Winter's age.
That long there doth not live.

When as the luscious smell
Of that delicious land
    Above the sea that flows
    The clear wind throws,
Your hearts to swell,
Approaching the dear strand;

In kenning of the shore
(Thanks to God first given)
    O you, the happiest men
    Be frolic then,
Let cannons roar,
Frighting the wide heaven.

And in regions far
Such heroes bring ye forth
    As those from whom we came,
    And plant our name
Under the star
Not known unto our North.

And as there plenty grows
Of Laurel everywhere,
    Apollo's sacred tree,
    You may it see
A Poet's brows
To crown, that may sing there.

Thy voyages attend
Industrious Hakluyt,
    Whose reading shall inflame
    Men to seek fame,
And much commend
To after-times thy wit.

68 Richard Hakluyt documented the exploits of the English overseas in his *Principall Navigations, Voiages, Traffics and Discoveries of the English Nation,* 1589 and 1598-1600.

Thomas Campion 1567–1620

HARK, ALL YOU LADIES

Hark, all you ladies that do sleep:
  The Fairie Queen Proserpina
Bids you awake and pity them that weep.
  You may do in the dark
What the day doth forbid;
  Fear not the dogs that bark,
    Night will have all hid.

But if you let your lovers moan,
  The Fairie Queen Proserpina
Will send abroad her Fairies ev'ry one,
  That shall pinch black and blue
Your white hands and fair arms
  That did not kindly rue
    Your Paramours' harms.

In Myrtle Arbors on the downs
  The Fairie Queen Proserpina,

From *Rosseter's Book of Airs* 1601. Appended to Sir Philip Sidney's *Astrophel and Stella* 1591.

The last four lines of each stanza are in sapphics; the notes show how the syllables are to be scanned for quantity.

This night by moon-shine leading merry rounds
  Holds a watch with sweet love,
Down the dale, up the hill;
  No plaints or groans may move
    Their holy vigil.

All you that will hold watch with love,
  The Fairie Queen Proserpina
Will make you fairer than Dione's dove;
  Roses red, lilies white,
And the clear damask hue,
  Shall on your cheeks alight:
    Love will adorn you.

All you that love, or loved before,
  The Fairie Queen Proserpina
Bids you increase that loving humor more:
  They that yet have not fed
On delight amorous,
  She vows that they shall lead
    Apes in Avernus.

24 *Dione's:* Venus's (she is given the name of her mother, the Titaness). 31 obsession 35 *Avernus:* the underworld. A jocular tradition had it that old maids would keep apes there because they refused to keep husbands here.

Ben Jonson 1572–1636

AN ODE. TO HIMSELF

Where dost thou careless lie,
  Buried in ease and sloth?
Knowledge, that sleeps, doth die;
And this Securitie,
  It is the common Moth,
That eats on wits, and Arts, and oft destroys them both.

Are all th'Aonian springs
  Dried up? lies Thespia waste?
Doth Clarius' Harp want strings,
That not a Nymph now sings?
  Or droop they as disgraced,
To see their Seats and Bowers by chattring Pies defaced?

If hence thy silence be,
  As 'tis too just a cause;
Let this thought quicken thee,
Minds that are great and free,
  Should not on fortune pause,
'Tis crown enough to virtue still, her own applause.

What though the greedy Fry
  Be taken with false Baits
Of worded Balladry,
And think it Poesie?
  They die with their conceits,
And only piteous scorn, upon their folly waits.

From *The Underworld*, 1640.

7-9 *Aonian springs:* associated with Mt. Helicon and the Muses. *Thespia:* a town near Helicon. *Clarius:* Apollo. 12 *Pies:* the Pierides, nine sisters so proud of their voices that they challenged the Muses to a singing contest. They lost but went on scolding and were changed into magpies.

Then take in hand thy Lyre,
  Strike in thy proper strain,
With Japhet's line, aspire
Sol's Chariot for new fire,
  To give the world again:
Who aided him, will thee, the issue of Jove's brain.

And since our Dainty age,
  Cannot endure reproof,
Make not thy self a Page,
To that strumpet the Stage,
  But sing high and aloof,
Safe from the wolf's black jaw, and the dull ass's hoof.

27 *Japhet's line:* Iapetus was the father of Prometheus; *aspire* [*to*].
30 *the issue . . . :* Minerva, goddess of wisdom, who sprang full-grown from Zeus's head.

Robert Herrick 1591–1674

THE HOCK-CART, OR HARVEST HOME

Come, sons of summer, by whose toil
We are the lords of wine and oil,
By whose tough labours and rough hands,
We rip up first, then reap our lands.
Crown'd with the ears of corn, now come,
And to the pipe sing harvest home.
Come forth my lord, and see the cart
Drest up with all the country art.
See here a Maukin, there a sheet,
As spotless pure as it is sweet:
The horses, mares, and frisking fillies,
Clad all in linen white as lilies.
The harvest swains and wenches bound
For joy, to see the Hock-cart crown'd.
About the cart, hear how the rout
Of rural younglings raise the shout:
Pressing before, some coming after,
Those with a shout, and these with laughter.
Some bless the cart, some kiss the sheaves,
Some prank them up with oaken leaves;
Some cross the fill-horse; some with great
Devotion, stroke the home-borne wheat
While other rusticks, less attent
To prayers than to merryment,
Run after with their breeches rent.
Well, on, brave boys, to your lord's hearth,
Glitt'ring with fire; where, for your mirth,
Ye shall see first the large and chief

From *Hesperides: or, The Works Both Human and Divine of Robert Herrick* 1648 (two poems). "The Hock-Cart" is inscribed "To the Right Honourable, Mildmay, Earle of Westmoreland."

The Hock-Cart: brought in the last load of the harvest; its arrival signaled the beginning of the harvest-home celebration.

9 an effigy

Foundation of your feast, fat beef:
With upper stories, mutton, veal,
And bacon, which makes full the meal,
With sev'ral dishes standing by,
As here a custard, there a pie,
And here all tempting frumentie.
And for to make the merry cheer,
If smirking wine be wanting here,
There's that which drowns all care, stout beer;
Which freely drink to your lord's health;
Then to the plough, the common-wealth;
Next to your flails, your fans, your fatts;
Then to the maids with wheaten hats:
To the rough sickle, and crookt scythe,
Drink, frollick boys, till all be blythe.
Feed, and grow fat; and as ye eat,
Be mindfull that the lab'ring neat,
As you, may have their fill of meat.
And know, besides, ye must revoke
The patient ox unto the yoke,
And all go back unto the plough
And harrow, though they'r hang'd up now.
And, you must know your lord's word's true,
Feed him ye must whose food fills you;
And that this pleasure is like rain,
Not sent ye for to drown your pain,
But for to make it spring again.

34 *frumentie:* a dish made of wheat boiled in milk, with sugar or spices. 36 sparkling 40 vats 45 oxen 47 call back

CORINNA'S GOING A-MAYING

Get up, get up for shame, the blooming morn
Upon her wings presents the god unshorn.
    See how Aurora throws her fair
    Fresh-quilted colours through the air!
    Get up, sweet slug-a-bed, and see
    The dew-bespangling herb and tree.
Each flower has wept, and bow'd toward the east,
Above an hour since; yet you not drest,
    Nay! not so much as out of bed?
    When all the birds have matins said,
    And sung their thankful hymns, 'tis sin,
    Nay, profanation to keep in,
When as a thousand virgins on this day,
Spring, sooner then the lark, to fetch in May.

Rise, and put on your foliage, and be seen
To come forth, like the spring-time, fresh and green
    And sweet as Flora. Take no care
    For jewels for your gown or hair.
    Fear not; the leaves will strew
    Gems in abundance upon you.
Besides, the childhood of the day has kept,
Against you come, some orient pearls unwept:
    Come, and receive them while the light
    Hangs on the dew-locks of the night,
    And Titan on the eastern hill
    Retires himself, or else stands still
Till you come forth. Wash, dress, be brief in praying:
Few beads are best, when once we go a Maying.

Come, my Corinna, come; and coming, mark
How each field turns a street, each street a park
    Made green, and trimm'd with trees: see how
    Devotion gives each house a bough
    Or branch: each porch, each door, ere this,

25 the sun

An ark, a tabernacle is,
Made up of white-thorn neatly interwove;
As if here were those cooler shades of love.
Can such delights be in the street
And open fields, and we not see't?
Come, we'll abroad; and let's obey
The proclamation made for May,
And sin no more, as we have done, by staying;
But, my Corinna, come, let's go a Maying.

There's not a budding boy, or girl, this day,
But is got up, and gone to bring in May.
A deal of youth, ere this, is come
Back, and with white-thorn laden home.
Some have dispatcht their cakes and cream,
Before that we have left to dream:
And some have wept, and woo'd, and plighted troth,
And chose their priest, ere we can cast off sloth.
Many a green-gown has been given;
Many a kiss, both odd and even;
Many a glance too has been sent
From out the eye, love's firmament;
Many a jest told of the keys betraying
This night, and locks pickt, yet w'are not a Maying.

Come, let us go, while we are in our prime,
And take the harmless folly of the time.
We shall grow old apace, and die
Before we know our liberty.
Our life is short, and our days run
As fast away as does the sun;
And as a vapour, or a drop of rain,
Once lost, can ne'er be found again,
So when or you or I are made
A fable, song, or fleeting shade,
All love, all liking, all delight,
Lies drown'd with us in endless night.
Then while time serves, and we are but decaying;
Come, my Corinna, come, let's go a Maying.

John Milton 1608–1674

ON THE MORNING OF CHRIST'S NATIVITY

I

This is the month, and this the happy morn,
Wherein the Son of Heaven's Eternal King,
Of wedded maid and virgin mother born,
Our great redemption from above did bring;
For so the holy sages once did sing,
  That he our deadly forfeit should release,
And with his Father work us a perpetual peace.

II

That glorious form, that light unsufferable,
And that far-beaming blaze of majesty,
Wherewith he wont at Heaven's high council-table
To sit the midst of Trinal Unity,
He laid aside, and, here with us to be,
  Forsook the courts of everlasting day,
And chose with us a darksome house of mortal clay.

III

Say, Heavenly Muse, shall not thy sacred vein
Afford a present to the Infant God?
Hast thou no verse, no hymn, or solemn strain,
To welcome him to this his new abode,
Now while the heaven, by the Sun's team untrod,
  Hath took no print of the approaching light,
And all the spangled host keep watch in squadrons bright?

From *Poems* 1645.

15 *Heavenly Muse:* Urania, originally the Muse of Astronomy, but whom Milton identified with divine wisdom and considered a source of poetic inspiration.

IV

See how from far upon the eastern road
The star-led wizards haste with odours sweet!
Oh! run; prevent them with thy humble ode,
And lay it lowly at his blessèd feet;
Have thou the honour first thy Lord to greet,
   And join thy voice unto the Angel Quire,
From out his secret altar touched with hallowed fire.

THE HYMN

I

      It was the winter wild,
      While the heaven-born child
   All meanly wrapt in the rude manger lies;
      Nature, in awe to him,
      Had doffed her gaudy trim,
   With her great Master so to sympathise:
It was no season then for her
To wanton with the Sun, her lusty paramour.

II

      Only with speeches fair
      She woos the gentle air
   To hide her guilty front with innocent snow,
      And on her naked shame,
      Pollute with sinful blame,
   The saintly veil of maiden white to throw;
Confounded, that her Maker's eyes
Should look so near upon her foul deformities.

III

      But he, her fears to cease,
      Sent down the meek-eyed Peace:
   She, crowned with olive green, came softly sliding
      Down through the turning sphere,
      His ready harbinger,

24 precede

With turtle wing the amorous clouds dividing;
And, waving wide her myrtle wand,
She strikes a universal peace through sea and land.

IV

No war, or battle's sound,
Was heard the world around;
The idle spear and shield were high uphung;
The hookèd chariot stood,
Unstained with hostile blood;
The trumpet spake not to the armèd throng;
And kings sat still with awful eye,
As if they surely knew their sovran Lord was by.

V

But peaceful was the night
Wherein the Prince of Light
His reign of peace upon the earth began.
The winds, with wonder whist,
Smoothly the waters kissed,
Whispering new joys to the mild Ocean,
Who now hath quite forgot to rave,
While birds of calm sit brooding on the charmèd wave.

VI

The stars, with deep amaze,
Stand fixed in steadfast gaze,
Bending one way their precious influence,
And will not take their flight,
For all the morning light,
Or Lucifer that often warned them thence;
But in their glimmering orbs did glow,
Until their Lord himself bespake, and bid them go.

50 turtledove 64 hushed 74 the morning star

VII

And, though the shady gloom
Had given day her room,
The Sun himself withheld his wonted speed,
And hid his head for shame,
As his inferior flame
The new-enlightened world no more should need:
He saw a greater Sun appear
Than his bright throne or burning axletree could bear.

VIII

The shepherds on the lawn,
Or ere the point of dawn,
Sat simply chatting in a rustic row;
Full little thought they than
That the mighty Pan
Was kindly come to live with them below:
Perhaps their loves, or else their sheep,
Was all that did their silly thoughts so busy keep.

IX

When such music sweet
Their hearts and ears did greet
As never was by mortal finger strook,
Divinely-warbled voice
Answering the stringèd noise,
As all their souls in blissful rapture took:
The air, such pleasure loth to lose,
With thousand echoes still prolongs each heavenly close.

X

Nature, that heard such sound
Beneath the hollow round
Of Cynthia's seat the Airy region thrilling,
Now was almost won
To think her part was done,

89 *Pan:* the god of Nature; God Himself, as understood by the rustic pagan shepherds of the pastoral convention. 92 simple

And that her reign had here its last fulfilling:
She knew such harmony alone
Could hold all Heaven and Earth in happier unïon.

XI

At last surrounds their sight
A globe of circular light,
That with long beams the shamefaced Night arrayed;
The helmèd cherubim
And sworded seraphim
Are seen in glittering ranks with wings displayed,
Harping in loud and solemn quire
With unexpressive notes, to Heaven's new-born Heir.

XII

Such music (as 'tis said)
Before was never made,
But when of old the Sons of Morning sung,
While the Creator great
His constellations set,
And the well-balanced World on hinges hung,
And cast the dark foundations deep,
And bid the weltering waves their oozy channel keep.

XIII

Ring out, ye crystal spheres!
Once bless our human ears,
If ye have power to touch our senses so;
And let your silver chime
Move in melodious time;
And let the bass of heaven's deep organ blow;
And with your ninefold harmony
Make up full consort to th' angelic symphony.

116 inexpressible 125 *crystal spheres:* according to Ptolemaic astronomy, there were nine concentric crystalline spheres which held the planets and the stars; harmoniously turning, they caused music which mortal ears were ordinarily too dulled by original sin to hear.

XIV

For, if such holy song
Enwrap our fancy long,
Time will run back and fetch the Age of Gold;
And speckled Vanity
Will sicken soon and die;
And leprous Sin will melt from earthly mould;
And Hell itself will pass away,
And leave her dolorous mansions to the peering day.

XV

Yea, Truth and Justice then
Will down return to men,
Orbed in a rainbow; and, like glories wearing,
Mercy will sit between,
Throned in celestial sheen,
With radiant feet the tissued clouds down steering;
And Heaven, as at some festival,
Will open wide the gates of her high palace-hall.

XVI

But wisest Fate says No,
This must not yet be so;
The Babe yet lies in smiling infancy
That on the bitter cross
Must redeem our loss,
So both himself and us to glorify:
Yet first, to those ychained in sleep,
The wakeful trump of doom must thunder through the deep,

XVII

With such a horrid clang
As on Mount Sinai rang,
While the red fire and smouldering clouds outbrake:
The aged Earth, aghast,
With terror of that blast,

Shall from the surface to the centre shake,
When, at the world's last session,
The dreadful Judge in middle air shall spread his throne.

XVIII

And then at last our bliss
Full and perfect is,
But now begins; for from this happy day
Th' Old Dragon under ground,
In straiter limits bound,
Not half so far casts his usurpèd sway,
And, wroth to see his kingdom fail,
Swingès the scaly horror of his folded tail.

XIX

The Oracles are dumb;
No voice or hideous hum
Runs through the archèd roof in words deceiving.
Apollo from his shrine
Can no more divine,
With hollow shriek the steep of Delphos leaving.
No nightly trance, or breathèd spell,
Inspires the pale-eyed priest from the prophetic cell.

XX

The lonely mountains o'er,
And the resounding shore,
A voice of weeping heard and loud lament;
From haunted spring, and dale
Edgèd with poplar pale,
The parting Genius is with sighing sent;
With flower-inwoven tresses torn
The Nymphs in twilight shade of tangled thickets mourn.

168 Satan 186 local spirit

XXI

In consecrated earth,
And on the holy hearth,
The Lars and Lemures moan with midnight plaint;
In urns, and altars round,
A drear and dying sound
Affrights the flamens at their service quaint;
And the chill marble seems to sweat,
While each peculiar Power forgoes his wonted seat.

XXII

Peor and Baälim
Forsake their temples dim,
With that twice-battered God of Palestine;
And moonèd Ashtaroth,
Heaven's queen and mother both,
Now sits not girt with tapers' holy shine:
The Libyc Hammon shrinks his horn;
In vain the Tyrian maids their wounded Thammuz mourn.

XXIII

And sullen Moloch, fled,
Hath left in shadows dread
His burning idol all of blackest hue;
In vain with cymbal's ring
They call the grisly king,
In dismal dance about the furnace blue;
The brutish gods of Nile as fast,
Isis, and Orus, and the dog Anubis, haste.

191 *Lars:* Roman minor gods associated with particular places; *Lemures:* spirits of dead who had gone unburied. 194 priests . . . elaborate 197-204 *Peor:* Baal, the highest Canaanite god. *Baälim:* lesser gods related to Baal. *twice-battered God:* Dagon, whose statue fell twice to the ground before the Ark of the Lord. *Ashtaroth:* Phoenician moon goddess, Astarte. *Hammon:* Ammon, the Egyptian god who was represented as a horned ram. *Thammuz:* God whose yearly death symbolized the coming of winter. 205-213 *Moloch:* a Canaanite god to whom children were sacrificed. Cymbals were clashed to cover their

XXIV

Nor is Osiris seen
In Memphian grove or green,
Trampling the unshowered grass with lowings loud;
Nor can he be at rest
Within his sacred chest;
Nought but profoundest Hell can be his shroud;
In vain, with timbreled anthems dark,
The sable-stolèd sorcerers bear his worshiped ark.

XXV

He feels from Juda's land
The dreaded Infant's hand;
The rays of Bethlehem blind his dusky eyn;
Nor all the gods beside
Longer dare abide,
Not Typhon huge ending in snaky twine:
Our Babe, to show his Godhead true,
Can in his swaddling bands control the damnèd crew.

XXVI

So, when the sun in bed,
Curtained with cloudy red,
Pillows his chin upon an orient wave,
The flocking shadows pale
Troop to th' infernal jail,
Each fettered ghost slips to his several grave,
And the yellow-skirted fays
Fly after the night-steeds, leaving their moon-loved maze.

cries. *Isis, Orus, Anubis, Osiris:* Egyptian gods represented by a cow, a hawk, a dog, and a bull respectively.

223 eyes 226 *Typhon:* a monster in Greek mythology whose body consisted of snakes from the hips down, and whose hands were serpent heads.

XXVII

But see! the Virgin blest
Hath laid her Babe to rest.
Time is our tedious song should here have ending:
Heaven's youngest-teemèd star
Hath fixed her polished car,
Her sleeping Lord with handmaid lamp attending;
And all about the courtly stable
Bright-harnessed Angels sit in order serviceable.

240 star of Bethlehem

Andrew Marvell 1621–1678

AN HORATIAN ODE UPON CROMWELL'S RETURN FROM IRELAND

The forward youth that would appear,
Must now forsake his Muses dear,
    Nor in the shadows sing
    His numbers languishing:

'Tis time to leave the books in dust,
And oil the unusèd armour's rust;
    Removing from the wall
    The corselet of the hall.

So restless Cromwell could not cease
In the inglorious arts of peace,
    But through adventurous war
    Urgèd his active star;

And, like the three-forked lightning, first
Breaking the clouds where it was nursed,
    Did thorough his own side
    His fiery way divide:

(For 'tis all one to courage high,
The emulous, or enemy;
    And with such, to enclose,
    Is more than to oppose;)

From *Miscellaneous Poems* 1681.

Cromwell's Return: In the end of May, 1650, Cromwell returned from a successful campaign in Ireland in order to direct a Scottish campaign.

4 poetry   16 *divide:* refers to Cromwell's rise through the ranks to become Parliamentary leader.

Then burning through the air he went,
And palaces and temples rent;
    And Caesar's head at last
    Did through his laurels blast.

'Tis madness to resist or blame
The face of angry Heaven's flame;
    And if we would speak true,
    Much to the man is due,

Who from his private gardens, where
He lived reservèd and austere,
    (As if his highest plot
    To plant the bergamot;)

Could by industrious valour climb
To ruin the great work of Time,
    And cast the kingdoms old,
    Into another mould;

Though Justice against Fate complain,
And plead the ancient rights in vain;
    (But those do hold or break,
    As men are strong or weak.)

Nature that hateth emptiness,
Allows of penetration less,
    And therefore must make room
    Where greater spirits come.

What field of all the civil war,
Where his were not the deepest scar?
    And Hampton shows what part
    He had of wiser art;

23 *Caesar:* Charles I. 32 pear tree 47 *Hampton:* Hampton Court, where Charles I was imprisoned, but from which Cromwell allowed him to escape in order to make him appear irresponsible. He escaped to Caresbrook Castle on the Isle of Wight.

Where, twining subtle fears with hope,
He wove a net of such a scope
That Charles himself might chase
To Caresbrooke's narrow case,

That thence the royal actor borne,
The tragic scaffold might adorn;
While round the armèd bands
Did clap their bloody hands.

He nothing common did; or mean,
Upon that memorable scene,
But with his keener eye
The axe's edge did try;

Nor called the gods with vulgar spite
To vindicate his helpless right;
But bowed his comely head
Down, as upon a bed.

This was that memorable hour,
Which first assured the forcèd power;
So, when they did design
The capitol's first line,

A bleeding head, where they begun,
Did fright the architects to run;
And yet in that the state
Foresaw its happy fate.

And now the Irish are ashamed
To see themselves in one year tamed;
So much one man can do,
That does both act and know.

57 *He:* Charles I 69 *bleeding head:* workmen digging the foundations for the Temple of Jupiter in Rome uncovered a bloody head which was taken to mean that Rome would be the "head" of an empire.

They can affirm his praises best,
And have, though overcome, confessed
    How good he is, how just,
    And fit for highest trust.

Nor yet grown stiffer with command,
But still in the republic's hand—
    How fit he is to sway,
    That can so well obey!

He to the Commons' feet presents
A kingdom for his first year's rents;
    And, what he may, forbears
    His fame, to make it theirs;

And has his sword and spoils ungirt,
To lay them at the public's skirt:
    So, when the falcon high
    Falls heavy from the sky,

She, having killed, no more doth search,
But on the next green bough to perch;
    Where, when he first does lure,
    The falconer has her sure.

What may not then our isle presume,
While victory his crest does plume?
    What may not others fear,
    If thus he crowns each year?

A Caesar, he, ere long, to Gaul,
To Italy an Hannibal,
    And to all states not free,
    Shall climactèric be.

90 feet

The Pict no shelter now shall find
Within his parti-coloured mind,
But, from this valour sad,
Shrink underneath the plaid;

Happy, if in the tufted brake,
The English hunter him mistake,
Nor lay his hounds in near
The Caledonian deer.

But thou, the war's and fortune's son,
March indefatigably on;
And for the last effect,
Still keep the sword erect;

Besides the force it has to fright
The spirits of the shady night,
The same arts that did gain
A power, must it maintain.

105 Scot 106 *parti-coloured:* factitious 112 Scottish

Alexander Pope 1688–1744

SOLITUDE. AN ODE

Happy the man whose wish and care
A few paternal acres bound,
Content to breathe his native air,
In his own ground.

Whose herds with milk, whose fields with bread,
Whose flocks supply him with attire,
Whose trees in summer yield him shade,
In winter fire.

Blest, who can unconcern'dly find
Hours, days, and years slide soft away,
In health of body, peace of mind,
Quiet by day,

Sound sleep by night; study and ease,
Together mixt; sweet recreation;
And Innocence, which most does please
With meditation.

Thus let me live, unseen, unknown,
Thus unlamented let me die,
Steal from the world, and not a stone
Tell where I lie.

From *Poems on Several Occasions* 1717.

Thomas Gray 1716–1771

ODE ON THE DEATH OF A FAVOURITE CAT, DROWNED IN A TUB OF GOLD FISHES

'Twas on a lofty vase's side,
Where China's gayest art had dyed
  The azure flowers, that blow;
Demurest of the tabby kind,
The pensive Selima, reclined,
  Gazed on the lake below.

Her conscious tail her joy declared;
The fair round face, the snowy beard,
  The velvet of her paws,
Her coat, that with the tortoise vies,
Her ears of jet, and emerald eyes,
  She saw; and purred applause.

Still had she gazed; but 'midst the tide
Two angel forms were seen to glide,
  The Genii of the stream;
Their scaly armour's Tyrian hue
Through richest purple to the view
  Betrayed a golden gleam.

The hapless nymph with wonder saw;
A whisker first and then a claw,
  With many an ardent wish,
She stretched in vain to reach the prize.
What female heart can gold despise?
  What Cat's averse to fish?

Presumptuous maid! with looks intent
Again she stretched, again she bent,
  Nor knew the gulf between.

From *Collection of Poems by Several Hands,* ed. Dodsley 1748.

(Malignant Fate sat by, and smiled)
The slippery verge her feet beguiled,
  She tumbled headlong in.

Eight times emerging from the flood
She mewed to every wat'ry god,
  Some speedy aid to send.
No Dolphin came, no Nereid stirred;
Nor cruel Tom, nor Susan heard.
  A fav'rite has no friend!

From hence, ye Beauties, undeceived,
Know, one false step is ne'er retrieved,
  And be with caution bold.
Not all that tempts your wand'ring eyes
And heedless hearts is lawful prize;
  Nor all, that glisters, gold.

William Collins 1721–1759

ODE TO EVENING

If aught of oaten stop, or pastoral song,
May hope, chaste Eve, to sooth thy modest ear,
  Like thy own solemn springs,
  Thy springs and dying gales,

O nymph reserv'd, while now the bright-hair'd sun
Sits in yon western tent, whose cloudy skirts,
  With brede ethereal wove,
  O'erhang his wavy bed:

Now air is hush'd, save where the weak-ey'd bat,
With short shrill shriek, flits by on leathern wing,
  Or where the beetle winds
  His small but sullen horn,

As oft he rises 'midst the twilight path,
Against the pilgrim borne in heedless hum:
  Now teach me, maid compos'd,
  To breathe some soften'd strain,

Whose numbers, stealing thro' thy dark'ning vale,
May not unseemly with its stillness suit,
  As, musing slow, I hail
  Thy genial lov'd return!

For when thy folding-star arising shews
His paly circlet, at his warning lamp
  The fragrant Hours, and elves
  Who slept in flow'rs the day,

From *Odes on Several Descriptive and Allegorical Subjects* 1746.
7 embroidery

And many a nymph who wreaths her brows with sedge,
And sheds the fresh'ning dew, and, lovelier still,
The pensive Pleasures sweet,
Prepare thy shadowy car.

Then lead, calm vot'ress, where some sheety lake
Cheers the lone heath, or some time-hallow'd pile
Or upland fallows grey
Reflect its last cool gleam.

But when chill blust'ring winds, or driving rain,
Forbid my willing feet, be mine the hut
That from the mountain's side
Views wilds, and swelling floods,

And hamlets brown, and dim-discover'd spires,
And hears their simple bell, and marks o'er all
Thy dewy fingers draw
The gradual dusky veil.

While Spring shall pour his show'rs, as oft he wont,
And bathe thy breathing tresses, meekest Eve;
While Summer loves to sport
Beneath thy ling'ring light;

While sallow Autumn fills thy lap with leaves;
Or Winter, yelling thro' the troublous air,
Affrights thy shrinking train,
And rudely rends thy robes;

So long, sure-found beneath the sylvan shed,
Shall Fancy, Friendship, Science, rose-lipp'd Health,
Thy gentlest influence own,
And hymn thy fav'rite name!

Samuel Taylor Coleridge 1772–1834

DEJECTION: AN ODE. WRITTEN 4 APRIL, 1802

Late, late yestreen I saw the new Moon,
With the old Moon in her arms;
And I fear, I fear, my Master dear!
We shall have a deadly storm.
Ballad of Sir Patrick Spence.

I

Well! If the Bard was weather-wise, who made
The grand old ballad of Sir Patrick Spence,
This night, so tranquil now, will not go hence
Unroused by winds, that ply a busier trade
Than those which mould yon cloud in lazy flakes,
Or the dull sobbing draft, that moans and rakes
Upon the strings of this Aeolian lute,
Which better far were mute.
For lo! the New-moon winter-bright!
And overspread with phantom light,
(With swimming phantom light o'erspread
But rimmed and circled by a silver thread)
I see the old Moon in her lap, foretelling
The coming-on of rain and squally blast.
And oh! that even now the gust were swelling,
And the slant night-shower driving loud and fast!
Those sounds which oft have raised me, whilst they awed,
And sent my soul abroad,
Might now perhaps their wonted impulse give,
Might startle this dull pain, and make it move and live!

II

A grief without a pang, void, dark, and drear,
A stifled, drowsy, unimpassioned grief,
Which finds no natural outlet, no relief,
In word, or sigh, or tear—

From *Sibylline Leaves* 1817.

O Lady! in this wan and heartless mood,
To other thoughts by yonder throstle wooed,
All this long eve, so balmy and serene,
Have I been gazing on the western sky,
And its peculiar tint of yellow green:
And still I gaze—and with how blank an eye!
And those thin clouds above, in flakes and bars,
That give away their motion to the stars;
Those stars, that glide behind them or between,
Now sparkling, now bedimmed, but always seen:
Yon crescent Moon, as fixed as if it grew
In its own cloudless, starless lake of blue,
I see them all so excellently fair,
I see, not feel, how beautiful they are!

III

My genial spirits fail;
And what can these avail
To lift the smothering weight from off my breast?
It were a vain endeavour,
Though I should gaze for ever
On that green light that lingers in the west:
I may not hope from outward forms to win
The passion and the life, whose fountains are within.

IV

O Lady! we receive but what we give
And in our life alone does Nature live:
Ours is her wedding garment, ours her shroud!
And would we aught behold, of higher worth,
Than that inanimate cold world allowed
To the poor loveless ever-anxious crowd,
Ah! from the soul itself must issue forth
A light, a glory, a fair luminous cloud
Enveloping the Earth—
And from the soul itself must there be sent
A sweet and potent voice, of its own birth,
Of all sweet sounds the life and element!

V

O pure of heart! thou need'st not ask of me
What this strong music in the soul may be!
What, and wherein it doth exist,
This light, this glory, this fair luminous mist,
This beautiful and beauty-making power.
  Joy, virtuous Lady! Joy that ne'er was given,
Save to the pure, and in their purest hour,
Life, and Life's effluence, cloud at once and shower,
Joy, Lady! is the spirit and the power,
Which wedding Nature to us gives in dower
  A new Earth and new Heaven,
Undreamt of by the sensual and the proud—
Joy is the sweet voice, Joy the luminous cloud—
    We in ourselves rejoice!
And thence flows all that charms or ear or sight,
  All melodies the echoes of that voice,
All colours a suffusion from that light.

VI

There was a time when, though my path was rough,
  This joy within me dallied with distress,
And all misfortunes were but as the stuff
  Whence Fancy made me dreams of happiness:
For hope grew round me, like the twining vine,
And fruits, and foliage, not my own, seemed mine.
But now afflictions bow me down to earth:
Nor care I that they rob me of my mirth;
    But oh! each visitation
Suspends what nature gave me at my birth,
  My shaping spirit of Imagination.
For not to think of what I needs must feel,
  But to be still and patient, all I can;
And haply by abstruse research to steal
  From my own nature all the natural man—
  This was my sole resource, my only plan:
Till that which suits a part infects the whole,
And now is almost grown the habit of my soul.

VII

Hence, viper thoughts, that coil around my mind,
Reality's dark dream!
I turn from you, and listen to the wind,
Which long has raved unnoticed. What a scream
Of agony by torture lengthened out
That lute sent forth! Thou Wind, that rav'st without,
Bare crag, or mountain-tairn, or blasted tree,
Or pine-grove whither woodman never clomb,
Or lonely house, long held the witches' home,
Methinks were fitter instruments for thee,
Mad Lutanist! who in this month of showers,
Of dark-brown gardens, and of peeping flowers,
Mak'st Devils' yule, with worse than wintry song,
The blossoms, buds, and timorous leaves among.
Thou Actor, perfect in all tragic sounds!
Thou mighty Poet, e'en to frenzy bold!
What tell'st thou now about?
'Tis of the rushing of an host in rout,
With groans of trampled men, with smarting wounds—
At once they groan with pain, and shudder with the cold!
But hush! there is a pause of deepest silence!
And all that noise, as of a rushing crowd,
With groans, and tremulous shudderings—all is over—
It tells another tale, with sounds less deep and loud!
A tale of less affright,
And tempered with delight,
As Otway's self had framed the tender lay,—
'Tis of a little child
Upon a lonesome wild,
Not far from home, but she hath lost her way:
And now moans low in bitter grief and fear,
And now screams loud, and hopes to make her mother hear.

VIII

'Tis midnight, but small thoughts have I of sleep:
Full seldom may my friend such vigils keep!
Visit her, gentle Sleep! with wings of healing,
   And may this storm be but a mountain-birth,
May all the stars hang bright above her dwelling,
   Silent as though they watched the sleeping Earth!
         With light heart may she rise,
         Gay fancy, cheerful eyes,
   Joy lift her spirit, joy attune her voice;
To her may all things live, from pole to pole,
Their life the eddying of her living soul!
   O simple spirit, guided from above,
Dear Lady! friend devoutest of my choice,
Thus mayest thou ever, evermore rejoice.

Percy Bysshe Shelley 1792–1822

ODE TO THE WEST WIND

I

O wild West Wind, thou breath of Autumn's being,
Thou, from whose unseen presence the leaves dead
Are driven, like ghosts from an enchanter fleeing,

Yellow, and black, and pale, and hectic red,
Pestilence-stricken multitudes: O thou,
Who chariotest to their dark wintry bed

The wingèd seeds, where they lie cold and low,
Each like a corpse within its grave, until
Thine azure sister of the spring shall blow

Her clarion o'er the dreaming earth, and fill
(Driving sweet buds like flocks to feed in air)
With living hues and odours plain and hill:

Wild Spirit, which art moving everywhere;
Destroyer and preserver; hear, oh hear!

II

Thou on whose stream, 'mid the steep sky's commotion,
Loose clouds like earth's decaying leaves are shed,
Shook from the tangled boughs of Heaven and Ocean,

Angels of rain and lightning: there are spread
On the blue surface of thine airy surge,
Like the bright hair uplifted from the head

Of some fierce Maenad, even from the dim verge
Of the horizon to the zenith's height,
The locks of the approaching storm. Thou dirge

From *Prometheus Unbound, With Other Poems* 1820.

Of the dying year, to which this closing night
Will be the doom of a vast sepulchre,
Vaulted with all thy congregated might

Of vapours, from whose solid atmosphere
Black rain, and fire, and hail, will burst: Oh hear!

III

Thou who didst waken from his summer dreams
The blue Mediterranean, where he lay,
Lulled by the coil of his crystalline streams,

Beside a pumice isle in Baiae's bay,
And saw in sleep old palaces and towers
Quivering within the wave's intenser day,

All overgrown with azure moss and flowers
So sweet, the sense faints picturing them! Thou
For whose path the Atlantic's level powers

Cleave themselves into chasms, while far below
The sea-blooms and the oozy woods which wear
The sapless foliage of the ocean, know

Thy voice, and suddenly grow gray with fear,
And tremble and despoil themselves: Oh hear!

IV

If I were a dead leaf thou mightest bear;
If I were a swift cloud to fly with thee;
A wave to pant beneath thy power, and share

The impulse of thy strength, only less free
Than thou, O uncontrollable! If even
I were as in my boyhood, and could be

32 *Baiae's bay:* west of Naples

The comrade of thy wanderings over heaven,
As then, when to outstrip the skyey speed
Scarce seemed a vision, I would ne'er have striven

As thus with thee in prayer in my sore need.
Oh! lift me as a wave, a leaf, a cloud!
I fall upon the thorns of life! I bleed!

A heavy weight of hours has chained and bowed
One too like thee: tameless, and swift, and proud.

V

Make me thy lyre, even as the forest is:
What if my leaves are falling like its own!
The tumult of thy mighty harmonies

Will take from both a deep autumnal tone,
Sweet though in sadness. Be thou, Spirit fierce,
My spirit! Be thou me, impetuous one!

Drive my dead thoughts over the universe
Like withered leaves to quicken a new birth!
And, by the incantation of this verse,

Scatter, as from an unextinguished hearth
Ashes and sparks, my words among mankind!
Be through my lips to unawakened earth

The trumpet of a prophecy! O wind,
If Winter comes, can Spring be far behind?

John Keats 1795–1821

ODE TO A NIGHTINGALE

1

My heart aches, and a drowsy numbness pains
  My sense, as though of hemlock I had drunk,
Or emptied some dull opiate to the drains
  One minute past, and Lethe-wards had sunk:
'Tis not through envy of thy happy lot,
  But being too happy in thine happiness,—
    That thou, light-wingèd Dryad of the trees,
      In some melodious plot
  Of beechen green, and shadows numberless,
    Singest of summer in full-throated ease.

2

O, for a draught of vintage! that hath been
  Cool'd a long age in the deep-delvèd earth,
Tasting of Flora and the country green,
  Dance, and Provençal song, and sunburnt mirth!
O for a beaker full of the warm South,
  Full of the true, the blushful Hippocrene,
    With beaded bubbles winking at the brim,
      And purple-stainèd mouth;
  That I might drink, and leave the world unseen,
    And with thee fade away into the forest dim:

3

Fade far away, dissolve, and quite forget
  What thou among the leaves hast never known,
The weariness, the fever, and the fret
  Here, where men sit and hear each other groan;
Where palsy shakes a few, sad, last gray hairs,
  Where youth grows pale, and spectre-thin, and dies;

From *Lamia, etc.* 1820 (three poems).
16 *Hippocrene:* fountain of the Muses on Mt. Helicon.

Where but to think is to be full of sorrow
And leaden-eyed despairs,
Where Beauty cannot keep her lustrous eyes,
Or new Love pine at them beyond to-morrow.

4

Away! away! for I will fly to thee,
Not charioted by Bacchus and his pards,
But on the viewless wings of Poesy,
Though the dull brain perplexes and retards:
Already with thee! tender is the night,
And haply the Queen-Moon is on her throne,
Cluster'd around by all her starry Fays;
But here there is no light,
Save what from heaven is with the breezes blown
Through verdurous glooms and winding mossy ways.

5

I cannot see what flowers are at my feet,
Nor what soft incense hangs upon the boughs,
But, in embalmèd darkness, guess each sweet
Wherewith the seasonable month endows
The grass, the thicket, and the fruit-tree wild;
White hawthorn, and the pastoral eglantine;
Fast fading violets cover'd up in leaves;
And mid-May's eldest child,
The coming musk-rose, full of dewy wine,
The murmurous haunt of flies on summer eves.

6

Darkling I listen; and, for many a time
I have been half in love with easeful Death,
Call'd him soft names in many a musèd rhyme,
To take into the air my quiet breath;
Now more than ever seems it rich to die,
To cease upon the midnight with no pain,

32 leopards 51 in the dark

While thou art pouring forth thy soul abroad
In such an ecstasy!
Still wouldst thou sing, and I have ears in vain—
To thy high requiem become a sod.

7

Thou wast not born for death, immortal Bird!
No hungry generations tread thee down;
The voice I hear this passing night was heard
In ancient days by emperor and clown:
Perhaps the self-same song that found a path
Through the sad heart of Ruth, when, sick for home,
She stood in tears amid the alien corn;
The same that oft-times hath
Charm'd magic casements, opening on the foam
Of perilous seas, in faery lands forlorn.

8

Forlorn! the very word is like a bell
To toll me back from thee to my sole self!
Adieu! the fancy cannot cheat so well
As she is fam'd to do, deceiving elf.
Adieu! adieu! thy plaintive anthem fades
Past the near meadows, over the still stream,
Up the hill-side; and now 'tis buried deep
In the next valley-glades:
Was it a vision, or a waking dream?
Fled is that music:—Do I wake or sleep?

ODE ON MELANCHOLY

I

No, no, go not to Lethe, neither twist
  Wolf's-bane, tight-rooted, for its poisonous wine;
Nor suffer thy pale forehead to be kiss'd
  By nightshade, ruby grape of Proserpine;
Make not your rosary of yew-berries,
  Nor let the beetle, nor the death-moth be
    Your mournful Psyche, nor the downy owl
A partner in your sorrow's mysteries;
  For shade to shade will come too drowsily,
    And drown the wakeful anguish of the soul.

2

But when the melancholy fit shall fall
  Sudden from heaven like a weeping cloud,
That fosters the droop-headed flowers all,
  And hides the green hill in an April shroud;
Then glut thy sorrow on a morning rose,
  Or on the rainbow of the salt sand-wave,
    Or on the wealth of globèd peonies;
Or if thy mistress some rich anger shows,
  Emprison her soft hand, and let her rave,
    And feed deep, deep upon her peerless eyes.

3

She dwells with Beauty—Beauty that must die;
  And Joy, whose hand is ever at his lips
Bidding adieu; and aching Pleasure nigh,
  Turning to poison while the bee-mouth sips:
Ay, in the very temple of Delight
  Veil'd Melancholy has her sovran shrine,
    Though seen of none save him whose strenuous tongue
  Can burst Joy's grape against his palate fine;
His soul shall taste the sadness of her might,
    And be among her cloudy trophies hung.

TO AUTUMN

I

Season of mists and mellow fruitfulness,
   Close bosom-friend of the maturing sun;
Conspiring with him how to load and bless
   With fruit the vines that round the thatch-eaves run;
To bend with apples the moss'd cottage-trees,
   And fill all fruit with ripeness to the core;
      To swell the gourd, and plump the hazel shells
   With a sweet kernel; to set budding more,
And still more, later flowers for the bees,
Until they think warm days will never cease,
      For Summer has o'er-brimm'd their clammy cells.

2

Who hath not seen thee oft amid thy store?
   Sometimes whoever seeks abroad may find
Thee sitting careless on a granary floor,
   Thy hair soft-lifted by the winnowing wind;
Or on a half-reap'd furrow sound asleep,
   Drows'd with the fume of poppies, while thy hook
      Spares the next swath and all its twinèd flowers:
And sometimes like a gleaner thou dost keep
   Steady thy laden head across a brook;
   Or by a cider-press, with patient look,
      Thou watchest the last oozings hours by hours.

3

Where are the songs of Spring? Ay, where are they?
   Think not of them, thou hast thy music too,—
While barrèd clouds bloom the soft-dying day,
   And touch the stubble-plains with rosy hue;
Then in a wailful choir the small gnats mourn
   Among the river sallows, borne aloft
      Or sinking as the light wind lives or dies;

28 willows

And full-grown lambs loud bleat from hilly bourn;
  Hedge-crickets sing; and now with treble soft
  The red-breast whistles from a garden-croft;
    And gathering swallows twitter in the skies.

John Clare 1793–1864

TO THE SNIPE

Lover of swamps
And quagmire overgrown
With hassock-tufts of sedge, where fear encamps
Around thy home alone,

The trembling grass
Quakes from the human foot,
Nor bears the weight of man to let him pass
Where thou, alone and mute,

Sittest at rest
In safety, near the clump
Of huge flag-forest that thy haunts invest
Or some old sallow stump,

Thriving on seams
That tiny islands swell,
Just hilling from the mud and rancid streams,
Suiting thy nature well;

For here thy bill,
Suited by wisdom good,
Of rude unseemly length, doth delve and drill
The jellied mass for food;

And here, mayhap,
When summer suns have drest
The moor's rude, desolate and spongy lap,
May hide thy mystic nest—

From *The Poems of John Clare*, ed. J. W. Tibble 1935.
12 willow

Mystic indeed;
For isles that oceans make
Are scarcely more secure for birds to build
Than this flag-hidden lake.

Boys thread the woods
To their remotest shades;
But in these marshy flats, these stagnant floods,
Security pervades.

From year to year
Places untrodden lie,
Where man nor boy nor stock hath ventured near,
Naught gazed on but the sky

And fowl that dread
They very breath of man,
Hiding in spots that never knew his tread,
A wild and timid clan,

Widgeon and teal
And wild duck—restless lot,
That from man's dreaded sight will ever steal
To the most dreary spot.

Here tempests howl
Around each flaggy plot,
Where they who dread man's sight, the water fowl,
Hide and are frightened not.

'Tis power divine
That heartens them to brave
The roughest tempest and at ease recline
On marshes or the wave.

Yet instinct knows
Not safety's bounds:—to shun
The firmer ground where skulking fowler goes
With searching dogs and gun,

By tepid springs
Scarcely one stride across
(Though bramble from its edge a shelter flings
Thy safety is at loss)

—And never choose
The little sinky foss,
Streaking the moors whence spa-red water spews
From pudges fringed with moss;

Freebooters there,
Intent to kill or slay,
Startle with cracking guns the trepid air,
And dogs thy haunts betray.

From danger's reach
Here thou art safe to roam,
Far as these washy flag-sown marshes stretch
A still and quiet home.

In these thy haunts
I've gleaned habitual love;
From the vague world where pride and folly taunts
I muse and look above.

Thy solitudes
The unbounded heaven esteems,
And here my heart warms into higher moods
And dignifying dreams.

62 ditch 64 puddles

I see the sky
Smile on the meanest spot,
Giving to all that creep or walk or fly
A calm and cordial lot.

Thine teaches me
Right feelings to employ—
That in the dreariest places peace will be
A dweller and a joy.

Alfred, Lord Tennyson 1809–1892

MILTON. ALCAICS

O mighty-mouth'd inventor of harmonies,
O skill'd to sing of Time or Eternity,
  God-gifted organ-voice of England,
    Milton, a name to resound for ages;
Whose Titan angels, Gabriel, Abdiel,
Starr'd from Jehovah's gorgeous armories,
  Tower as the deep-domed empyrëan
    Rings to the roar of an angel onset—
Me rather all that bowery loneliness,
The brooks of Eden mazily murmuring,
  And bloom profuse and cedar arches
    Charm, as a wanderer out in ocean,
Where some refulgent sunset of India
Streams o'er a rich ambrosial ocean isle,
  And crimson-hued the stately palm-woods
    Whisper in odorous heights of even.

From *Cornhill Magazine,* December 1863.

Alcaics: after Alcaeus, a lyric poet of Mytilene, c. 600 B.C. Tennyson strictly follows the form, four four-line strophes scanned according to quantity thus:

–|–∪|– –| |–∪∪|–∪–|
–|–∪|– –| |–∪∪|–∪–|
–|–∪|– –|–∪|–∪
–∪∪|–∪∪|–∪|–∪

Walt Whitman 1809–1892

OUT OF THE CRADLE ENDLESSLY ROCKING

Out of the cradle endlessly rocking,
Out of the mocking-bird's throat, the musical shuttle,
Out of the Ninth-month midnight,
Over the sterile sands and the fields beyond, where the child leaving his bed wander'd alone, bareheaded, barefoot,
Down from the shower'd halo,
Up from the mystic play of shadows twining and twisting as if they were alive,
Out from the patches of briers and blackberries,
From the memories of the bird that chanted to me,
From your memories sad brother, from the fitful risings and fallings I heard,
From under that yellow half-moon late-risen and swollen as if with tears,
From those beginning notes of yearning and love there in the mist,
From the thousand responses of my heart never to cease,
From the myriad thence-arous'd words,
From the word stronger and more delicious than any,
From such as now they start the scene revisiting,
As a flock, twittering, rising, or overhead passing,
Borne hither, ere all eludes me, hurriedly,
A man, yet by these tears a little boy again,
Throwing myself on the sand, confronting the waves,
I, chanter of pains and joys, uniter of here and hereafter,
Taking all hints to use them, but swiftly leaping beyond them,
A reminiscence sing.

Once Paumanok,
When the lilac-scent was in the air and Fifth-month grass was growing,
Up this seashore in some briers,

From *Leaves of Grass,* 8th edition 1881.

Two feather'd guests from Alabama, two together,
And their nest, and four light-green eggs spotted with brown,
And every day the he-bird to and fro near at hand,
And every day the she-bird crouch'd on her nest, silent, with bright eyes,
And every day I, a curious boy, never too close, never disturbing them,
Cautiously peering, absorbing, translating.

Shine! shine! shine!
Pour down your warmth, great sun!
While we bask, we two together.

Two together!
Winds blow south, or winds blow north,
Day come white, or night come black,
Home, or rivers and mountains from home,
Singing all time, minding no time,
While we two keep together.

Till of a sudden,
May-be kill'd, unknown to her mate,
One forenoon the she-bird crouch'd not on the nest,
Nor return'd that afternoon, nor the next,
Nor ever appear'd again.

And thenceforward all summer in the sound of the sea,
And at night under the full of the moon in calmer weather,
Over the hoarse surging of the sea,
Or flitting from brier to brier by day,
I saw, I heard at intervals the remaining one, the he-bird,
The solitary guest from Alabama.

Blow! blow! blow!
Blow up sea-winds along Paumanok's shore;
I wait and I wait till you blow my mate to me.

Yes, when the stars glisten'd,
All night long on the prong of a moss-scallop'd stake,
Down almost amid the slapping waves,
Sat the lone singer wonderful causing tears.

He call'd on his mate,
He pour'd forth the meanings which I of all men know.

Yes my brother I know,
The rest might not, but I have treasur'd every note,
For more than once dimly down to the beach gliding,
Silent, avoiding the moonbeams, blending myself with the shadows,
Recalling now the obscure shapes, the echoes, the sounds and sights after their sorts,
The white arms out in the breakers tirelessly tossing,
I, with bare feet, a child, the wind wafting my hair,
Listen'd long and long.

Listen'd to keep, to sing, now translating the notes,
Following you my brother.

Soothe! soothe! soothe!
Close on its wave soothes the wave behind,
And again another behind embracing and lapping, every one close,
But my love soothes not me, not me.

Low hangs the moon, it rose late,
It is lagging—O I think it is heavy with love, with love.

O madly the sea pushes upon the land,
With love, with love.

O night! do I not see my love fluttering out among the breakers?
What is that little black thing I see there in the white?

Loud! loud! loud!
Loud I call to you, my love!
High and clear I shoot my voice over the waves,
Surely you must know who is here, is here,
You must know who I am, my love.

Low-hanging moon!
What is that dusky spot in your brown yellow?
O it is the shape, the shape of my mate!
O moon do not keep her from me any longer.

Land! land! O land!
Whichever way I turn, O I think you could give me my mate back again if you only would,
For I am almost sure I see her dimly whichever way I look.

O rising stars!
Perhaps the one I want so much will rise, will rise with some of you.

O throat! O trembling throat!
Sound clearer through the atmosphere!
Pierce the woods, the earth,
Somewhere listening to catch you must be the one I want.

Shake out carols!
Solitary here, the night's carols!
Carols of lonesome love! death's carols!
Carols under that lagging, yellow, waning moon!
O under that moon where she droops almost down into the sea!
O reckless despairing carols.

But soft! sink low!
Soft! let me just murmur,
And do you wait a moment you husky-nois'd sea,
For somewhere I believe I heard my mate responding to me,

So faint, I must be still, be still to listen,
But not altogether still, for then she might not come immediately to me.

Hither my love!
Here I am! here!
With this just-sustain'd note I announce myself to you,
This gentle call is for you my love, for you.

Do not be decoy'd elsewhere,
That is the whistle of the wind, it is not my voice,
That is the fluttering, the fluttering of the spray,
Those are the shadows of leaves.

O darkness! O in vain!
O I am very sick and sorrowful.

O brown halo in the sky near the moon, drooping upon the sea!
O troubled reflection in the sea!
O throat! O throbbing heart!
And I singing uselessly, uselessly all the night.

O past! O happy life! O songs of joy!
In the air, in the woods, over fields,
Loved! loved! loved! loved! loved!
But my mate no more, no more with me!
We two together no more.

The aria sinking,
All else continuing, the stars shining,
The winds blowing, the notes of the bird continuous echoing,
With angry moans the fierce old mother incessantly moaning,
On the sands of Paumanok's shore gray and rustling,
The yellow half-moon enlarged, sagging down, drooping, the face of the sea almost touching,
The boy ecstatic, with his bare feet the waves, with his hair the atmosphere dallying,
The love in the heart long pent, now loose, now at last tumultuously bursting,

The aria's meaning, the ears, the soul, swiftly depositing,
The strange tears down the cheeks coursing,
The colloquy there, the trio, each uttering,
The undertone, the savage old mother incessantly crying,
To the boy's soul's questions sullenly timing, some drown'd secret hissing,
To the outsetting bard.

Demon or bird! (said the boy's soul,)
Is it indeed toward your mate you sing? or is it really to me?
For I, that was a child, my tongue's use sleeping, now I have heard you,
Now in a moment I know what I am for, I awake,
And already a thousand singers, a thousand songs, clearer, louder and more sorrowful than yours,
A thousand warbling echoes have started to life within me, never to die.

O you singer solitary, singing by yourself, projecting me,
O solitary me listening, never more shall I cease perpetuating you,
Never more shall I escape, never more the reverberations,
Never more the cries of unsatisfied love be absent from me,
Never again leave me to be the peaceful child I was before what there in the night,
By the sea under the yellow and sagging moon,
The messenger there arous'd, the fire, the sweet hell within,
The unknown want, the destiny of me.

O give me the clew! (it lurks in the night here somewhere,)
O if I am to have so much, let me have more!

A word then, (for I will conquer it,)
The word final, superior to all,
Subtle, sent up—what is it?—I listen;
Are you whispering it, and have been all the time, you sea waves?
Is that it from your liquid rims and wet sands?

Whereto answering, the sea,
Delaying not, hurrying not,
Whisper'd me through the night, and very plainly before daybreak,
Lisp'd to me the low and delicious word death,
And again death, death, death, death,
Hissing melodious, neither like the bird nor like my arous'd child's heart,
But edging near as privately for me rustling at my feet,
Creeping thence steadily up to my ears and laving me softly all over,
Death, death, death, death, death.

Which I do not forget,
But fuse the song of my dusky demon and brother,
That he sang to me in the moonlight on Paumanok's gray beach,
With the thousand responsive songs at random,
My own songs awaked from that hour,
And with them the key, the word up from the waves,
The word of the sweetest song and all songs,
That strong and delicious word which, creeping to my feet,
(Or like some old crone rocking the cradle, swathed in sweet garments, bending aside,)
The sea whisper'd me.

William Butler Yeats 1865–1939

EASTER 1916

I have met them at close of day
Coming with vivid faces
From counter or desk among grey
Eighteenth-century houses.
I have passed with a nod of the head
Or polite meaningless words,
Or have lingered awhile and said
Polite meaningless words,
And thought before I had done
Of a mocking tale or a gibe
To please a companion
Around the fire at the club,
Being certain that they and I
But lived where motley is worn:
All changed, changed utterly:
A terrible beauty is born.

That woman's days were spent
In ignorant good-will,
Her nights in argument
Until her voice grew shrill.
What voice more sweet than hers
When, young and beautiful,
She rode to harriers?
This man had kept a school
And rode our wingèd horse;
This other his helper and friend
Was coming into his force;
He might have won fame in the end,
So sensitive his nature seemed,
So daring and sweet his thought.

From *Michael Robartes and the Dancer* 1921.

This other man I had dreamed
A drunken, vainglorious lout.
He had done most bitter wrong
To some who are near my heart,
Yet I number him in the song;
He, too, has resigned his part
In the casual comedy;
He, too, has been changed in his turn,
Transformed utterly:
A terrible beauty is born.

Hearts with one purpose alone
Through summer and winter seem
Enchanted to a stone
To trouble the living stream.
The horse that comes from the road,
The rider, the birds that range
From cloud to tumbling cloud,
Minute by minute they change;
A shadow of cloud on the stream
Changes minute by minute;
A horse-hoof slides on the brim,
And a horse plashes within it;
The long-legged moor-hens dive,
And hens to moor-cocks call;
Minute by minute they live:
The stone's in the midst of all.

Too long a sacrifice
Can make a stone of the heart.
O when may it suffice?
That is Heaven's part, our part
To murmur name upon name,
As a mother names her child
When sleep at last has come
On limbs that had run wild.
What is it but nightfall?

No, no, not night but death;
Was it needless death after all?
For England may keep faith
For all that is done and said.
We know their dream; enough
To know they dreamed and are dead;
And what if excess of love
Bewildered them till they died?
I write it out in a verse—
MacDonagh and MacBride
And Connolly and Pearse
Now and in time to be,
Wherever green is worn,
Are changed, changed utterly:
A terrible beauty is born.

Pablo Neruda 1904—

ODE TO MY SOCKS

Maru Mori brought me
a pair
of socks
which she knitted herself
with her sheep-herder's hands,
two socks as soft
as rabbits.
I slipped my feet
into them
as though into
two
cases
knitted
with threads of
twilight
and goatskin.
Violent socks,
my feet were
two fish made
of wool,
two long sharks
seablue, shot
through
by one golden thread,
two immense blackbirds,
two cannons,
my feet
were honored
in this way
by
these
heavenly
socks.

From *Odas Elementales* 1954-1957. Translated by Robert Bly 1926—.

They were
so handsome
for the first time
my feet seemed to me
unacceptable
like two decrepit
firemen, firemen
unworthy
of that woven
fire,
of those glowing
socks.

Nevertheless
I resisted
the sharp temptation
to save them somewhere
as schoolboys
keep
fireflies,
as learned men
collect
sacred texts,
I resisted
the mad impulse
to put them
in a golden
cage
and each day give them
birdseed
and pieces of pink melon.
Like explorers
in the jungle who hand
over the very rare
green deer
to the spit
and eat it
with remorse,

I stretched out
my feet
and pulled on
the magnificent
socks
and then my shoes.

The moral
of my ode is this:
beauty is twice
beauty
and what is good is doubly
good
when it is a matter of two socks
made of wool
in winter.

Robert Duncan 1919—

A POEM BEGINNING WITH A LINE BY PINDAR

I

The light foot hears you and the brightness begins
god-step at the margins of thought,
    quick adulterous tread at the heart.
Who is it that goes there?
    Where I see your quick face
notes of an old music pace the air,
torso-reverberations of a Grecian lyre.

In Goya's canvas Cupid and Psyche
have a hurt voluptuous grace
bruised by redemption. The copper light
falling upon the brown boy's slight body
is carnal fate that sends the soul wailing
up from blind innocence, ensnared
    by dimness
into the deprivations of desiring sight.

But the eyes in Goya's painting are soft,
diffuse with rapture absorb the flame.
Their bodies yield out of strength.
    Waves of visual pleasure
wrap them in a sorrow previous to their impatience.

A bronze of yearning, a rose that burns
    the tips of their bodies, lips,
ends of fingers, nipples. He is not wingd.
His thighs are flesh, are clouds
    lit by the sun in its going down,
hot luminescence at the loins of the visible.

From *The Opening of the Field* 1960.

But they are not in a landscape.
They exist in an obscurity.

The wind spreading the sail serves them.
The two jealous sisters eager for her ruin
serve them.
That she is ignorant, ignorant of what Love will be,
serves them.
The dark serves them.
The oil scalding his shoulder serves them,
serves their story. Fate, spinning,
knots the threads for Love.

Jealousy, ignorance, the hurt . . . serve them.

II

This is magic. It is passionate dispersion.
What if they grow old? The gods
would not allow it.
Psyche is preserved.

In time we see a tragedy, a loss of beauty
the glittering youth
of the god retains—but from this threshold
it is age
that is beautiful. It is toward the old poets
we go, to their faltering,
their unaltering wrongness that has style,
their variable truth,
the old faces,
words shed like tears from
a plenitude of powers time stores.

A stroke. These little strokes. A chill.
The old man, feeble, does not recoil.
Recall. A phase so minute,
only a part of the word in- jerrd.

The Thundermakers descend,

damerging a nuv. A nerb.
The present dented of the U
nighted stayd. States. The heavy clod?
Cloud. Invades the brain. What
if lilacs last in *this* dooryard bloomd?

Hoover, Roosevelt, Truman, Eisenhower—
where among these did the power reside
that moves the heart? What flower of the nation
bride-sweet broke to the whole rapture?
Hoover, Coolidge, Harding, Wilson
hear the factories of human misery turning out commodities.
For whom are the holy matins of the heart ringing?
Noble men in the quiet of morning hear
Indians singing the continent's violent requiem.
Harding, Wilson, Taft, Roosevelt,
idiots fumbling at the bride's door,
hear the cries of men in meaningless debt and war.
Where among these did the spirit reside
that restores the land to productive order?
McKinley, Cleveland, Harrison, Arthur,
Garfield, Hayes, Grant, Johnson,
dwell in the roots of the heart's rancor.
How sad "amid lanes and through old woods"
echoes Whitman's love for Lincoln!

There is no continuity then. Only a few
posts of the good remain. I too
that am a nation sustain the damage
where smokes of continual ravage
obscure the flame.
It is across great scars of wrong
I reach toward the song of kindred men
and strike again the naked string
old Whitman sang from. Glorious mistake!
that cried:

"The theme is creative and has vista."
"He is the president of regulation."

I see always the under side turning,
fumes that injure the tender landscape.
From which up break
lilac blossoms of courage in daily act
striving to meet a natural measure.

III

for Charles Olson

Psyche's tasks—the sorting of seeds
wheat   barley   oats   poppy   coriander
anise   beans   lentils   peas   —every grain
in its right place
before nightfall;

gathering the gold wool from the cannibal sheep
(for the soul must weep
and come near upon death);

harrowing Hell for a casket Proserpina keeps
that must not
be opend . . . containing beauty?

no! Melancholy coild like a serpent
that is deadly sleep
we are not permitted
to succumb to.

These are the old tasks.
You've heard them before.

They must be impossible. Psyche
must despair, be brought to her
insect instructor;
must obey the counsels of the green reed;

saved from suicide by a tower speaking,
must follow to the letter
freakish instructions.

In the story the ants help. The old man at Pisa
mixd in whose mind
(to draw the sorts) are all seeds
as a lone ant from a broken ant-hill
had part restored by an insect, was
upheld by a lizard

(to draw the sorts)
the wind is part of the process
defines a nation of the wind—

father of many notions,
Who?
let the light into the dark? began
the many movements of the passion?
West
from east men push.
The islands are blessd
(cursed) that swim below the sun,

man upon whom the sun has gone down!

There is the hero who struggles east
widdershins to free the dawn and must
woo Night's daughter,
sorcery, black passionate rage, covetous queens,
so that the fleecy sun go back from Troy,
Colchis, India . . . all the blazing armies
spent, he must struggle alone toward the pyres of Day.

124 *The old man at Pisa:* Ezra Pound, whose *Pisan Cantos* echo through this passage.

The light that is Love
rushes on toward passion. It verges upon dark.
Roses and blood flood the clouds.
Solitary first riders advance into legend.

This land, where I stand, was all legend
in my grandfathers' time: cattle raiders,
animal tribes, priests, gold.
It was the West. Its vistas painters saw
in diffuse light, in melancholy,
in abysses left by glaciers as if they had been the sun
primordial carving empty enormities
out of the rock.

Snakes lurkd
guarding secrets. Those first ones
survived solitude.

Scientia
holding the lamp, driven by doubt;
Eros naked in foreknowledge
smiling in his sleep; and the light
spilld, burning his shoulder—the outrage
that conquers legend—
passion, dismay, longing, search
flooding up where
the Beloved is lost. Psyche travels
life after life, my life, station
after station,
to be tried

without break, without
news, knowing only—but what did she know?
The oracle at Miletus had spoken
truth surely: that he was Serpent-Desire
that flies thru the air,
a monster-husband. But she saw him fair

whom Apollo's mouthpiece said spread
      pain
beyond cure   to those
      wounded by his arrows.

Rilke torn by a rose thorn
blackend toward Eros.   Cupidinous Death!
      that will not take no for an answer.

IV

      Oh yes!   Bless the footfall where
step by step   the boundary walker
(in Maverick Road   the snow
thud by thud   from the roof
circling the house—another tread)

   that foot   informd
by the weight of all things
      that can be elusive
no more than a nearness to the mind
      of a single image

         Oh yes!   this
most dear
      the catalyst force that renders clear
the days of a life from the surrounding medium!

            Yes, beautiful rare wilderness!
wildness that verifies strength of my tame mind,
      clearing held against indians,
health that prepared to meet death,
      the stubborn hymns going up
into the ramifications of the hostile air

      that, deceptive, gives way.

Who is there?   O, light the light!
      The Indians give way,   the clearing falls.

Great Death gives way   and unprepares us.
      Lust gives way.   The Moon gives way.
Night gives way.   Minutely,   the Day gains.

She saw the body of her beloved
      dismemberd in waking . . . or was it
in sight?   *Finders Keepers* we sang
      when we were children   or were taught to sing
before our histories began   and we began
      who were beloved   our animal life
toward the Beloved,   sworn to be Keepers.

      On the hill before the wind came
the grass moved toward the one sea,
      blade after blade dancing in waves.

There the children turn the ring to the left.
There the children turn the ring to the right.
      Dancing . . . Dancing . . .

And the lonely psyche goes up thru the boy to the king
      that in the caves of history dreams.
Round and round the children turn.
      London Bridge that is a kingdom falls.

We have come so far that all the old stories
whisper once more.
Mount Segur, Mount Victoire, Mount Tamalpais . . .
      rise to adore the mystery of Love!

(An ode? Pindar's art, the editors tell us, was not a statue but a mosaic, an accumulation of metaphor. But if he was archaic, not classic, a survival of obsolete mode, there may have been old voices in the survival that directed the heart. So, a line from a hymn came in a novel I was reading to help me. Psyche, poised to leap—and Pindar too, the editors write, goes too far, topples over—listened to a tower that said, *Listen to me!* The oracle had said, *Despair! The Gods themselves abhor his power.* And then the virgin flower of the dark falls back flesh of our flesh from which everywhere . . .

the information flows
   that is yearning. A line of Pindar
moves from the area of my lamp
   toward morning.

In the dawn that is nowhere
   I have seen the willful children
clockwise and counter-clockwise turning.

Frank O'Hara 1926–1966

ODE TO WILLEM DE KOONING

Beyond the sunrise
where the black begins
                    an enormous city
                    is sending up its shutters

and just before the last lapse of nerve which I am already sorry for,
that friends describe as "just this once" in a temporary hell, I hope

I try to seize upon greatness
which is available to me
                    through generosity and
                    lavishness of spirit, yours
not to be inimitably weak
and picturesque, my self
                    but to be standing clearly
                    alone in the orange wind

while our days tumble and rant through Gotham and the Easter narrows
and I have not the courage to convict myself of cowardice or care

for now a long history slinks over the sill, of patent absurdities
and the fathomless miseries of a small person upset by personality

and I look to the flags
in your eyes as they go up
                    on the enormous walls
                    as the brave must always ascend

From *Odes* 1969 (two poems).

into the air, always the musts
like banderillas dangling

and jingling jewel-like amidst the red drops on the shoulders
of men
who lead us not forward or backward, but on as we must go on

out into the mesmerized world
of inanimate voices like traffic
noises, hewing a clearing
in the crowded abyss of the West

2

Stars of all passing sights,
language, thought and reality,
"I am assuming that one knows
what it is to be ashamed"
and that the light we seek
is broad and pure, not winking
and that the evil inside us
now and then strolls into a field
and sits down like a forgotten rock
while we walk on to a horizon
line that's beautifully keen,
precarious and doesn't sag
beneath our variable weight

In this dawn as in the first
it's the Homeric rose, its scent
that leads us up the rocky path
into the pass where death
can disappear or where the face
of future senses may appear
in a white night that opens
after the embattled hours of day

And the wind tears up the rose
fountains of prehistoric light
falling upon the blinded heroes

who did not see enough or were not
mad enough or felt too little
when the blood began to pour down
the rocky slopes into pink seas

3

Dawn must always recur
to blot out stars and the terrible systems
of belief
Dawn, which dries out the web so the wind can blow it, spider and all, away

Dawn,
erasing blindness from an eye inflamed,
reaching for its
morning cigarette in Promethean inflection
after the blames
and desperate conclusions of the dark
where messages were intercepted
by an ignorant horde of thoughts
and all simplicities perished in desire

A bus crashes into a milk truck
and the girl goes skating up the avenue
with streaming hair
roaring through fluttering newspapers
and their Athenian contradictions
for democracy is joined
with stunning collapsible savages, all natural and relaxed and free

as the day zooms into space and only darkness lights our lives,

with few flags flaming, imperishable courage and the gentle will
which is the individual dawn of genius rising from its bed

"maybe they're wounds, but maybe they are rubies"
each painful as a sun

ODE ON LUST

Asking little more than
a squeal of satisfaction
from a piece of shrapnel,
the hero of a demi-force
pounces cheerfully upon
an exalted height which shall
hereafter be called Bath

Where in the magnified panorama of hysterical pageantry upon the heights
stands Bath? he is standing in a lovely crater near the topmost peak!

Mildly frowning Bath adjourns
to the crystal lake of his
conception, but
if he imitates his father he
is bathed in sin no matter
how high he climbs and bends
he loses his pearls on the
slopes he finds them again
"meanwhile, back at the crater"
Poor Bath! and poorer still
are his pursuers, seeking only
the momentary smile of clouds
and underneath, a small
irresponsible glory that fits

In pursuing glory are they not wise to take the path of pale eschewment?
for who seeks Bath is the lover of lightning, burnt rather than burning

The avoidance of misery and
pity is a harrowing task for
one who must picture humanity
upside down and singing A
smile then freezes in its charcoal
and, like a girl in Conrad,
one is the slave of an image
or, like Aïda, begins a slave
and ends singing under a stone
where only the other was to sing

Who has tears for any but these, though they hate them, these whose greed
is simply an over-prodigal need of dispersal, whose individuality is silver,
whose attention is solely upon the fragments of love as they die, one by one?
who, like Theodora, are stripped of their seeds by the whiteness of doves
till they stand with their arms spread, nude in the arena; become Empresses

Masks and Voices

IN THE SPHERE of the moon Dante, journeying outward, sees for the first time souls in heaven:

As in a clear pane
  or say a shallow,
  clear, smoothrunning stream,
we see our faces faintly
  reflected, as a pearl on a fair forehead,
  white upon white, can barely be seen,
so saw I many faces eager to speak;
  and my mistake then was just the reverse
  of the one a man made so he fell in love with a fountain.
Thinking they were reflections
  I turned to see
  who it was behind me:
No one. When I turned again
  it was to the light of my tender teacher
  whose blessed eyes were shining with mirth.
"Don't be surprised if I laugh,"
  she said, "when your childish thought
  doesn't yet trust its foot's weight on truth
but turns you back, as it always has,
  to vanity. What you see
  are the true substances."

Paradiso III 10-29

The joke is that these disembodied spirits are more real than anyone Dante has ever seen, their identities purified, as Piccarda explains by and by, in the divine will. In the next sphere the souls are glimpsed within the light; in the sphere of Venus and beyond, their light conceals their forms.

Who any of us is, itself a vexed question, takes on another sort of urgency when we write a poem. Who speaks?

A Victorian solution to the problem was the dramatic monologue, in which the poet himself says nothing while his character, someone imagined or drawn from history, speaks as the dead speak in Homer, called to the foss and infused with living blood. The art of this form is in its convincing diction, something with the thrust of real speech, in its vivid revelation of personality, setting, and so on, revealing as the final artful touch the reactions of the silent interlocutor, and, above all, giving away, as it were unwittingly, the secrets of the objectified speaker. Its satisfactions are those of the theatre, as its name implies, or even of the novel, in a dramatization of the individual defined by his passions and possessions asserting his own will in the face of whatever stands before him: not like Piccarda and the others transparent in the moon, but like the memorable damned in hell whose fear has changed to desire.

Romantic individualism is one of the great intellectual commonplaces of the nineteenth century, an assumption that colors all thought; with its near kin imperialism and aestheticism, it is one of the great errors. We are still sorting ourselves out of it.

Pound began with the idea of the persona, a mask to speak through; translations too were masks. The quest for dramatic objectivity leads to documentation: *The Ring and the Book,* then *Ulysses, Paterson,* Pound's *Cantos* where the sole ego carves away at all history. Quoting verbatim, the poet contributes not words but his specialized attention; this leads ultimately to the found poem, to composition by chance operations, and so on: outward ways to get rid of the interfering individual ego.

Another quest leads inward, avoiding all evasions, ignoring the details of the mask while concentrating on the nascent voice, the very point where language happens, the poet's own involuntary utterance or perhaps some other voice produced in a trance.

It is true too that a speech changes the speaker, and that poetry is a kind of powerful speech. If trances produce poems, poems can also cause trances. Chants, spells, curses, incantations, blessings, syllabic seeds of holiness. I haven't included any pure example of the like in this book—you wouldn't want to learn them from a book anyway—but the poems here, though they offer other satisfactions, rightly pronounced have power enough themselves.

Anonymous, Old English

THE WANDERER

"The mercy of God may often come to a homeless hermit,
though heart-sick from long lonely travel over land and sea,
stirring with his own hands the icecold ocean, rowing,
or on foot, following the frozen path of exile to its end.
Life's course is determined." So spoke the Wanderer,
remembering hardships, fierce slaughters, loss of friends.
"Alone in the hour before each dawn I bewail my sorrows.
No one now lives to whom I dare open my heart in confidence.
Yet, a noble custom in man is the firm binding of his breast
to contain his heart and in privacy his freedom of thought.
With weary heart and troubled mind, one cannot withstand
fate.
Thus, those who seek glory are often sad in secret.
I am; my heart is careworn without comfort of my native land.
Memories of noble kinsmen far away fasten fetters to my heart.
Long ago my generous lord was beneath earth's darkness
blinded,
and abject, I went desolate as winter across waves' expanse.
Mourning the loss of my benefactor, I sought near and far
for friends who had known affection for me in the meadhall
or for one who might wish to comfort my friendlessness
in his service, surrounded by precious objects as enticements.
Only he who has endured the trials of this trail knows
how cruel sorrow is as a companion. He who has no friends
knows the path of exile is not paved with golden bricks.
His frozen breast is not full of earth's glory but grief.
He remembers his retainer distributing treasures in the hall
and himself as a youth feasting at the table of his generosity.

Translated from the Old English by Andrew Hoyem 1935—; from *Articles* 1969. Because the original manuscript is unpunctuated, the distribution of speeches between the poet's own voice, the Wanderer's, and that of the sad survivor of lines 66ff. has been construed by the translator.

Painful knowledge persists that all this perished in the past,
that he must forever forgo the cherished counsels of his lord.
When sorrow and sleep together bed down for the night
this solitary one is blanketed in wretchedness. He dreams
he embraces his liege lord, kissing him as in former times,
lays hands and head on his knee at the throne with pride.
Then this friendless man perceives himself awake once more,
standing before the ominous approach of yellow green waves.
Seabirds bathing spread wings, preen their feathers.
Frost, hail and snow fall, forming rime and rigor over all.
His heart wounds are sore from longing for the beloved prince.
Sorrow returns when recollections of kinsmen pervade his mind.
In eager imagination he sees spirits of seafarers swimming away
into extinction; their utterances unfamiliar, then inaudible.
Sorrow returns to the one who has often had to journey alone
across waves' expanse with weary heart. Why in this world
should my heart not darken in meditation on life's transiency,
how men suddenly abandon their hall and noble retainer.
Thus this world decays day by day and falls away forever.
Indeed, no kinsman grows wise until he has aged sufficiently
in the winter of life's seasons and in the realm of this world.
The wise man is patient, not too impulsive or hasty of speech,
not lacking in moral strength, nor too reckless, not too afraid,
neither too happy, nor too avaricious, not too eager for glory
before he has once known glory and seen clearly within himself.
A man should wait when about to utter a vow until resolute
and certain whither the mind's thought wishes to go.
A wise man must absorb and understand the pervasive ghastliness
which occupies a locale where this world's wealth is deserted.
Even now in various places ruined walls stand exposed to storm.
Wind blows upon them; frost covers them; winehalls moulder.
Their rulers lie dead, deprived of the joys we once shared.
Bodies of mature men fell proud beside these walls.
Wars account for some; others were carried off by a bird
over high seas or were eaten by the grey wolf as his share.

The remainder are underground, buried by sad-faced men in
graves.
So it is that man's creator destroys our dwelling places.
Abandoned by inhabitants, our old giants' creations stand
silent.
With wisdom of experience he would survey these wall
foundations.
Pondering their significance, meditating upon this dark life,
recounting incidents of innumerable slaughters, he might ask:
Where went my youth? And with it my war horse and war lord?
Where are the joys of the meadhall? Where are the feasts?
The good days of old grow dark under the shadow of night
as if they had not been but were only dreams or empty hopes.
Standing in the tracks of departed warrior kin is a wall
wonderfully high, stones carved with variegated serpentine
motif.
Here, slain by mighty spears, weapons hungry for slaughter,
men were destroyed by a fate famous for frequency and
honor.
Now, storms dash against these stone walls, snow falls;
earth is bound by winter's harbinger, the onset of long nights.
Fierce northerly hailstorms are driven down upon vexed
mankind.
The kingdom of this world is fraught with hardship, and fate
changes our ordained course of events beneath the heavens.
Here, property is transitory; here, friends are transitory;
here, man is transitory; here, kinsmen are transitory.
The framework of this world falls to earth eventually."
So spoke the wise man to his mind alone, seated in meditation.
"He is good who keeps faith, only gradually coming to grief,
who knows the remedy prior to speech, then acts courageously.
He is well who seeks mercy and solace from our Father
in the heavens, where our only stability stands."

Anonymous, Early Irish

EVE'S LAMENT

I am Eve, great Adam's wife,
'Tis I that outraged Jesus of old;
'Tis I that robbed my children of Heaven,
By rights 'tis I that should have gone upon the cross.

I had a kingly house to please me,
Grievous the evil choice that disgraced me,
Grievous the wicked advice that withered me!
Alas! my hand is not pure.

'Tis I that plucked the apple,
Which went across my gullet:
So long as they endure in the light of day,
So long women will not cease from folly.

There would be no ice in any place,
There would be no glistening windy winter,
There would be no hell, there would be no sorrow,
There would be no fear, if it were not for me.

Three anonymous poems translated by Kuno Meyer, 1858-1919, in *Selections from Ancient Irish Poetry* 1911.
Eve's Lament: Late tenth or early eleventh century.

THE TRYST AFTER DEATH

Fothad Canann, the leader of a Connaught warrior-band, had carried off the wife of Alill of Munster with her consent. The outraged husband pursued them and a fierce battle was fought, in which Fothad and Alill fell by each other's hand. The lovers had engaged to meet in the evening after the battle. Faithful to his word, the spirit of the slain warrior kept the tryst and thus addressed his paramour:

Hush, woman, do not speak to me! My thoughts are not with thee.
My thoughts are still in the encounter at Feic.

My bloody corpse lies by the side of the Slope of two Brinks;
My head all unwashed is among warrior-bands in fierce slaughter.

It is blindness for any one making a tryst to set aside the tryst with Death:
The tryst that we made at Claragh has been kept by me in pale death.

It was destined for me,—unhappy journey! at Feic my grave had been marked out;
It was ordained for me—O sorrowful fight! to fall by warriors of another land.

'Tis not I alone who in the fulness of desires has gone astray to meet a woman—
No reproach to thee, though it was for thy sake—wretched is our last meeting!

From afar I have come to my tryst; my noble mate is horror-stricken:
Had we known it would be thus, it had not been hard to desist.

My men, the noble-faced, grey-horsed warrior-band have not betrayed me.

The Tryst after Death: ninth century.

Alas! for the wonderful yew-forest, that they should have
gone into the abode of clay!

Had they been alive, they would have revenged their lords;
Had mighty death not intervened, I ween this warrior-band had
not been unavenged.

To their very end they were brave; they ever strove for victory
over their foes;
They would still sing a stave—a deep-toned shout—they
sprang from the race of a noble lord.

That was a joyous, lithe-limbed band to the very hour when
they were slain:
The green-leaved forest has received them—it was an all-fierce
slaughter.

Well-armed Donall, he of the red draught, he was the Lugh
of the well-accoutred hosts:
By him in the ford—it was doom of death—fell Congal the
Slender.

The three Eogans, the three Flanns, they were renowned
outlaws;
By each of them four men fell, it was not a coward's portion.

Swiftly Cu-Domna reached us, making for his namesake:
On the hill of the encounter will be found the body of Flann
the Little.

With him where his bloody bed is thou wilt find eight men:
Though we thought them feeble, the leavings of the weapon of
Mughirne's son.

Not feebly fights Falvey the Red; the play of his spear-strings
withers the host;

14 *yew-forest:* A kenning for a band of warriors. (K. M.) 21 *Lugh:* A mythical hero. (K. M.)

Ferchorb of radiant body leapt upon the field and dealt seven murderous blows.

Front to front twelve warriors stood against me in mutual fight:
Not one remains of them all that I did not leave in slaughter.

Then we two exchanged spears, I and Alill, Eogan's son:
We both perished—O the fierceness of those stout thrusts!
We fell by each other,—though it was senseless, it was the encounter of two heroes.

Do not await the terror of night upon the battle-field among the slain warriors:
One should not hold converse with ghosts! betake thee home, carry my spoils with thee!

Every one will tell thee that mine was not the raiment of a churl:
A crimson cloak and a white tunic, a belt of silver, no paltry work!

My five-edged spear, a murderous lance, whose slaughters have been many;
A shield with five circles and a boss of bronze, by which they used to swear binding oaths.

The white cup of my cup-bearer, a shining gem, will glitter before thee;
My golden finger-ring, my bracelets, treasures without a flaw, King Nia Nar has brought them over the sea.

Cailte's brooch, a pin with luck, it was one of his marvellous treasures:
Two heads of silver round a head of gold, a goodly piece, though small.

My draught-board—no mean treasure!—is thine; take it with thee.
Noble blood drips on its rim, it lies not far hence.

Around its crimson woof many a body of the spear-armed host lies here and there,
A dense bush of the ruddy oak-wood conceals it by the side of the grave.

As thou searchest carefully for it thou shouldst not speak much:
Earth never covered anything so marvellous.

One half of its pieces are yellow gold, the other are white bronze;
Its woof is of pearls; it is the wonder of smiths how it was wrought.

The bag for its pieces,—'tis a marvel of a story—its rim is embroidered with gold;
The master-smith has left a lock upon it which no ignorant person can open.

A four-cornered casket,—it is but tiny—made of coils of red gold;
One hundred ounces of white bronze have been put into it firmly.

For it is of a coil of firm red gold, Dinoll the gold-smith brought it over the sea;
Even one of its clasps only has been priced at seven slave-women.

Memories describe it as one of Turvey's masterworks:
In the time of Art—he was a luxurious king—'tis then Turvey, lord of many herds, made it.

Smiths never made any work comparable with it;
Earth never hid a king's jewel so marvellous.

59 *slave-women:* A slave-woman (rated at three cows) was the standard of value among the ancient Irish. (K. M.)

If thou be cunning as to its price, I know thy children will
never be in want;
If thou hoard it, a close treasure, none of thy off-spring will
ever be destitute.

There are around us here and there many spoils of famous
luck:
Horrible are the huge entrails which the Morrigan washes.

From the edge of a spear she came to us, 'tis she that egged
us on.
Many are the spoils she washes, terrible the hateful laugh she
laughs.

She has flung her mane over her back—it is a stout heart that
will not quail at her:
Though she is so near to us, do not let fear overcome thee!

In the morning I shall part from all that is human, I shall
follow the warrior-band;
Go to thy house, stay not here, the end of the night is at hand.

Some one will at all times remember this song of Fothad
Canann;
My discourse with thee shall not be unrenowned, if thou
remember my bequest.

Since my grave will be frequented, let a conspicuous tomb be
raised;
Thy trouble for thy love is no loss of labour.

My riddled body must now part from thee awhile, my soul to
be tortured by the black Demon.
Save for the worship of Heaven's King, love of this world is
folly.

67 *Morrigan:* a battle-goddess. (K. M.)

I hear the dusky ousel that sends a joyous greeting to all the faithful:
My speech, my shape are spectral—hush, woman, do not speak to me!

THE LAMENT OF THE OLD WOMAN OF BEARE

The reason why she was called the Old Woman of Beare was that she had fifty foster-children in Beare. She had seven periods of youth one after another, so that every man who had lived with her came to die of old age, and her grandsons and great-grandsons were tribes and races. For a hundred years she wore the veil which Cumine had blessed upon her head. Thereupon old age and infirmity came to her. 'Tis then she said:

Ebb-tide to me as of the sea!
Old age causes me reproach.
Though I may grieve thereat—
Happiness comes out of fat.

I am the old Woman of Beare,
An ever-new smock I used to wear:
To-day—such is my mean estate—
I wear not even a cast-off smock.

It is riches
Ye love, it is not men:
In the time when *we* lived
It was men we loved.

Swift chariots,
And steeds that carried off the prize,—
Their day of plenty has been,
A blessing on the King who lent them!

The Lament . . . : late tenth century.

My body with bitterness has dropt
Towards the abode we know:
When the Son of God deems it time
Let Him come to deliver His behest.

My arms when they are seen
Are bony and thin:
Once they would fondle,
They would be round glorious kings.

When my arms are seen,
And they bony and thin,
They are not fit, I declare,
To be uplifted over comely youths.

The maidens rejoice
When May-day comes to them:
For me sorrow is meeter,
For I am wretched, I am an old hag.

I hold no sweet converse,
No wethers are killed for my wedding-feast,
My hair is all but grey,
The mean veil over it is no pity.

I do not deem it ill
That a white veil should be on my head:
Time was when many cloths of every hue
Bedecked my head as we drank the good ale.

The Stone of the Kings on Femen,
The Chair of Ronan in Bregon,
'Tis long since storms have reached them:
The slabs of their tombs are old and decayed.

The wave of the great sea talks aloud,
Winter has arisen:
Fermuid the son of Mugh to-day
I do not expect on a visit.

I know what they are doing:
They row and row across
The reeds of the Ford of Alma—
Cold is the dwelling where they sleep.

'Tis "O my God!"
To me to-day, whatever will come of it.
I must take my garment even in the sun:
The time is at hand that shall renew me.

Youth's summer in which we were
I have spent with its autumn:
Winter-age which overwhelms all men,
To me has come its beginning.

Amen! Woe is me!
Every acorn has to drop.
After feasting by shining candles
To be in the gloom of a prayer-house!

I had my day with kings
Drinking mead and wine:
To-day I drink whey-water
Among shrivelled old hags.

I see upon my cloak the hair of old age,
My reason has beguiled me:
Grey is the hair that grows through my skin—
'Tis thus I am an old hag.

The flood-wave
And the second ebb-tide—
They have all reached me,
So that I know them well.

The flood-wave
Will not reach the silence of my kitchen:
Though many are my company in darkness,
A hand has been laid upon them all.

O happy the isle of the great sea
Which the flood reaches after the ebb!
As for me, I do not expect
Flood after ebb to come to me.

There is scarce a little place to-day
That I can recognise:
What was on flood
Is all on ebb.

Dante Alighieri 1265–1321

ULYSSES

Then of the antique flame the greater horn,
  Murmuring, began to wave itself about
  Even as a flame doth which the wind fatigues.
Thereafterward, the summit to and fro
  Moving as if it were the tongue that spake,
  It uttered forth a voice, and said: "When I
From Circe had departed, who concealed me
  More than a year there near unto Gaëta,
  Or ever yet Aeneas named it so,
Nor fondness for my son, nor reverence
  For my old father, nor the due affection
  Which joyous should have made Penelope,
Could overcome within me the desire
  I had to be experienced of the world,
  And of the vice and virtue of mankind;
But I put forth on the high open sea
  With one sole ship, and that small company
  By which I never had deserted been.
Both of the shores I saw as far as Spain,
  Far as Morocco, and the isle of Sardes,
  And the others which that sea bathes round about.
I and my company were old and slow
  When at that narrow passage we arrived
  Where Hercules his landmarks set as signals,
That man no farther onward should adventure.

From *The Divine Comedy, Inferno*. Translated by Henry Wadsworth Longfellow 1807-1882. In the eighth foss of the Malebolge, Dante and Virgil encounter the evil counselors hidden in flames.

Ulysses (*Inferno* xxvi) replies to Virgil's courteous request.

1 *greater horn:* Ulysses and Diomedes are joined beneath a single flame parted at the top, "together under vengeance as they were in wrath." 9 before 24 *Hercules his landmarks:* The Pillars of Hercules, Gibraltar and Mt. Abyla in Africa, marked the limit of the known world.

On the right hand behind me left I Seville,
And on the other already had left Ceuta.
'O brothers, who amid a hundred thousand
Perils,' I said, 'have come unto the West,
To this so inconsiderable vigil
Which is remaining of your senses still,
Be ye unwilling to deny the knowledge,
Following the sun, of the unpeopled world.
Consider ye the seed from which ye sprang;
Ye were not made to live like unto brutes,
But for pursuit of virtue and of knowledge.'
So eager did I render my companions,
With this brief exhortation, for the voyage,
That then I hardly could have held them back.
And having turned our stern unto the morning,
We of the oars made wings for our mad flight,
Evermore gaining on the larboard side.
Already all the stars of the other pole
The night beheld, and ours so very low
It did not rise above the ocean floor.
Five times rekindled and as many quenched
Had been the splendor underneath the moon,
Since we had entered into the deep pass,
When there appeared to us a mountain, dim
From distance, and it seemed to me so high
As I had never any one beheld.
Joyful were we, and soon it turned to weeping;
For out of the new land a whirlwind rose,
And smote upon the fore part of the ship.
Three times it made it whirl with all the waters,
At the fourth time it made the stern uplift,
And the prow downward go, as pleased Another,
Until the sea above us closed again."

GUIDO DA MONTEFELTRO

"If I believed that my reply were made
To one who to the world would e'er return,
This flame without more flickering should stand still;
But inasmuch as never from this depth
Did any one return, if I hear true,
Without the fear of infamy I answer,
I was a man of arms, then Cordelier,
Believing thus begirt to make amends;
And truly my belief had been fulfilled
But for the High Priest, whom may ill betide,
Who put me back into my former sins;
And how and wherefore I will have thee hear.
While I was still the form of bone and pulp
My mother gave to me, the deeds I did
Were not those of a lion, but a fox.
The machinations and the covert ways
I knew them all, and practised so their craft,
That to the ends of earth the sound went forth.
When now unto that portion of mine age
I saw myself arrived, when each one ought
To lower the sails, and coil away the ropes,
That which before had pleased me then displeased me;
And penitent and confessing I surrendered,
Ah woe is me! and it would have bestead me.
The Leader of the modern Pharisees
Having a war near unto Lateran,
And not with Saracens nor with the Jews

Guido da Montefeltro (*Inferno* xxvii) is another of the evil counselors who speaks to Dante.

7 *Cordelier:* Franciscan monk, "a corded friar." 10 *High Priest:* Pope Boniface VIII. 25 *The Leader:* Boniface was waging war against the Colonna family, because two of them, cardinals, had refused to ratify Boniface's election. In 1297, they were entrenched in their stronghold at Palestrina about 24 miles from Rome and visible from the Lateran hill. Boniface excommunicated them, and ordered them to surrender. They surrendered Palestrina, and on Guido's advice, Boniface broke faith with them and destroyed it.

(For each one of his enemies was Christian,
And none of them had been to conquer Acre,
Nor merchandising in the Sultan's land),
Nor the high office, nor the sacred orders,
In him regarded, nor in me that cord
Which used to make those girt with it more meagre;
But even as Constantine sought out Sylvester
To cure his leprosy, within Soracte,
So this one sought me out as an adept
To cure him of the fever of his pride.
Counsel he asked of me, and I was silent,
Because his words appeared inebriate.
And then he said: 'Be not thy heart afraid;
Henceforth I thee absolve; and thou instruct me
How to raze Palestrina to the ground.
Heaven have I power to lock and to unlock,
As thou dost know; therefore the keys are two,
The which my predecessor held not dear.'
Then urged me on his weighty arguments
There, where my silence was the worst advice;
And said I: 'Father, since thou washest me
Of that sin into which I now must fall,
The promise long with the fulfilment short
Will make thee triumph in thy lofty seat.'
Francis came afterward, when I was dead,
For me; but one of the black Cherubim
Said to him: 'Take him not; do me no wrong;
He must come down among my servitors,
Because he gave the fraudulent advice
From which time forth I have been at his hair;
For who repents not cannot be absolved,

29 *Acre:* The last Christian stronghold in Palestine fell to the Saracens in 1291. An earlier pope, Nicholas IV, forbade Christians to trade with the Saracens, and the point here is that Boniface is waging war against Christians, even though they had broken no such commands.
34 *Constantine:* According to legend, Pope Sylvester was called from his refuge on Mt. Soracte to heal the Emperor Constantine of leprosy, which he did by baptizing him.

Nor can one both repent and will at once,
Because of the contradiction which consents not.'
O miserable me! how I did shudder
When he seized on me, saying: 'Peradventure
Thou didst not think that I was a logician!'
He bore me unto Minos, who entwined
Eight times his tail about his stubborn back,
And after he had bitten it in great rage,
Said: 'Of the thievish fire a culprit this;'
Wherefore, here where thou seest, am I lost,
And vested thus in going I bemoan me."
When it had thus completed its recital,
The flame departed uttering lamentations,
Writhing and flapping its sharp-pointed horn.

64 *Minos:* one of the three judges in the classical underworld; at the rim of the second circle of Dante's hell, he sentences sinners to their final destination, which he signifies with his tail.

Christopher Marlowe 1564–1593

THE PASSIONATE SHEPHERD TO HIS LOVE

Come live with me, and be my love,
And we will all the pleasures prove
That hills and valleys, dales and fields,
Woods, or steepy mountain yields.

And we will sit upon the rocks,
Seeing the shepherds feed their flocks
By shallow rivers, to whose falls
Melodious birds sing madrigals.

And I will make thee beds of roses,
And a thousand fragrant posies;
A cap of flowers, and a kirtle
Embroidered all with leaves of myrtle.

A gown made of the finest wool,
Which from our pretty lambs we pull,
Fair-linèd slippers for the cold:
With buckles of the purest gold;

A belt of straw and ivy-buds,
With coral clasps and amber studs:
And if these pleasures may thee move,
Come live with me, and be my love.

The shepherd swains shall dance and sing
For thy delight each May-morning;
If these delights thy mind may move,
Then live with me, and be my love.

From *The Passionate Pilgrim* 1599.
11 skirt

Sir Walter Ralegh 1552?–1618

THE NYMPH'S REPLY TO THE SHEPHERD

If all the world and love were young,
And truth in every shepherd's tongue,
These pretty pleasures might me move,
To live with thee, and be thy love.

Time drives the flocks from field to fold,
When rivers rage, and rocks grow cold,
And Philomel becometh dumb,
The rest complains of cares to come.

The flowers do fade, and wanton fields,
To wayward winter reckoning yields,
A honey tongue, a heart of gall,
Is fancy's spring, but sorrow's fall.

Thy gowns, thy shoes, thy bed of roses,
Thy cap, thy kirtle, and thy posies,
Soon break, soon wither, soon forgotten:
In folly ripe, in reason rotten.

Thy belt of straw and ivy buds,
Thy coral clasps and amber studs,
All those in me no means can move,
To come to thee, and be thy love.

But could youth last, and love still breed;
Had joys no date, nor age no need;
Then those delights my mind might move,
To live with thee, and be thy love.

From *England's Helicon* 1600.

John Donne 1572–1631

THE CANONIZATION

For Godsake hold your tongue and let me love,
  Or chide my palsy or my gout,
My five grey hairs or ruin'd fortune flout;
With wealth your state, your mind with arts improve,
  Take you a course, get you a place,
  Observe his Honor, or his Grace,
Or the king's real or his stampèd face
  Contemplate, what you will, approve,
    So you will let me love.

Alas, alas, who's injur'd by my love?
  What merchant's ships have my sighs drown'd?
Who says my tears have overflow'd his ground?
When did my colds a forward spring remove?
  When did the heats which my veins fill
  Add one more to the plaguy bill?
Soldiers find wars, and lawyers find out still
  Litigious men, which quarrels move,
    Though she and I do love.

Call us what you will, we'are made such by love.
  Call her one, me another fly,
We're tapers too, and at our own cost die,
And we in us find th' Eagle and the Dove.
  The Phoenix riddle hath more wit
  By us, we two being one, are it.
So to one neutral thing both sexes fit,
  We die and rise the same, and prove
    Mysterious by his love.

We can die by it, if not live by love,
  And if unfit for tombs and hearse

From *Poems* 1623: *Songs and Sonnets* (two poems).
15 *plaguy bill:* the weekly list of plague victims.

Our legend be, it will be fit for verse;
And if no piece of chronicle we prove,
We'll build in sonnets pretty rooms;
As well a well-wrought urn becomes
The greatest ashes, as half-acre tombs,
And by these hymns all shall approve
Us canoniz'd for love,

And thus invoke us: You whom reverent love
Made one another's hermitage,
You to whom love was peace, that now is rage,
Who did the whole world's soul contract, and drove
Into the glasses of your eyes
(So made such mirrors and such spies
That they did all to you epitomize)
Countries, towns, courts: Beg from above
A pattern of your love!

A LECTURE UPON THE SHADOW

Stand still, and I will read to thee
A lecture, love, in Love's philosophy.
These three hours that we have spent
Walking here, two shadows went
Along with us, which we ourselves produc'd;
But, now the sun is just above our head,
We do those shadows tread;
And to brave clearness all things are reduc'd.
So whilst our infant loves did grow,
Disguises did, and shadows, flow
From us, and our cares; but now 'tis not so.

That love hath not attain'd the high'st degree,
Which is still diligent lest others see.

Except our loves at this noon stay,
We shall new shadows make the other way.
As the first were made to blind
Others, these which come behind
Will work upon ourselves, and blind our eyes.
If our loves faint, and westwardly decline;
To me thou falsely thine,
And I to thee mine actions shall disguise.
The morning shadows wear away,
But these grow longer all the day.
But O, love's day is short if love decay.

Love is a growing, or full constant light,
And his first minute after noon is night.

Andrew Marvell 1621–1678

TO HIS COY MISTRESS

Had we but World enough, and Time,
This coyness Lady were no crime.
We would sit down, and think which way
To walk, and pass our long Love's Day.
Thou by the Indian Ganges' side
Should'st Rubies find: I by the Tide
Of Humber would complain. I would
Love you ten years before the Flood:
And you should if you please refuse
Till the Conversion of the Jews.
My vegetable Love should grow
Vaster than Empires, and more slow.
An hundred years should go to praise
Thine Eyes, and on thy Forehead Gaze.
Two hundred to adore each Breast:
But thirty thousand to the rest.
An Age at least to every part,
And the last Age should show your Heart.
For Lady you deserve this State;
Nor would I love at lower rate.
  But at my back I always hear
Time's wingèd Chariot hurrying near:
And yonder all before us lie
Desarts of vast Eternity.
Thy Beauty shall no more be found;
Nor, in thy marble Vault, shall sound
My echoing Song: then Worms shall try
That long preserv'd Virginity:

From *Miscellaneous Poems* 1681 (two poems).

11 *vegetable:* alludes to a traditional classification of souls. The vegetable excels in duration of life and extent of growth but lacks sense and motion (in which the animal excels) as well as reason (the unique property of the rational soul).

And your quaint Honour turn to dust;
And into ashes all my Lust.
The Grave's a fine and private place,
But none I think do there embrace.
  Now therefore, while the youthful hew
Sits on thy skin like morning dew,
And while thy willing Soul transpires
At every pore with instant Fires,
Now let us sport us while we may;
And now, like am'rous birds of prey,
Rather at once our Time devour,
Than languish in his slow-chapt pow'r.
Let us roll all our Strength, and all
Our sweetness, up into one Ball:
And tear our Pleasures with rough strife,
Thoròugh the Iron gates of Life.
Thus, though we cannot make our Sun
Stand still, yet we will make him run.

THE NYMPH COMPLAINING FOR THE DEATH OF HER FAUN

The wanton troopers riding by
Have shot my Faun, and it will die.
Ungentle men! they cannot thrive
Who killed thee. Thou ne'er didst alive
Them any harm: alas nor could
Thy death yet do them any good.
I'm sure I never wished them ill;
Nor do I for all this, nor will:
But, if my simple prayers may yet
Prevail with Heaven to forget

34 *dew:* the correction *lew,* "warmth," was suggested by H. M. Margoliouth in the Oxford edition (1927); I prefer the error of the intervening centuries. 40 -jawed

. . . *Her Faun:* In the seventeenth century the spellings *faun* and *fawn* were not consistently distinguished.

Thy murder, I will join my tears
Rather than fail. But, O my fears!
It cannot die so. Heaven's king
Keeps register of everything,
And nothing may we use in vain;
Even beasts must be with justice slain;
Else men are made their Deodands.
Though they should wash their guilty hands
In this warm life-blood which doth part
From thine, and wound me to the heart,
Yet could they not be clean; their stain
Is dyed in such a purple grain.
There is not such another in
The world, to offer for their sin.
  Unconstant SYLVIO, when yet
I had not found him counterfeit,
One morning (I remember well),
Tied in his silver chain and bell,
Gave it to me: nay and I know
What he said then; I'm sure I do:
Said he, "Look how your huntsman here
Hath taught a Faun to hunt his Dear."
But SYLVIO soon had me beguiled;
This waxèd tame, while he grew wild,
And quite regardless of my smart,
Left me his Faun, but took his Heart.
  Thenceforth I set myself to play
My solitary time away
With this; and, very well content,
Could so mine idle life have spent;
For it was full of sport, and light
Of foot and heart, and did invite
Me to its game: it seemed to bless
Itself in me; how could I less
Than love it? O, I cannot be

17 *Deodands:* Under English law, any personal property which caused someone's death was forfeited to the crown to be used for good purposes.

Unkind to a beast that loveth me.
  Had it lived long, I do not know
Whether it too might have done so
As SYLVIO did; his gifts might be
Perhaps as false, or more, than he;
But I am sure, for aught that I
Could in so short a time espy,
Thy love was far more better then
The love of false and cruel men.
  With sweetest milk and sugar first
I it at mine own fingers nursed;
And as it grew, so every day
It waxed more white and sweet than they.
It had so sweet a breath! And oft
I blushed to see its foot more soft
And white, shall I say than my hand?
Nay, any lady's of the land.
  It is a wondrous thing how fleet
'Twas on those little silver feet;
With what a pretty skipping grace
It oft would challenge me the race;
And when't had left me far away,
'Twould stay, and run again, and stay.
For it was nimbler much than hinds,
And trod, as on the four Winds.
  I have a garden of my own,
But so with roses overgrown,
And lilies, that you would it guess
To be a little wilderness;
And all the spring time of the year
It only lovèd to be there.
Among the beds of lilies I
Have sought it oft, where it should lie,
Yet could not, till itself would rise,
Find it, although before mine eyes;
For, in the flaxen lilies' shade,
It like a bank of lilies laid.

53 *then: than*

Upon the roses it would feed,
Until its lips ev'n seem to bleed
And then to me 'twould boldly trip,
And print those roses on my lip.
But all its chief delight was still
On roses thus itself to fill,
And its pure virgin limbs to fold
In whitest sheets of lilies cold:
Had it lived long, it would have been
Lilies without, roses within.
  O help! O help! I see it faint:
And die as calmly as a saint.
See how it weeps. The tears do come
Sad, slowly, dropping like a gum.
So weeps the wounded balsam; so
The holy frankincense doth flow.
The brotherless Heliades
Melt in such amber tears as these.
  I in a golden vial will
Keep these two crystal tears; and fill
It till it do o'erflow with mine;
Then place it in DIANA's shrine.
  Now my sweet Faun is vanished to
Whither the swans and turtles go;
In fair Elysium to endure,
With milk-white lambs, and ermines pure.
O do not run too fast: for I
Will but bespeak thy grave, and die.
  First my unhappy statue shall
Be cut in marble; and withal,
Let it be weeping too; but there
Th'engraver sure his art may spare;
For I so truly thee bemoan,
That I shall weep though I be stone:

99 *Heliades:* the daughters of the sun, sisters to Phaeton, who recklessly drove his father's chariot and had to be struck dead by Zeus because he let the sun come too close to the earth. 106 turtledoves

Until my tears, still dropping, wear
My breast, themselves engraving there.
There at my feet shalt thou be laid,
Of purest alabaster made;
For I would have thine image be
White as I can, though not as Thee.

Jonathan Swift 1667–1745

THE HUMBLE PETITION OF FRANCES HARRIS, WHO MUST STARVE, AND DIE A MAID IF IT MISCARRIES

Humbly Sheweth.

That I went to warm my self in Lady *Betty*'s Chamber, because I was cold,
And I had in a Purse, seven Pound, four Shillings and six Pence, besides Farthings, in Money, and Gold;
So because I had been buying things for my *Lady* last Night,
I was resolved to tell my Money, to see if it was right:
Now you must know, because my Trunk has a very bad Lock,
Therefore all the Money, I have, which, *God* knows, is a very small Stock,
I keep in a Pocket ty'd about my Middle, next my Smock.
So when I went to put up my Purse, as *God* would have it, my Smock was unript,
And, instead of putting it into my Pocket, down it slipt:
Then the Bell rung, and I went down to put my *Lady* to Bed,
And, *God* knows, I thought my Money was as safe as my Maidenhead.
So when I came up again, I found my Pocket feel very light,
But when I search'd, and miss'd my Purse, *Lord!* I thought I should have sunk outright:
Lord! Madam, says *Mary,* how d'ye do? Indeed, says I, never worse;
But pray, *Mary,* can you tell what I have done with my Purse!
Lord help me, said *Mary,* I never stirr'd out of this Place!
Nay, said I, I had it in Lady *Betty*'s Chamber, that's a plain Case.
So *Mary* got me to Bed, and cover'd me up warm,
However, she stole away my Garters, that I might do my self no Harm:

From *A Meditation upon a Broomstick, and Somewhat Beside* 1710.
4 count

So I tumbl'd and toss'd all Night, as you may very well think,
But hardly ever set my Eyes together, or slept a Wink.
So I was a-dream'd, methought, that we went and search'd the Folks round,
And in a Corner of Mrs. *Dukes*'s Box, ty'd in a Rag, the Money was found.
So next Morning we told *Whittle,* and he fell a Swearing;
Then my Dame *Wadgar* came, and she, you know, is thick of Hearing;
Dame, said I, as loud as I could bawl, do you know what a Loss I have had?
Nay, said she, my Lord *Collway*'s Folks are all very sad,
For my Lord *Dromedary* comes a *Tuesday* without fail;
Pugh! said I, but that's not the Business that I ail.
Says *Cary,* says he, I have been a Servant this Five and Twenty Years, come Spring,
And in all the Places I liv'd, I never heard of such a Thing.
Yes, says the *Steward,* I remember when I was at my Lady *Shrewsbury*'s,
Such a thing as this happen'd, just about the time of *Goosberries*.
So I went to the Party suspected, and I found her full of Grief;
(Now you must know, of all Things in the World, I hate a Thief.)
However, I was resolv'd to bring the Discourse slily about,
Mrs. *Dukes,* said I, here's an ugly Accident has happen'd out;
'Tis not that I value the Money three Skips of a Louse;
But the Thing I stand upon, is the Credit of the House;
'Tis true, seven Pound, four Shillings, and six Pence, makes a great Hole in my Wages,
Besides, as they say, Service is no Inheritance in these Ages.
Now, Mrs. *Dukes,* you know, and every Body understands,
That tho' 'tis hard to judge, yet Money can't go without Hands.
The *Devil* take me, said she, (blessing her self,) if I ever saw't!
So she roar'd like a *Bedlam,* as tho' I had call'd her all to naught;
So you know, what could I say to her any more,
I e'en left her, and came away as wise as I was before.

Well: But then they would have had me gone to the Cunning Man;
No, said I, 'tis the same Thing, the *Chaplain* will be here anon.
So the *Chaplain* came in; now the Servants say, he is my Sweet-heart,
Because he's always in my Chamber, and I always take his Part;
So, as the *Devil* would have it, before I was aware, out I blunder'd,
Parson, said I, can you cast a *Nativity,* when a Body's plunder'd?
(Now you must know, he hates to be call'd *Parson,* like the *Devil.*)
Truly, says he, Mrs. *Nab,* it might become you to be more civil:
If your Money be gone, as a Learned *Divine* says, d'ye see,
You are no *Text* for my Handling, so take that from me:
I was never taken for a *Conjurer* before, I'd have you to know.
Lord, said I, don't be angry, I'm sure I never thought you so;
You know, I honour the Cloth, I design to be a *Parson*'s Wife,
I never took one in *Your Coat* for a *Conjurer* in all my Life.
With that, he twisted his Girdle at me like a Rope, as who should say,
Now you may go hang your self for me, and so went away.
Well; I thought I should have swoon'd; *Lord,* said I, what shall I do?
I have lost my *Money,* and shall lose my *True-Love* too.
Then my *Lord* call'd me; *Harry,* said my *Lord,* don't cry,
I'll give something towards thy Loss; and says my *Lady,* so will I.
Oh but, said I, what if after all my Chaplain won't *come to?*
For that, he said, (an't please your *Excellencies*) I must Petition You.

The Premises tenderly consider'd, I desire your *Excellencies* Protection,

48 fortune teller

And that I may have a Share in next *Sunday*'s Collection:
And over and above, that I may have your *Excellencies* Letter,
With an Order for the *Chaplain* aforesaid; or instead of Him, a Better:
And then your poor *Petitioner,* both Night and Day,
Or the *Chaplain,* (for 'tis his *Trade*) as in Duty bound, shall ever *Pray.*

Robert Burns 1759–1796

THE PRAYER OF HOLY WILLIE, A CANTING, HYPOCRITICAL KIRK ELDER 1789

And send the godly in a pet to pray.—POPE.

I

O Thou that in the Heavens does dwell,
Wha, as it pleases best Thysel,
Sends ane to Heaven an' ten to Hell
A' for Thy glory,
And no for onie guid or ill
They've done before Thee!

II

I bless and praise Thy matchless might,
When thousands Thou hast left in night,
That I am here before Thy sight,
For gifts an' grace
A burning and a shining light
To a' this place.

III

What was I, or my generation,
That I should get sic exaltation?
I, wha deserv'd most just damnation
For broken laws
Sax thousand years ere my creation,
Thro' Adam's cause!

IV

When from my mither's womb I fell,
Thou might hae plung'd me deep in hell
To gnash my gooms, and weep, and wail

First published separately 1789.

In burning lakes,
Whare damnèd devils roar and yell,
Chain'd to their stakes

V

Yet I am here, a chosen sample,
To show Thy grace is great and ample:
I'm here a pillar o' Thy temple,
Strong as a rock,
A guide, a buckler, and example
To a' thy flock!

VI

But yet, O Lord! confess I must:
At times I'm fash'd wi' fleshly lust;
An' sometimes, too, in warldly trust,
Vile self gets in;
But Thou remembers we are dust,
Defiled wi' sin.

VII

O Lord! yestreen, Thou kens, wi' Meg—
Thy pardon I sincerely beg—
O, may 't ne'er be a living plague
To my dishonour!
An' I'll ne'er lift a lawless leg
Again upon her.

VIII

Besides, I farther maun avow—
Wi' Leezie's lass, three times, I trow—
But, Lord, that Friday I was fon,
When I cam near her,
Or else, Thou kens, Thy servant true
Wad never steer her.

32 troubled 45 drunk 48 molest

IX

Maybe Thou lets this fleshly thorn
Buffet Thy servant e'en and morn,
Lest he owre proud and high should turn
That he's sae gifted:
If sae, Thy han' maun e'en be borne
Until Thou lift it.

X

Lord, bless Thy chosen in this place,
For here Thou has a chosen race!
But God confound their stubborn face
An' blast their name,
Wha bring Thy elders to disgrace
An' open shame!

XI

Lord, mind Gau'n Hamilton's deserts:
He drinks, an' swears, an' plays at cartes,
Yet has sae monie takin arts
Wi' great and sma',
Frae God's ain Priest the people's hearts
He steals awa.

XII

And when we chasten'd him therefore,
Thou kens how he bred sic a splore,
And set the warld in a roar
O' laughin at us:
Curse Thou his basket and his store,
Kail an' potatoes!

68 riot 72 cabbage

XIII

Lord, hear my earnest cry and pray'r
Against that Presbyt'ry of Ayr!
Thy strong right hand, Lord, mak it bare
        Upo' their heads!
Lord, visit them, an' dinna spare,
        For their misdeeds!

XIV

O Lord, my God! that glib-tongu'd Aiken,
My vera heart and flesh are quakin
To think how we stood sweatin, shakin,
        An' pish'd wi' dread,
While he, wi' hingin lip an' snakin,
        Held up his head.

XV

Lord, in Thy day o' vengeance try him!
Lord, visit him wha did employ him!
And pass not in Thy mercy by them,
        Nor hear their pray'r,
But for Thy people's sake destroy them,
        An' dinna spare!

XVI

But, Lord, remember me and mine
Wi' mercies temporal and divine,
That I for grace an' gear may shine
        Excell'd by nane;
And a' the glory shall be Thine—
        Amen, Amen!

82 pissed   92 possessions

William Blake 1757–1827

from TIRIEL

5

And aged Tiriel stood & said: "Where does the thunder sleep?
Where doth he hide his terrible head? & his swift & fiery daughters,
Where do they shroud their fiery wings & the terrors of their hair?
Earth, thus I stamp thy bosom! rouse the earthquake from his den,
To raise his dark & burning visage thro' the cleaving ground,
To thrust these towers with his shoulders! let his fiery dogs
Rise from the center, belching flames & roarings, dark smoke!
Where art thou, Pestilence, that bathest in fogs & standing lakes?
Rise up thy sluggish limbs & let the loathsomest of poisons
Drop from thy garments as thou walkest, wrapt in yellow clouds!
Here take thy seat in this wide court; let it be strown with dead;
And sit & smile upon these cursed sons of Tiriel!
Thunder & fire & pestilence, hear you not Tiriel's curse?"

He ceast: the heavy clouds confus'd roll'd round the lofty towers,
Discharging their enormous voices at the father's curse.

From a unique manuscript first published in *The Complete Writings of William Blake* 1925, ed. Geoffrey Keynes. The present selection is about a third of the whole, three sections out of eight, or 107 septenarii out of 354 (fourteeners, Blake's characteristic later line, adapted from the ballad half-couplet and from the great Elizabethan translators). The poem begins with the death of Tiriel's wife and ends with his own. He is perhaps, like Urizen, a type of the vengeful rationalistic Jehovah of deism Blake hated, influenced no doubt by King Lear and his own mad senile King George III.

The earth trembled; fires belched from the yawning clefts;
And when the shaking ceast, a fog possest the accursed clime.

The cry was great in Tiriel's palace: his five daughters ran
And caught him by the garments, weeping with cries of bitter woe.

"Aye, now you feel the curse, you cry! but may all ears be deaf
As Tiriel's, & all eyes as blind as Tiriel's to your woes!
May never stars shine on your roofs! may never sun nor moon
Visit you, but eternal fogs hover around your walls!
Hela, my youngest daughter, you shall lead me from this place,
And let the curse fall on the rest & wrap them up together!"

He ceast, & Hela led her father from the noisom place.
In haste they fled, while all the sons & daughters of Tiriel,
Chain'd in thick darkness, utter'd cries of mourning all the night;
And in the morning, Lo! an hundred men in ghastly death!
The four daughters stretch'd on the marble pavement, silent all,
Fall'n by the pestilence!—the rest moped round in guilty fears;
And all the children in their beds were cut off in one night.
Thirty of Tiriel's sons remain'd, to wither in the palace,
Desolate, Loathed, Dumb, Astonish'd, waiting for black death.

6

And Hela led her father thro' the silent of the night,
Astonish'd, silent, till the morning beams began to spring.

"Now, Hela, I can go with pleasure & dwell with Har & Heva,
Now that the curse shall clean devour all those guilty sons.
This is the right & ready way; I know it by the sound
That our feet make. Remember, Hela, I have sav'd thee from death;
Then be obedient to thy father, for the curse is taken off thee.
I dwelt with Myratana five years in the desolate rock,
And all that time we waited for the fire from heaven,

Or for the torrents of the sea to overwhelm you all.
But now my wife is dead & all the time of grace is past:
You see the parent's curse. Now lead me where I have commanded."

"O leagued with evil spirits, thou accursed man of sin!
True, I was born thy slave! who ask'd thee to save me from death?
'Twas for thy self, thou cruel man, because thou wantest eyes."

"True, Hela, this is the desert of all those cruel ones.
Is Tiriel cruel? look! his daughter & his youngest daughter
Laughs at affection, glories in rebellion, scoffs at Love.
I have not eat these two days; lead me to Har & Heva's tent,
Or I will wrap thee up in such a terrible father's curse
That thou shalt feel worms in thy marrow creeping thro' thy bones.
Yet thou shalt lead me! Lead me, I command, to Har & Heva!"

"O cruel! O destroyer! O consumer! O avenger!
To Har & Heva I will lead thee: then would that they would curse!
Then would they curse as thou hast cursed! but they are not like thee!
O! they are holy & forgiving, fill'd with loving mercy,
Forgetting the offences of their most rebellious children,
Or else thou wouldest not have liv'd to curse thy helpless children."

"Look on my eyes, Hela, & see, for thou hast eyes to see,
The tears swell from my stony fountains: wherefore do I weep?
Wherefore from my blind orbs art thou not seiz'd with pois'nous stings?
Laugh, serpent, youngest venomous reptile of the flesh of Tiriel!
Laugh! for thy father Tiriel shall give thee cause to laugh,
Unless thou lead me to the tent of Har, child of the curse!"

"Silence thy evil tongue, thou murderer of thy helpless children!
I lead thee to the tent of Har; not that I mind thy curse,

But that I feel they will curse thee & hang upon thy bones
Fell shaking agonies, & in each wrinkle of that face
Plant worms of death to feast upon the tongue of terrible curses."

"Hela, my daughter, listen! thou art the daughter of Tiriel.
Thy father calls. Thy father lifts his hand unto the heavens,
For thou hast laughed at my tears & curst thy aged father.
Let snakes rise from thy bedded locks & laugh among thy curls!"

He ceast: her dark hair upright stood, while snakes infolded round
Her madding brows: her shrieks appall'd the soul of Tiriel.

"What have I done, Hela, my daughter? fear'st thou now the curse,
Or wherefore dost thou cry? Ah, wretch, to curse thy aged father!
Lead me to Har & Heva, & the curse of Tiriel
Shall fail. If thou refuse, howl in the desolate mountains!"

7

She, howling, led him over mountains & thro' frighted vales,
Till to the caves of Zazel they approach'd at even tide.
Forth from their caves old Zazel & his sons ran; when they saw
Their tyrant prince blind, & his daughter howling & leading him,
They laugh'd & mocked; some threw dirt & stones as they pass'd by;

But when Tiriel turn'd around & rais'd his awful voice,
Some fled away; but Zazel stood still, & thus begun:

"Bald tyrant, wrinkled, cunning, listen to Zazel's chains!
'Twas thou that chain'd thy brother Zazel! where are now thine eyes?
Shout, beautiful daughter of Tiriel! thou singest a sweet song!

Where are you going? come & eat some roots & drink some water
Thy crown is bald, old man; the sun will dry thy brains away,
And thou wilt be as foolish as thy foolish brother Zazel."

The blind man heard, & smote his breast, & trembling passed on.
They threw dirt after them, till to the covert of a wood
The howling maiden led her father, where wild beasts resort,
Hoping to end her woes; but from her cries the tygers fled.
All night they wander'd thro' the wood, & when the sun arose,
They enter'd on the mountains of Har: at Noon the happy tents
Were frighted by the dismal cries of Hela on the mountains.

But Har & Heva slept fearless as babes on loving breasts.
Mnetha awoke: she ran & stood at the tent door, & saw
The aged wanderer led towards the tents; she took her bow,
And chose her arrows, then advanc'd to meet the terrible pair.

Alfred, Lord Tennyson 1809–1892

ULYSSES

It little profits that an idle king,
By this still hearth, among these barren crags,
Match'd with an agèd wife, I mete and dole
Unequal laws unto a savage race,
That hoard, and sleep, and feed, and know not me.
I cannot rest from travel: I will drink
Life to the lees: all times I have enjoy'd
Greatly, have suffer'd greatly, both with those
That loved me, and alone; on shore, and when
Thro' scudding drifts the rainy Hyades
Vext the dim sea: I am become a name;
For always roaming with a hungry heart
Much have I seen and known; cities of men
And manners, climates, councils, governments,
Myself not least, but honour'd of them all;
And drunk delight of battle with my peers,
Far on the ringing plains of windy Troy.
I am a part of all that I have met;
Yet all experience is an arch wherethro'
Gleams that untravell'd world, whose margin fades
For ever and for ever when I move.
How dull it is to pause, to make an end,
To rust unburnish'd, not to shine in use!
As tho' to breathe were life. Life piled on life
Were all too little, and of one to me
Little remains: but every hour is saved
From that eternal silence, something more,
A bringer of new things; and vile it were
For some three suns to store and hoard myself,

From *Poems* 1842, *English Idylls and Other Poems.*

10 *Hyades:* the seven stars in the head of the constellation Taurus. Their rise in the sky marks the beginning of the rainy season.

And this gray spirit yearning in desire
To follow knowledge like a sinking star,
Beyond the utmost bound of human thought.

This is my son, mine own Telemachus,
To whom I leave the sceptre and the isle—
Well-loved of me, discerning to fulfil
This labour, by slow prudence to make mild
A rugged people, and thro' soft degrees
Subdue them to the useful and the good.
Most blameless is he, centred in the sphere
Of common duties, decent not to fail
In offices of tenderness, and pay
Meet adoration to my household gods,
When I am gone. He works his work, I mine.

There lies the port; the vessel puffs her sail:
There gloom the dark broad seas. My mariners,
Souls that have toil'd, and wrought, and thought with me—
That ever with a frolic welcome took
The thunder and the sunshine, and opposed
Free hearts, free foreheads—you and I are old;
Old age hath yet his honour and his toil;
Death closes all: but something ere the end,
Some work of noble note, may yet be done,
Not unbecoming men that strove with Gods.
The lights begin to twinkle from the rocks:
The long day wanes: the slow moon climbs: the deep
Moans round with many voices. Come, my friends,
'Tis not too late to seek a newer world.
Push off, and sitting well in order smite
The sounding furrows; for my purpose holds
To sail beyond the sunset, and the baths
Of all the western stars, until I die.
It may be that the gulfs will wash us down:
It may be we shall touch the Happy Isles,
And see the great Achilles, whom we knew.
Tho' much is taken, much abides; and tho'
We are not now that strength which in old days

Moved earth and heaven; that which we are, we are;
One equal temper of heroic hearts,
Made weak by time and fate, but strong in will
To strive, to seek, to find, and not to yield.

Robert Browning 1812–1889

THE BISHOP ORDERS HIS TOMB AT SAINT PRAXED'S CHURCH

ROME, 15—

Vanity, saith the preacher, vanity!
Draw round my bed: is Anselm keeping back?
Nephews—sons mine . . . ah God, I know not! Well—
She, men would have to be your mother once,
Old Gandolf envied me, so fair she was!
What 's done is done, and she is dead beside,
Dead long ago, and I am Bishop since,
And as she died so must we die ourselves,
And thence ye may perceive the world 's a dream.
Life, how and what is it? As here I lie
In this state-chamber, dying by degrees,
Hours and long hours in the dead night, I ask
"Do I live, am I dead?" Peace, peace seems all.
Saint Praxed's ever was the church for peace;
And so, about this tomb of mine. I fought
With tooth and nail to save my niche, ye know:
—Old Gandolf cozened me, despite my care;
Shrewd was that snatch from out the corner South
He graced his carrion with, God curse the same!
Yet still my niche is not so cramped but thence
One sees the pulpit o' the epistle-side,
And somewhat of the choir, those silent seats,
And up into the aery dome where live
The angels, and a sunbeam 's sure to lurk:
And I shall fill my slab of basalt there,
And 'neath my tabernacle take my rest,
With those nine columns round me, two and two,

From *Dramatic Romances* 1845, and *Men and Women* 1863; first published in *Hood's Magazine,* March 1845.

21 *epistle-side:* the right hand of the church as you face the altar.

The odd one at my feet where Anselm stands:
Peach-blossom marble all, the rare, the ripe
As fresh-poured red wine of a mighty pulse.
—Old Gandolf with his paltry onion-stone,
Put me where I may look at him! True peach,
Rosy and flawless: how I earned the prize!
Draw close: that conflagration of my church
—What then? So much was saved if aught were missed!
My sons, ye would not be my death? Go dig
The white-grape vineyard where the oil-press stood,
Drop water gently till the surface sink,
And if ye find . . . Ah God, I know not, I ! . . .
Bedded in store of rotten fig-leaves soft,
And corded up in a tight olive-frail,
Some lump, ah God, of *lapis lazuli,*
Big as a Jew's head cut off at the nape,
Blue as a vein o'er the Madonna's breast . . .
Sons, all have I bequeathed you, villas, all,
That brave Frascati villa with its bath,
So, let the blue lump poise between my knees,
Like God the Father's globe on both his hands
Ye worship in the Jesu Church so gay,
For Gandolf shall not choose but see and burst!
Swift as a weaver's shuttle fleet our years:
Man goeth to the grave, and where is he?
Did I say basalt for my slab, sons? Black—
'T was ever antique-black I meant! How else
Shall ye contrast my frieze to come beneath?
The bas-relief in bronze ye promised me,
Those Pans and Nymphs ye wot of, and perchance
Some tripod, thyrsus, with a vase or so,
The Saviour at his sermon on the mount,
Saint Praxed in a glory, and one Pan
Ready to twitch the Nymph's last garment off,
And Moses with the tables . . . but I know

41 olive basket 58 *thyrsus:* staff ornamented with ivy or grapevines, carried by Dionysus and his followers.

Ye mark me not! What do they whisper thee,
Child of my bowels, Anselm? Ah, ye hope
To revel down my villas while I gasp
Bricked o'er with beggar's mouldy travertine
Which Gandolf from his tomb-top chuckles at!
Nay, boys, ye love me—all of jasper, then!
'T is jasper ye stand pledged to, lest I grieve
My bath must needs be left behind, alas!
One block, pure green as a pistachio-nut,
There 's plenty jasper somewhere in the world—
And have I not Saint Praxed's ear to pray
Horses for ye, and brown Greek manuscripts,
And mistresses with great smooth marbly limbs?
—That 's if ye carve my epitaph aright,
Choice Latin, picked phrase, Tully's every word,
No gaudy ware like Gandolf's second line—
Tully, my masters? Ulpian serves his need!
And then how I shall lie through centuries,
And hear the blessed mutter of the mass,
And see God made and eaten all day long,
And feel the steady candle-flame, and taste
Good strong thick stupefying incense-smoke!
For as I lie here, hours of the dead night,
Dying in state and by such slow degrees,
I fold my arms as if they clasped a crook,
And stretch my feet forth straight as stone can point,
And let the bedclothes, for a mortcloth, drop
Into great laps and folds of sculptor's-work:
And as yon tapers dwindle, and strange thoughts
Grow, with a certain humming in my ears,
About the life before I lived this life,
And this life too, popes, cardinals and priests,
Saint Praxed at his sermon on the mount,
Your tall pale mother with her talking eyes,
And new-found agate urns as fresh as day,

66 limestone 77 Cicero 79 *Ulpian:* Domitius Ulpianus, a Roman jurist, d. 228 A.D., whose Latin would be considered inferior to Cicero's.

And marble's language, Latin pure, discreet,
—Aha, ELUCESCEBAT quoth our friend?
No Tully, said I, Ulpian at the best!
Evil and brief hath been my pilgrimage.
All *lapis,* all, sons! Else I give the Pope
My villas! Will ye ever eat my heart?
Ever your eyes were as a lizard's quick,
They glitter like your mother's for my soul,
Or ye would heighten my impoverished frieze,
Piece out its starved design, and fill my vase
With grapes, and add a vizor and a Term,
And to the tripod ye would tie a lynx
That in his struggle throws the thyrsus down,
To comfort me on my entablature
Whereon I am to lie till I must ask
"Do I live, am I dead?" There, leave me, there!
For ye have stabbed me with ingratitude
To death—ye wish it—God, ye wish it! Stone—
Gritstone, a-crumble! Clammy squares which sweat
As if the corpse they keep were oozing through—
And no more *lapis* to delight the world!
Well, go! I bless ye. Fewer tapers there,
But in a row: and, going, turn your backs
—Ay, like departing altar-ministrants,
And leave me in my church, the church for peace,
That I may watch at leisure if he leers—
Old Gandolf, at me, from his onion-stone,
As still he envied me, so fair she was!

99 *Elucescebat:* "he shone forth." Cicero would have said "elucebat."
108 mask . . . pillar

SOLILOQUY OF THE SPANISH CLOISTER

I

Gr-r-r—there go, my heart's abhorrence!
  Water your damned flower-pots, do!
If hate killed men, Brother Lawrence,
  God's blood, would not mine kill you!
What? your myrtle-bush wants trimming?
  Oh, that rose has prior claims—
Needs its leaden vase filled brimming?
  Hell dry you up with its flames!

II

At the meal we sit together:
  Salve tibi! I must hear
Wise talk of the kind of weather,
  Sort of season, time of year:
Not a plenteous cork-crop: scarcely
  Dare we hope oak-galls, I doubt:
What's the Latin name for "parsley"?
  What's the Greek name for Swine's Snout?

III

Whew! We'll have our platter burnished,
  Laid with care on our own shelf!
With a fire-new spoon we 're furnished,
  And a goblet for ourself,
Rinsed like something sacrificial
  Ere 't is fit to touch our chaps—
Marked with L. for our initial!
  (He-he! There his lily snaps!)

From *Dramatic Lyrics* 1842.
10 *Salve tibi:* "Hail to thee."

IV

Saint, forsooth! While brown Dolores
  Squats outside the Convent bank
With Sanchicha, telling stories,
  Steeping tresses in the tank,
Blue-black, lustrous, thick like horsehairs,
  —Can't I see his dead eye glow,
Bright as 't were a Barbary corsair's?
  (That is, if he 'd let it show!)

V

When he finishes refection,
  Knife and fork he never lays
Cross-wise, to my recollection,
  As do I, in Jesu's praise.
I the Trinity illustrate,
  Drinking watered orange-pulp—
In three sips the Arian frustrate;
  While he drains his at one gulp.

VI

Oh, those melons? If he 's able
  We 're to have a feast! so nice!
One goes to the Abbot's table,
  All of us get each a slice.
How go on your flowers? None double?
  Not one fruit-sort can you spy?
Strange!—And I, too, at such trouble,
  Keep them close-nipped on the sly!

39 *Arian:* follower of the heretic Arius, who denied the Trinity.

VII

There 's a great text in Galatians,
  Once you trip on it, entails
Twenty-nine distinct damnations,
  One sure, if another fails:
If I trip him just a-dying,
  Sure of heaven as sure can be,
Spin him round and send him flying
  Off to hell, a Manichee?

VIII

Or, my scrofulous French novel
  On grey paper with blunt type!
Simply glance at it, you grovel
  Hand and foot in Belial's gripe:
If I double down its pages
  At the woeful sixteenth print,
When he gathers his greengages,
  Ope a sieve and slip it in 't?

IX

Or, there's Satan!—one might venture
  Pledge one's soul to him, yet leave
Such a flaw in the indenture
  As he 'd miss till, past retrieve,
Blasted lay that rose-acacia
  We 're so proud of! *Hy, Zy, Hine* . . .
'St, there 's Vespers! *Plena gratiâ*
  Ave, Virgo! Gr-r-r—you swine!

56 *Manichee:* follower of the heretic Manes, a dualist. 71-72 *Plena gratiâ* . . . : "Hail, Virgin, full of grace."

Matthew Arnold 1822–1888

DOVER BEACH

The sea is calm to-night.
The tide is full, the moon lies fair
Upon the straits;—on the French coast the light
Gleams and is gone; the cliffs of England stand,
Glimmering and vast, out in the tranquil bay.
Come to the window, sweet is the night-air!
Only, from the long line of spray
Where the sea meets the moon-blanch'd land,
Listen! you hear the grating roar
Of pebbles which the waves draw back, and fling,
At their return, up the high strand,
Begin, and cease, and then again begin,
With tremulous cadence slow, and bring
The eternal note of sadness in.

Sophocles long ago
Heard it on the Aegaean, and it brought
Into his mind the turbid ebb and flow
Of human misery; we
Find also in the sound a thought,
Hearing it by this distant northern sea.

The Sea of Faith
Was once, too, at the full, and round earth's shore
Lay like the folds of a bright girdle furl'd.
But now I only hear
Its melancholy, long, withdrawing roar,
Retreating, to the breath
Of the night-wind, down the vast edges drear
And naked shingles of the world.

From *New Poems* 1867.

Ah, love, let us be true
To one another! for the world, which seems
To lie before us like a land of dreams,
So various, so beautiful, so new,
Hath really neither joy, nor love, nor light,
Nor certitude, nor peace, nor help for pain;
And we are here as on a darkling plain
Swept with confused alarms of struggle and flight,
Where ignorant armies clash by night.

William Butler Yeats 1865–1939

AN IRISH AIRMAN FORESEES HIS DEATH

I know that I shall meet my fate
Somewhere among the clouds above;
Those that I fight I do not hate,
Those that I guard I do not love;
My country is Kiltartan Cross,
My countrymen Kiltartan's poor,
No likely end could bring them loss
Or leave them happier than before.
Nor law, nor duty bade me fight,
Nor public men, nor cheering crowds,
A lonely impulse of delight
Drove to this tumult in the clouds;
I balanced all, brought all to mind,
The years to come seemed waste of breath,
A waste of breath the years behind
In balance with this life, this death.

AMONG SCHOOL CHILDREN

I

I walk through the long schoolroom questioning;
A kind old nun in a white hood replies;
The children learn to cipher and to sing,
To study reading-books and histories,
To cut and sew, be neat in everything
In the best modern way—the children's eyes
In momentary wonder stare upon
A sixty-year-old smiling public man.

From *The Wild Swans at Coole* 1919.
From *The Tower* 1928.

II

I dream of a Ledaean body, bent
Above a sinking fire, a tale that she
Told of a harsh reproof, or trivial event
That changed some childish day to tragedy—
Told, and it seemed that our two natures blent
Into a sphere from youthful sympathy,
Or else, to alter Plato's parable,
Into the yolk and white of the one shell.

III

And thinking of that fit of grief or rage
I look upon one child or t'other there
And wonder if she stood so at that age—
For even daughters of the swan can share
Something of every paddler's heritage—
And had that colour upon cheek or hair,
And thereupon my heart is driven wild:
She stands before me as a living child.

IV

Her present image floats into the mind—
Did Quattrocento finger fashion it
Hollow of cheek as though it drank the wind
And took a mess of shadows for its meat?
And I though never of Ledaean kind
Had pretty plumage once—enough of that,
Better to smile on all that smile, and show
There is a comfortable kind of old scarecrow.

V

What youthful mother, a shape upon her lap
Honey of generation had betrayed,
And that must sleep, shriek, struggle to escape
As recollection or the drug decide,
Would think her son, did she but see that shape
With sixty or more winters on its head,
A compensation for the pang of his birth,
Or the uncertainty of his setting forth?

VI

Plato thought nature but a spume that plays
Upon a ghostly paradigm of things;
Solider Aristotle played the taws
Upon the bottom of a king of kings;
World-famous golden-thighed Pythagoras
Fingered upon a fiddle-stick or strings
What a star sang and careless Muses heard:
Old clothes upon old sticks to scare a bird.

VII

Both nuns and mothers worship images,
But those the candles light are not as those
That animate a mother's reveries,
But keep a marble or a bronze repose.
And yet they too break hearts—O Presences
That passion, piety or affection knows,
And that all heavenly glory symbolise—
O self-born mockers of man's enterprise;

VIII

Labour is blossoming or dancing where
The body is not bruised to pleasure soul,
Nor beauty born out of its own despair,
Nor blear-eyed wisdom out of midnight oil.
O chestnut-tree, great-rooted blossomer,
Are you the leaf, the blossom or the bole?
O body swayed to music, O brightening glance,
How can we know the dancer from the dance?

CRAZY JANE ON GOD

That lover of a night
Came when he would,
Went in the dawning light
Whether I would or no;
Men come, men go;
All things remain in God.

Banners choke the sky;
Men-at-arms tread;
Armoured horses neigh
Where the great battle was
In the narrow pass:
All things remain in God.

Before their eyes a house
That from childhood stood
Uninhabited, ruinous,
Suddenly lit up
From door to top:
All things remain in God.

I had wild Jack for a lover:
Though like a road
That men pass over
My body makes no moan
But sings on:
All things remain in God.

From *The Winding Stair and Other Poems 1933* (two poems).

FOR ANNE GREGORY

"Never shall a young man,
Thrown into despair
By those great honey-coloured
Ramparts at your ear,
Love you for yourself alone
And not your yellow hair."

"But I can get a hair-dye
And set such colour there,
Brown, or black, or carrot,
That young men in despair
May love me for myself alone
And not my yellow hair."

"I heard an old religious man
But yesternight declare
That he had found a text to prove
That only God, my dear,
Could love you for yourself alone
And not your yellow hair."

Robert Frost 1874–1963

A SERVANT TO SERVANTS

I didn't make you know how glad I was
To have you come and camp here on our land.
I promised myself to get down some day
And see the way you lived, but I don't know!
With a houseful of hungry men to feed
I guess you'd find. . . . It seems to me
I can't express my feelings, any more
Than I can raise my voice or want to lift
My hand (oh, I can lift it when I have to).
Did ever you feel so? I hope you never.
It's got so I don't even know for sure
Whether I *am* glad, sorry, or anything.
There's nothing but a voice-like left inside
That seems to tell me how I ought to feel,
And would feel if I wasn't all gone wrong.
You take the lake. I look and look at it.
I see it's a fair, pretty sheet of water.
I stand and make myself repeat out loud
The advantages it has, so long and narrow,
Like a deep piece of some old running river
Cut short off at both ends. It lies five miles
Straightaway through the mountain notch
From the sink window where I wish the plates,
And all our storms come up toward the house,
Drawing the slow waves whiter and whiter and whiter.
It took my mind off doughnuts and soda biscuit
To step outdoors and take the water dazzle
A sunny morning, or take the rising wind
About my face and body and through my wrapper,
When a storm threatened from the Dragon's Den,
And a cold chill shivered across the lake.

From *North of Boston* 1914 (two poems).

I see it's a fair, pretty sheet of water,
Our Willoughby! How did you hear of it?
I expect, though, everyone's heard of it.
In a book about ferns? Listen to that!
You let things more like feathers regulate
Your going and coming. And you like it here?
I can see how you might. But I don't know!
It would be different if more people came,
For then there would be business. As it is,
The cottages Len built, sometimes we rent them,
Sometimes we don't. We've a good piece of shore
That ought to be worth something, and may yet.
But I don't count on it as much as Len.
He looks on the bright side of everything,
Including me. He thinks I'll be all right
With doctoring. But it's not medicine—
Lowe is the only doctor's dared to say so—
It's rest I want—there, I have said it out—
From cooking meals for hungry hired men
And washing dishes after them—from doing
Things over and over that just won't stay done.
By good rights I ought not to have so much
Put on me, but there seems no other way.
Len says one steady pull more ought to do it.
He says the best way out is always through.
And I agree to that, or in so far
As that I can see no way out but through—
Leastways for me—and then they'll be convinced.
It's not that Len don't want the best for me.
It was his plan our moving over in
Beside the lake from where that day I showed you
We used to live—ten miles from anywhere.
We didn't change without some sacrifice,
But Len went at it to make up the loss.
His work's a man's, of course, from sun to sun,
But he works when he works as hard as I do—
Though there's small profit in comparisons.
(Women and men will make them all the same.)
But work ain't all. Len undertakes too much.

He's into everything in town. This year
It's highways, and he's got too many men
Around him to look after that make waste.
They take advantage of him shamefully,
And proud, too, of themselves for doing so.
We have four here to board, great good-for-nothings,
Sprawling about the kitchen with their talk
While I fry their bacon. Much they care!
No more put out in what they do or say
Than if I wasn't in the room at all.
Coming and going all the time, they are:
I don't learn what their names are, let alone
Their characters, or whether they are safe
To have inside the house with doors unlocked.
I'm not afraid of them, though, if they're not
Afraid of me. There's two can play at that.
I have my fancies: it runs in the family.
My father's brother wasn't right. They kept him
Locked up for years back there at the old farm.
I've been away once—yes, I've been away.
The State Asylum. I was prejudiced;
I wouldn't have sent anyone of mine there;
You know the old idea—the only asylum
Was the poorhouse, and those who could afford,
Rather than send their folks to such a place,
Kept them at home; and it does seem more human.
But it's not so: the place is the asylum.
There they have every means proper to do with,
And you aren't darkening other people's lives—
Worse than no good to them, and they no good
To you in your condition; you can't know
Affection or the want of it in that state.
I've heard too much of the old-fashioned way.
My father's brother, he went mad quite young.
Some thought he had been bitten by a dog,
Because his violence took on the form
Of carrying his pillow in his teeth;
But it's more likely he was crossed in love,
Or so the story goes. It was some girl.

Anyway all he talked about was love.
They soon saw he would do someone a mischief
If he wa'n't kept strict watch of, and it ended
In father's building him a sort of cage,
Or room within a room, of hickory poles,
Like stanchions in the barn, from floor to ceiling—
A narrow passage all the way around.
Anything they put in for furniture
He'd tear to pieces, even a bed to lie on.
So they made the place comfortable with straw,
Like a beast's stall, to ease their consciences.
Of course they had to feed him without dishes.
They tried to keep him clothed, but he paraded
With his clothes on his arm—all of his clothes.
Cruel—it sounds. I s'pose they did the best
They knew. And just when he was at the height,
Father and mother married, and mother came,
A bride, to help take care of such a creature,
And accommodate her young life to his.
That was what marrying father meant to her.
She had to lie and hear love things made dreadful
By his shouts in the night. He'd shout and shout
Until the strength was shouted out of him,
And his voice died down slowly from exhaustion.
He'd pull his bars apart like bow and bowstring,
And let them go and make them twang, until
His hands had worn them smooth as any oxbow.
And then he'd crow as if he thought that child's play—
The only fun he had. I've heard them say, though,
They found a way to put a stop to it.
He was before my time—I never saw him;
But the pen stayed exactly as it was,
There in the upper chamber in the ell,
A sort of catchall full of attic clutter.
I often think of the smooth hickory bars.
It got so I would say—you know, half fooling—
"It's time I took my turn upstairs in jail"—
Just as you will till it becomes a habit.
No wonder I was glad to get away.

Mind you, I waited till Len said the word.
I didn't want the blame if things went wrong.
I was glad though, no end, when we moved out,
And I looked to be happy, and I was,
As I said, for a while—but I don't know!
Somehow the change wore out like a prescription.
And there's more to it than just window views
And living by a lake. I'm past such help—
Unless Len took the notion, which he won't,
And I won't ask him—it's not sure enough.
I s'pose I've got to go the road I'm going:
Other folks have to, and why shouldn't I?
I almost think if I could do like you,
Drop everything and live out on the ground—
But it might be, come night, I shouldn't like it,
Or a long rain. I should soon get enough,
And be glad of a good roof overhead.
I've lain awake thinking of you, I'll warrant,
More than you have yourself, some of these nights.
The wonder was the tents weren't snatched away
From over you as you lay in your beds.
I haven't courage for a risk like that.
Bless you, of course you're keeping me from work,
But the thing of it is, I need to *be* kept.
There's work enough to do—there's always that;
But behind's behind. The worst that you can do
Is set me back a little more behind.
I shan't catch up in this world, anyway.
I'd *rather* you'd not go unless you must.

AFTER APPLE-PICKING

My long two-pointed ladder's sticking through a tree
Toward heaven still,
And there's a barrel that I didn't fill
Beside it, and there may be two or three
Apples I didn't pick upon some bough.
But I am done with apple-picking now.

Essence of winter sleep is on the night,
The scent of apples: I am drowsing off.
I cannot rub the strangeness from my sight
I got from looking through a pane of glass
I skimmed this morning from the drinking trough
And held against the world of hoary grass.
It melted, and I let it fall and break.
But I was well
Upon my way to sleep before it fell,
And I could tell
What form my dreaming was about to take.
Magnified apples appear and disappear,
Stem end and blossom end,
And every fleck of russet showing clear.
My instep arch not only keeps the ache,
It keeps the pressure of a ladder-round.
I feel the ladder sway as the boughs bend.
And I keep hearing from the cellar bin
The rumbling sound
Of load on load of apples coming in.
For I have had too much
Of apple-picking: I am overtired
Of the great harvest I myself desired.
There were ten thousand thousand fruit to touch,
Cherish in hand, lift down, and not let fall.
For all
That struck the earth,
No matter if not bruised or spiked with stubble,
Went surely to the cider-apple heap
As of no worth.
One can see what will trouble
This sleep of mine, whatever sleep it is.
Were he not gone,
The woodchuck could say whether it's like his
Long sleep, as I describe its coming on,
Or just some human sleep.

William Carlos Williams 1883–1963

THIS IS JUST TO SAY

I have eaten
the plums
that were in
the icebox

and which
you were probably
saving
for breakfast

Forgive me
they were delicious
so sweet
and so cold

A UNISON

The grass is very green, my friend.
and tousled, like the head of—
your grandson, yes? And the mountain,
the mountain we climbed
twenty years since for the last
time (I write this thinking
of you) is saw-horned as then
upon the sky's edge—an old barn
is peaked there also, fatefully,
against the sky. And there it is
and we can't shift it or change
it or parse it or alter it
in any way. Listen! Do you not hear

From *Selected Poems* 1949 (three poems).

them? the singing? There it is and
we'd better acknowledge it and
write it down that way, not otherwise.
Not twist the words to mean
what we should have said but to mean
—what cannot be escaped: the
mountain riding the afternoon as
it does, the grass matted green,
green underfoot and the air—
rotten wood. Hear! Hear them!
the Undying. The hill slopes away,
then rises in the middleground,
you remember, with a grove of gnarled
maples centering the bare pasture,
sacred, surely—for what reason?
I cannot say. Idyllic!
a shrine cinctured there by
the trees, a certainty of music!
a unison and a dance, joined
at this death's festival: Something
of a shed snake's skin, the beginning
goldenrod. Or, best, a white stone,
you have seen it: *Mathilda Maria*
Fox—and near the ground's lip,
all but undecipherable, *Aet Suae,*
Anno 9—still there, the grass
dripping of last night's rain—and
welcome! The thin air, the near,
clear brook water!—and could not,
and died, unable; to escape
what the air and the wet grass—
through which, tomorrow, bejeweled,
the great sun will rise—the
unchanging mountains, forced on them—
and they received, willingly!
Stones, stones of a difference
joining the others at pace. Hear!
Hear the unison of their voices. . . .

FROM THE WANDERER: A ROCOCO STUDY

PATERSON—THE STRIKE

At the first peep of dawn she roused me!
I rose trembling at the change which the night saw!
For there, wretchedly brooding in a corner
From which her old eyes glittered fiercely—
"Go!" she said, and I hurried shivering
Out into the deserted streets of Paterson.
That night she came again, hovering
In rags within the filmy ceiling—
"Great Queen, bless me with thy tatters!"
"You are blest, go on!"
                                        "Hot for savagery,
Sucking the air! I went into the city,
Out again, baffled onto the mountain!
Back into the city!
                                        Nowhere
The subtle! Everywhere the electric!"

"A short bread line before a hitherto empty tea shop:
No questions—all stood patiently,
Dominated by one idea: something
That carried them as they are always wanting to be carried,
'But what is it,' I asked those nearest me,
'This thing heretofore unobtainable
That they seem so clever to have put on now!'

"Why since I have failed them can it be anything but their own
      brood?
Can it be anything but brutality?
On that at least they're united! That at least
Is their bean soup, their calm bread and a few luxuries!

"But in me, more sensitive, marvelous old queen
It sank deep into the blood, that I rose upon
The tense air enjoying the dusty fight!
Heavy drink where the low, sloping foreheads

The flat skulls with the unkempt black or blond hair,
The ugly legs of the young girls, pistons
Too powerful for delicacy!
The women's wrists, the men's arms red
Used to heat and cold, to toss quartered beeves
And barrels, and milk-cans, and crates of fruit!
"Faces all knotted up like burls on oaks,
Grasping, fox-snouted, thick-lipped,
Sagging breasts and protruding stomachs,
Rasping voices, filthy habits with the hands.
Nowhere you! Everywhere the electric!

"Ugly, venomous, gigantic!
Tossing me as a great father his helpless
Infant till it shriek with ecstasy
And its eyes roll and its tongue hangs out!—

"I am at peace again, old queen, I listen clearer now."

Ezra Pound 1885—

MARVOIL

A poor clerk, "Arnaut the less" they call me,
And because I have small mind to sit
Day long, long day cooped on a stool
A-jumbling o' figures for Maître Jacques Polin,
I ha' taken to rambling the South here.

The Vicomte of Beziers 's not such a bad lot.
I made rimes to his lady this three year:
Vers and canzone, till that damn'd son of Aragon,
Alfonso the half-bald, took to hanging
His helmet at Beziers.
Then came what might come, to wit: three men and one woman,
Beziers off at Mont-Ausier, I and his lady
Singing the stars in the turrets of Beziers,
And one lean Aragonese cursing the seneschal
To the end that you see, friends:

Aragon cursing in Aragon, Beziers busy at Beziers—
Bored to an inch of extinction,
Tibors all tongue and temper at Mont-Ausier,
Me! in this damn'd inn of Avignon,
Stringing long verse for the Burlatz;
All for one half-bald, knock-knee'd king of the Aragonese,
Alfonso, Quattro, poke-nose.

From *Personae* 1908-1910.

Marvoil: Arnaut de Marvoil, or Mareuil (c. 1170-1200), was born in Périgord, and trained as a notary (ll. 2-5), but gave that up and became poet at the court of Roger II, Viscount of Béziers, and his wife Adelaide. Roger died in 1194, around which time Arnaut left the court of Béziers, because of the rivalry of Alfonso of Aragon who came as a suitor to Adelaide. He then went to the court of William VIII, Count of Montpelier.

And if when I am dead
They take the trouble to tear out this wall here,
They'll know more of Arnaut of Marvoil
Than half his canzoni say of him.
As for will and testament I leave none,
Save this: "Vers and canzone to the Countess of Beziers
In return for the first kiss she gave me."
May her eyes and her cheek be fair
To all men except the King of Aragon,
And may I come speedily to Beziers
Whither my desire and my dream have preceded me.

O hole in the wall here! be thou my jongleur
As ne'er had I other, and when the wind blows,
Sing thou the grace of the Lady of Beziers,
For even as thou art hollow before I fill thee with this parchment,
So is my heart hollow when she filleth not mine eyes,
And so were my mind hollow, did she not fill utterly my thought.

Wherefore, O hole in the wall here,
When the wind blows sigh thou for my sorrow
That I have not the Countess of Beziers
Close in my arms here.
Even as thou shalt soon have this parchment.

O hole in the wall here, be thou my jongleur,
And though thou sighest my sorrow in the wind,
Keep yet my secret in thy breast here;
Even as I keep her image in my heart here.

Mihi pergamena deest

Mihi . . . : My parchment is not with me.

from HOMAGE TO SEXTUS PROPERTIUS

V

I

Now if ever it is time to cleanse Helicon;
                                        to lead Emathian horses afield,
And to name over the census of my chiefs in the Roman camp.
If I have not the faculty, "The bare attempt would be praiseworthy."
"In things of similar magnitude
                                        the mere will to act is sufficient."

The primitive ages sang Venus,
                                        the last sings of a tumult,
And I also will sing war when this matter of a girl is exhausted.
I with my beak hauled ashore would proceed in a more stately manner,
My Muse is eager to instruct me in a new gamut, or gambetto,
Up, up my soul, from your lowly cantilation,
                                        put on a timely vigour.

Oh august Pierides! Now for a large-mouthed product.
Thus:
"The Euphrates denies its protection to the Parthian and apologizes for Crassus,"
And "It is, I think, India which now gives necks to your triumph,"
And so forth, Augustus. "Virgin Arabia shakes in her inmost dwelling."
If any land shrink into a distant seacoast,
                    it is a mere postponement of your domination,

These poems proceed from the elegies of Sextus Propertius: V from II, 10, II, 1; VI from II, 13, III, 4-5 *passim*. The book is "not a translation" (Pound) but a persona, an antique mask for the living poet to speak through. "Now if ever it is time."

And I shall follow the camp, I shall be duly celebrated for
 singing the affairs of your cavalry.
May the fates watch over my day.

2

Yet you ask on what account I write so many love-lyrics
And whence this soft book comes into my mouth.
Neither Calliope nor Apollo sung these things into my ear,
 My genius is no more than a girl.

If she with ivory fingers drive a tune through the lyre,
 We look at the process.
How easy the moving fingers; if hair is mussed on her forehead,
If she goes in a gleam of Cos, in a slither of dyed stuff,
There is a volume in the matter; if her eyelids sink into sleep,
There are new jobs for the author;
And if she plays with me with her shirt off,
 We shall construct many Iliads.
And whatever she does or says
 We shall spin long yarns out of nothing.

Thus much the fates have allotted me, and if, Maecenas,
I were able to lead heroes into armour, I would not,
Neither would I warble of Titans, nor of Ossa
 spiked onto Olympus,
Nor of causeways over Pelion,
Nor of Thebes in its ancient respectability,
 nor of Homer's reputation in Pergamus,
Nor of Xerxes' two-barreled kingdom, nor of Remus and his
 royal family,
Nor of dignified Carthaginian characters,
Nor of Welsh mines and the profit Marus had out of them.

I should remember Caesar's affairs . . .
 for a background,
Although Callimachus did without them,
 and without Theseus,
Without an inferno, without Achilles attended of gods,

Without Ixion, and without the sons of Menoetius and the Argo
and without Jove's grave and the Titans.

And my ventricles do not palpitate to Caesarial *ore rotundos,*
Nor to the tune of the Phrygian fathers.
Sailor, of winds; a plowman, concerning his oxen;
Soldier, the enumeration of wounds; the sheep-feeder, of ewes;
We, in our narrow bed, turning aside from battles:
Each man where he can, wearing out the day in his manner.

3

It is noble to die of love, and honourable to remain
uncuckolded for a season.
And she speaks ill of light women
and will not praise Homer
Because Helen's conduct is "unsuitable."

VI

When, when, and whenever death closes our eyelids,

Moving naked over Acheron
Upon the one raft, victor and conquered together,
Marius and Jugurtha together,
one tangle of shadows.
Caesar plots against India,
Tigris and Euphrates shall, from now on, flow at his bidding,
Tibet shall be full of Roman policemen,
The Parthians shall get used to our statuary
and acquire a Roman religion;
One raft on the veiled flood of Acheron,
Marius and Jugurtha together.

Nor at my funeral either will there be any long trail,
bearing ancestral lares and images;
No trumpets filled with my emptiness,
Nor shall it be on an Atalic bed;
The perfumed cloths shall be absent.
A small plebeian procession.

Enough, enough and in plenty
There will be three books at my obsequies
Which I take, my not unworthy gift, to Persephone.

You will follow the bare scarified breast
Nor will you be weary of calling my name, nor too weary
To place the last kiss on my lips
When the Syrian onyx is broken.

"He who is now vacant dust
"Was once the slave of one passion:"
Give that much inscription
"Death why tardily come?"

You, sometimes, will lament a lost friend,
For it is a custom:
This care for past men,

Since Adonis was gored in Idalia, and the Cytharean
Ran crying with out-spread hair,
In vain, you call back the shade,
In vain, Cynthia. Vain call to unanswering shadow,
Small talk comes from small bones.

from THE CANTOS

III

I sat on the Dogana's steps
For the gondolas cost too much, that year,
And there were not "those girls", there was one face,
And the Buccentoro twenty yards off, howling "Stretti",
And the lit cross-beams, that year, in the Morosini,
And peacocks in Koré's house, or there may have been.
        Gods float in the azure air,
Bright gods and Tuscan, back before dew was shed.
Light: and the first light, before ever dew was fallen.
Panisks, and from the oak, dryas,
And from the apple, maelid,
Through all the wood, and the leaves are full of voices,
A-whisper, and the clouds bowe over the lake,
And there are gods upon them,
And in the water, the almond-white swimmers,
The silvery water glazes the upturned nipple,
        As Poggio has remarked.
Green veins in the turquoise,
Or, the gray steps lead up under the cedars.

My Cid rode up to Burgos,
Up to the studded gate between two towers,
Beat with his lance butt, and the child came out,
Una niña de nueve años,
To the little gallery over the gate, between the towers,
Reading the writ, voce tinnula:
That no man speak to, feed, help Ruy Diaz,
On pain to have his heart out, set on a pike spike
And both his eyes torn out, and all his goods sequestered,
"And here, Myo Cid, are the seals,
The big seal and the writing."
And he came down from Bivar, Myo Cid,

23 a nine-year-old girl   25 in a ringing voice

With no hawks left there on their perches,
And no clothes there in the presses,
And left his trunk with Raquel and Vidas,
That big box of sand, with the pawn-brokers,
To get pay for his menie;
Breaking his way to Valencia.
Ignez da Castro murdered, and a wall
Here stripped, here made to stand.
Drear waste, the pigment flakes from the stone,
Or plaster flakes, Mantegna painted the wall.
Silk tatters, "Nec Spe Nec Metu."

36 following *Nec . . . :* Neither hope nor fear.

T. S. Eliot 1888–1965

THE LOVE SONG OF J. ALFRED PRUFROCK

S'io credesse che mia risposta fosse
A persona che mai tornasse al mondo,
Questa fiamma staria senza piu scosse.
Ma perciocche giammai di questo fondo
Non torno vivo alcun, s'i'odo il vero,
Senza tema d'infamia ti rispondo.

Let us go then, you and I,
When the evening is spread out against the sky
Like a patient etherised upon a table;
Let us go, through certain half-deserted streets,
The muttering retreats
Of restless nights in one-night cheap hotels
And sawdust restaurants with oyster-shells:
Streets that follow like a tedious argument
Of insidious intent
To lead you to an overwhelming question. . .
Oh, do not ask, "What is it?"
Let us go and make our visit.

In the room the women come and go
Talking of Michelangelo.

The yellow fog that rubs its back upon the window-panes,
The yellow smoke that rubs its muzzle on the window-panes
Licked its tongue into the corners of the evening,
Lingered upon the pools that stand in drains,
Let fall upon its back the soot that falls from chimneys,
Slipped by the terrace, made a sudden leap,
And seeing that it was a soft October night,
Curled once about the house, and fell asleep.

From *Prufrock and Other Observations* 1917.
S'io credesse: Inferno, Canto 27, ll. 61-66, Guido da Montefeltro speaking. See Longfellow's translation, ll. 1-6, page 369 in this book.

And indeed there will be time
For the yellow smoke that slides along the street,
Rubbing its back upon the window-panes;
There will be time, there will be time
To prepare a face to meet the faces that you meet;
There will be time to murder and create,
And time for all the works and days of hands
That lift and drop a question on your plate;
Time for you and time for me,
And time yet for a hundred indecisions,
And for a hundred visions and revisions,
Before the taking of a toast and tea.

In the room the women come and go
Talking of Michelangelo.

And indeed there will be time
To wonder, "Do I dare?" and, "Do I dare?"
Time to turn back and descend the stair,
With a bald spot in the middle of my hair—
[They will say: "How his hair is growing thin!"]
My morning coat, my collar mounting firmly to the chin,
My necktie rich and modest, but asserted by a simple pin—
[They will say: "But how his arms and legs are thin!"]
Do I dare
Disturb the universe?
In a minute there is time
For decisions and revisions which a minute will reverse.

For I have known them all already, known them all:—
Have known the evenings, mornings, afternoons,
I have measured out my life with coffee spoons;
I know the voices dying with a dying fall
Beneath the music from a farther room.
  So how should I presume?

And I have known the eyes already, known them all—
The eyes that fix you in a formulated phrase,
And when I am formulated, sprawling on a pin,

When I am pinned and wriggling on the wall,
Then how should I begin
To spit out all the butt-ends of my days and ways?
   And how should I presume?

And I have known the arms already, known them all—
Arms that are braceleted and white and bare
[But in the lamplight, downed with light brown hair!]
Is it perfume from a dress
That makes me so digress?
Arms that lie along a table, or wrap about a shawl.
   And should I then presume?
   And how should I begin?

. . . . .

Shall I say, I have gone at dusk through narrow streets
And watched the smoke that rises from the pipes
Of lonely men in shirt-sleeves, leaning out of windows? . . .

I should have been a pair of ragged claws
Scuttling across the floors of silent seas.

. . . . .

And the afternoon, the evening, sleeps so peacefully!
Smoothed by long fingers,
Asleep . . . tired . . . or it malingers,
Stretched on the floor, here beside you and me.
Should I, after tea and cakes and ices,
Have the strength to force the moment to its crisis?
But though I have wept and fasted, wept and prayed,
Though I have seen my head [grown slightly bald] brought in upon a platter,
I am no prophet—and here's no great matter;
I have seen the moment of my greatness flicker,
And I have seen the eternal Footman hold my coat, and snicker,
And in short, I was afraid.

And would it have been worth it, after all,
After the cups, the marmalade, the tea,

Among the porcelain, among some talk of you and me,
Would it have been worth while,
To have bitten off the matter with a smile,
To have squeezed the universe into a ball
To roll it toward some overwhelming question,
To say: "I am Lazarus, come from the dead,
Come back to tell you all, I shall tell you all"—
If one, settling a pillow by her head,
  Should say: "That is not what I meant at all.
  That is not it, at all."

And would it have been worth it, after all,
Would it have been worth while,
After the sunsets and the dooryards and the sprinkled streets,
After the novels, after the teacups, after the skirts that trail along the floor—
And this, and so much more?—
It is impossible to say just what I mean!
But as if a magic lantern threw the nerves in patterns on a screen:
Would it have been worth while
If one, settling a pillow or throwing off a shawl,
And turning toward the window, should say:
  "That is not it at all,
  That is not what I meant, at all."

. . . . .

No! I am not Prince Hamlet, nor was meant to be;
Am an attendant lord, one that will do
To swell a progress, start a scene or two,
Advise the prince; no doubt, an easy tool,
Deferential, glad to be of use,
Politic, cautious, and meticulous;
Full of high sentence, but a bit obtuse;
At times, indeed, almost ridiculous—
Almost, at times, the Fool.

113 *progress:* i.e., add to the number of the people who accompany royalty on a journey, like Polonius.

I grow old . . . I grow old . . .
I shall wear the bottoms of my trousers rolled.

Shall I part my hair behind? Do I dare to eat a peach?
I shall wear white flannel trousers, and walk upon the beach.
I have heard the mermaids singing, each to each.

I do not think that they will sing to me.

I have seen them riding seaward on the waves
Combing the white hair of the waves blown back
When the wind blows the water white and black.

We have lingered in the chambers of the sea
By sea-girls wreathed with seaweed red and brown
Till human voices wake us, and we drown.

Theodore Roethke 1908–1963

from MEDITATIONS OF AN OLD WOMAN

I'M HERE

I

Is it enough?—
The sun loosening the frost on December windows,
The glitter of wet in the first of morning?
The sound of voices, young voices, mixed with sleighbells,
Coming across snow in early evening?

Outside, the same sparrows bicker in the eaves.
I'm tired of tiny noises:
The April cheeping, the vireo's insistence,
The prattle of the young no longer pleases.
Behind the child's archness
Lurks the bad animal.

—How needles and corners perplex me!
Dare I shrink to a hag,
The worst surprise a corner could have,
A witch who sleeps with her horse?
Some fates are worse.

2

I was queen of the vale—
For a short while,
Living all my heart's summer alone,
Ward of my spirit,
Running through high grasses,
My thighs brushing against flower-crowns;
Leaning, out of all breath,
Bracing my back against a sapling,
Making it quiver with my body;
At the stream's edge, trailing a vague finger;

From *Words for the Wind* 1958.

Flesh-awkward, half-alive,
Fearful of high places, in love with horses;
In love with stuffs, silks,
Rubbing my nose in the wool of blankets;
Bemused; pleased to be;
Mindful of cries,
The meaningful whisper,
The wren, the catbird.

So much of adolescence is an ill-defining dying,
An intolerable waiting,
A longing for another place and time,
Another condition.

I stayed: a willow to the wind.
The bats twittered at noon.
The swallows flew in and out of the smokeless chimneys.
I sang to the edges of flame,
My skin whiter in the soft weather,
My voice softer.

3

I remember walking down a path,
Down wooden steps toward a weedy garden;
And my dress caught on a rose-brier.
When I bent to untangle myself,
The scent of the half-opened buds came up over me.
I thought I was going to smother.

In the slow coming-out of sleep,
On the sill of the eyes, something flutters,
A thing we feel at evening, and by doors,
Or when we stand at the edge of a thicket,
And the ground-chill comes closer to us,
From under the dry leaves,
A beachy wetness.

The body, delighting in thresholds,
Rocks in and out of itself.
A bird, small as a leaf,
Sings in the first
Sunlight.

And the time I was so sick—
The whole place shook whenever I got a chill—
I closed my eyes, and saw small figures dancing,
A congress of tree-shrews and rats,
Romping around a fire,
Jumping up and down on their hind feet,
Their forepaws joined together, like hands—
They seemed very happy.

In my grandmother's inner eye,
So she told me when I was little,
A bird always kept singing.
She was a serious woman.

4

My geranium is dying, for all I can do,
Still leaning toward the last place the sun was.
I've tried I don't know how many times to replant it.
But these roses: I can wear them by looking away.
The eyes rejoice in the act of seeing and the fresh after-image;
Without staring like a lout, or a moping adolescent;
Without commotion.
Looking at the far trees at the end of the garden.
The flat branch of that hemlock holds the last of the sun,
Rocking it, like a sun-struck pond,
In a light wind.

I prefer the still joy:
The wasp drinking at the edge of my cup;
A snake lifting its head;
A snail's music.

5

What's weather to me? Even carp die in this river.
I need a pond with small eels. And a windy orchard.
I'm no midge of that and this. The dirt glitters like salt.
Birds are around. I've all the singing I would.
I'm not far from a stream.
It's not my first dying.
I can hold this valley,
Loose in my lap,
In my arms.

If the wind means me,
I'm here!
Here.

William Stafford 1914—

BELIEVING WHAT I KNOW

A lake on the map of Canada
may forget in the snow—
in the spring be gone.

Imagine the flower-eyes
nodding a little breeze,
looking at the land where the lake was.

Many things that were true
disappeared, grew up in grass,
and now hide from flowers that stare.

I learn from the land. Some day
like a field I may take the next thing
so well that whatever is will be me.

AT OUR HOUSE

Home late, one lamp turned low,
crumpled pillow on the couch,
wet dishes in the sink (late snack),
in every child's room the checked,
slow, sure breath—

Suddenly in this doorway where I stand
in this house I see this place again,
this time the night as quiet, the house
as well secured, all breath but mine borne
gently on the air—

And where I stand, no one.

From *Allegiances* 1970 (three poems).

SO LONG

At least at night, a streetlight
is better than a star.
And better good shoes on a
long walk, than a good friend.

Often in winter with my old
cap I slip away into the gloom
like a happy fish, at home
with all I touch, at the level of love.

No one can surface till far,
far on, and all that we'll have
to love may be what's near
in the cold, even then.

Denise Levertov 1923—

HYPOCRITE WOMEN

Hypocrite women, how seldom we speak
of our own doubts, while dubiously
we mother man in his doubt!

And if at Mill Valley perched in the trees
the sweet rain drifting through western air
a white sweating bull of a poet told us

our cunts are ugly—why didn't we
admit we have thought so too? (And
what shame? They are not for the eye!)

No, they are dark and wrinkled and hairy,
caves of the Moon . . .   And when a
dark humming fills us, a

coldness towards life,
we are too much women to
own to such unwomanliness.

Whorishly with the psychopomp
we play and plead—and say
nothing of this later.   And our dreams,

with what frivolity we have pared them
like toenails, clipped them like ends of
split hair.

From *O Taste and See* 1962 (two poems).

IN MIND

There's in my mind a woman
of innocence, unadorned but

fair-featured, and smelling of
apples or grass. She wears

a utopian smock or shift, her hair
is light brown and smooth, and she

is kind and very clean without
ostentation—
                    but she has
no imagination.
                    And there's a
turbulent moon-ridden girl

or old woman, or both,
dressed in opals and rags, feathers

and torn taffeta,
who knows strange songs—

but she is not kind.

Allen Ginsberg 1926—

AMERICA

America I've given you all and now I'm nothing.
America two dollars and twentyseven cents January 17, 1956.
I can't stand my own mind.
America when will we end the human war?
Go fuck yourself with your atom bomb.
I don't feel good don't bother me.
I won't write my poem till I'm in my right mind.
America when will you be angelic?
When will you take off your clothes?
When will you look at yourself through the grave?
When will you be worthy of your million Trotskyites?
America why are your libraries full of tears?
America when will you send your eggs to India?
I'm sick of your insane demands.
When can I go into the supermarket and buy what I need with my good looks?
America after all it is you and I who are perfect not the next world.
Your machinery is too much for me.
You made me want to be a saint.
There must be some other way to settle this argument.
Burroughs is in Tangiers I don't think he'll come back it's sinister.
Are you being sinister or is this some form of practical joke?
I'm trying to come to the point.
I refuse to give up my obsession.
America stop pushing I know what I'm doing.
America the plum blossoms are falling.
I haven't read the newspapers for months, everyday somebody goes on trial for murder.
America I feel sentimental about the Wobblies.
America I used to be a communist when I was a kid I'm not sorry.

From *Howl and Other Poems* 1956.

I smoke marijuana every chance I get.
I sit in my house for days on end and stare at the roses in the closet.
When I go to Chinatown I get drunk and never get laid.
My mind is made up there's going to be trouble.
You should have seen me reading Marx.
My psychoanalyst thinks I'm perfectly right.
I won't say the Lord's Prayer.
I have mystical visions and cosmic vibrations.
America I still haven't told you what you did to Uncle Max after he came over from Russia.

I'm addressing you.
Are you going to let your emotional life be run by Time Magazine?
I'm obsessed by Time Magazine.
I read it every week.
Its cover stares at me every time I slink past the corner candystore.
I read it in the basement of the Berkeley Public Library.
It's always telling me about responsibility. Businessmen are serious. Movie producers are serious. Everybody's serious but me.
It occurs to me that I am America.
I am talking to myself again.

Asia is rising against me.
I haven't got a chinaman's chance.
I'd better consider my national resources.
My national resources consist of two joints of marijuana millions of genitals an unpublishable private literature that goes 1400 miles an hour and twentyfive-thousand mental institutions.
I say nothing about my prisons nor the millions of underprivileged who live in my flowerpots under the light of five hundred suns.
I have abolished the whorehouses of France, Tangiers is the next to go.

My ambition is to be President despite the fact that I'm a Catholic.

America how can I write a holy litany in your silly mood?
I will continue like Henry Ford my strophes are as individual as his automobiles more so they're all different sexes.
America I will sell you strophes $2500 apiece $500 down on your old strophe
America free Tom Mooney
America save the Spanish Loyalists
America Sacco & Vanzetti must not die
America I am the Scottsboro boys.
America when I was seven momma took me to Communist Cell meetings they sold us garbanzos a handful per ticket a ticket costs a nickel and the speeches were free everybody was angelic and sentimental about the workers it was all so sincere you have no idea what a good thing the party was in 1835 Scott Nearing was a grand old man a real mensch Mother Bloor made me cry I once saw Israel Amter plain. Everybody must have been a spy.
America you don't really want to go to war.
America it's them bad Russians.
Them Russians them Russians and them Chinamen. And them Russians.
The Russia wants to eat us alive. The Russia's power mad. She wants to take our cars from out our garages.
Her wants to grab Chicago. Her needs a Red Readers' Digest. Her wants our auto plants in Siberia. Him big bureaucracy running our fillingstations.
That no good. Ugh. Him make Indians learn read. Him need big black niggers. Hah. Her make us all work sixteen hours a day. Help.
America this is quite serious.
America this is the impression I get from looking in the television set.
America is this correct?
I'd better get right down to the job.

61 *in 1835:* 1935?

It's true I don't want to join the Army or turn lathes in precision parts factories, I'm nearsighted and psychopathic anyway.
America I'm putting my queer shoulder to the wheel.

Gregory Corso 1930—

ZIZI'S LAMENT

I am in love with the laughing sickness
it would do me a lot of good if I had it—
I have worn the splendid gowns of Sudan,
carried the magnificent halivas of Boudodin Bros.,
kissed the singing Fatimas of the pimp of Aden,
wrote glorious psalms in Hakhaliba's cafe,
but I've never had the laughing sickness,
so what good am I?

The fat merchant offers me opium, kief, hashish, even camel juice,
all is unsatisfactory—
O bitter damned night! you again! must I yet
pluck out my unreal teeth
undress my unlaughable self
put to sleep this melancholy head?
I am nothing without the laughing sickness.

My father's got it, my grandfather had it;
surely my Uncle Fez will get it, but me, me
who it would do the most good,
will I ever get it?

From *Gasoline* 1958.

Robert Creeley 1926—

I KNOW A MAN

As I sd to my
friend, because I am
always talking,—John, I

sd, which was not his
name, the darkness sur-
rounds us, what

can we do against
it, or else, shall we &
why not, buy a goddamn big car,

drive, he sd, for
christ's sake, look
out where yr going.

NOT NOW

I can see you,
hairy, extended, vulnerable,
but how did you get up there.
Where were you going all alone,

why didn't you wait
for the others to come home
to go too, they would
have gone with you.

From *A Form of Women* 1959.
From *For Love* 1962.

THE FRIENDS

I want to help you
by understanding what
you want me to
understand by saying so.

·

I listen. I had
an ego once upon
a time—I do still,
for you listen to me.

Let's be very still.
Do you hear? Hear
what, I will say when-
ever you ask me to listen.

·

I wouldn't joke about
your wife wanting to wash
her hair at eleven o'clock
at night supposing she

wants to I'd consider her
thoughts on the matter equally
with yours wherever you were
and for whatever reason.

·

Don't think I'm
so awful you can
afford my company
so as not to
put me down more.

From *Pieces* 1969.

God, I hate
simplistic logic like—
I like it. Who cares.

·

Liking is as
liking does
for you, for me.

·

The "breathtaking banalities"
one only accomplishes in
retrospect. Hindsight—

they call it—like the
backend of a horse. *Horse's*
ass, would be the way.

Sylvia Plath 1932–1963

LADY LAZARUS

I have done it again.
One year in every ten
I manage it—

A sort of walking miracle, my skin
Bright as a Nazi lampshade,
My right foot

A paperweight,
My face a featureless, fine
Jew linen.

Peel off the napkin
O my enemy.
Do I terrify?—

The nose, the eye pits, the full set of teeth?
The sour breath
Will vanish in a day.

Soon, soon the flesh
The grave cave ate will be
At home on me

And I a smiling woman.
I am only thirty.
And like the cat I have nine times to die.

This is Number Three.
What a trash
To annihilate each decade.

From *Ariel* 1961.

What a million filaments.
The peanut-crunching crowd
Shoves in to see

Them unwrap me hand and foot—
The big strip tease.
Gentleman, ladies,

These are my hands,
My knees.
I may be skin and bone,

Nevertheless, I am the same, identical woman.
The first time it happened I was ten.
It was an accident.

The second time I meant
To last it out and not come back at all.
I rocked shut

As a seashell.
They had to call and call
And pick the worms off me like sticky pearls.

Dying
Is an art, like everything else.
I do it exceptionally well.

I do it so it feels like hell.
I do it so it feels real.
I guess you could say I've a call.

It's easy enough to do it in a cell.
It's easy enough to do it and stay put.
It's the theatrical

Comeback in broad day
To the same place, the same face, the same brute
Amused shout:

"A miracle!"
That knocks me out.
There is a charge

For the eyeing of my scars, there is a charge
For the hearing of my heart—
It really goes.

And there is a charge, a very large charge,
For a word or a touch
Or a bit of blood

Or a piece of my hair or my clothes.
So, so, Herr Doktor.
So, Herr Enemy.

I am your opus,
I am your valuable,
The pure gold baby

That melts to a shriek.
I turn and burn.
Do not think I underestimate your great concern.

Ash, ash—
You poke and stir.
Flesh, bone, there is nothing there—

A cake of soap,
A wedding ring,
A gold filling.

Herr God, Herr Lucifer,
Beware
Beware.

Out of the ash
I rise with my red hair
And I eat men like air.

John Ashbery 1927—

DEFINITION OF BLUE

The rise of capitalism parallels the advance of romanticism
And the individual is dominant until the close of the nineteenth century.
In our own time, mass practices have sought to submerge the personality
By ignoring it, which has caused it instead to branch out in all directions
Far from the permanent tug that used to be its notion of "home."
These different impetuses are recieved from everywhere
And are as instantly snapped back, hitting through the cold atmosphere
In one steady, intense line.

There is no remedy for this "packaging" which has supplanted the old sensations.
Formerly there would have been architectural screens at the point where the action became most difficult
As a path trails off into shrubbery—confusing, forgotten, yet continuing to exist.
But today there is no point in looking to imaginative new methods
Since all of them are in constant use. The most that can be said for them further
Is that erosion produces a kind of dust or exaggerated pumice
Which fills space and transforms it, becoming a medium
In which it is possible to recognize oneself.

Each new diversion adds its accurate touch to the ensemble, and so
A portrait, smooth as glass, is built up out of multiple corrections
And it has no relation to the space or time in which it was lived.

From *The Double Dream of Spring* 1970.

Only its existence is a part of all being, and is therefore, I suppose, to be prized
Beyond chasms of night that fight us
By being hidden and present.

And yet it results in a downward motion, or rather a floating one
In which the blue surroundings drift slowly up and past you
To realize themselves some day, while, you, in this nether world that could not be better
Waken each morning to the exact value of what you did and said, which remains.

Gary Snyder 1930—

from BURNING

I

SECOND SHAMAN SONG

Squat in swamp shadows.
        mosquitoes sting;
        high light in cedar above.
Crouched in a dry vain frame
      —thirst for cold snow
      —green slime of bone marrow
Seawater fills each eye

Quivering in nerve and muscle
Hung in the pelvic cradle
Bones propped against roots
A blind flicker of nerve

Still hand moves out alone
Flowering and leafing
            turning to quartz
Streaked rock   congestion of karma
The long body of the swamp.
A mud-streaked thigh.

Dying carp biting air
          in the damp grass,
River recedes. No matter.

Limp fish sleep in the weeds
The sun dries me as I dance

Burning: Section III of *Myths and Texts* 1960.

6

My clutch and your clutch
            batter the same bough
Elliptical bird-light
            stink of spilled wine.
Whirling hills, lost out of mind.

When Red Hand came to the river he saw
a man sitting on the other side of the river
pointing with his arm. So Red Hand
sat and pointed with his arm until nightfall
when he suddenly realized that it was
only a dead tree with a stretched out limb
and he got up and crossed the river.

March wind
      blows the bright dawn
      apricot blossoms down.
      salty bacon smoking on the stove
      (sitting on Chao-chou's *wu*
                  my feet sleep)

Ananda, grieving all night in the square
   gave up & went to bed & just then woke
The big trucks go by in the half-asleep night,
Ah, butterflies
Granite rots and crumbles
Warm seas & simple life slops on the ranges
Mayflies glitter for a day
Like Popes!

            where the sword is kept sharp
            the VOID
            gnashes its teeth

8

John Muir on Mt. Ritter:

After scanning its face again and again,
I began to scale it, picking my holds
With intense caution. About half-way
To the top, I was suddenly brought to
A dead stop, with arms outspread
Clinging close to the face of the rock
Unable to move hand or foot
Either up or down. My doom
Appeared fixed. I MUST fall.
There would be a moment of
Bewilderment, and then,
A lifeless rumble down the cliff
To the glacier below.
My mind seemed to fill with a
Stifling smoke. This terrible eclipse
Lasted only a moment, when life blazed
Forth again with preternatural clearness.
I seemed suddenly to become possessed
Of a new sense. My trembling muscles
Became firm again, every rift and flaw in
The rock was seen as through a microscope,
My limbs moved with a positiveness and precision
With which I seemed to have
Nothing at all to do.

17

THE TEXT

Sourdough mountain called a fire in:
Up Thunder Creek, high on a ridge.
Hiked eighteen hours, finally found
A snag and a hundred feet around on fire:
All afternoon and into night
Digging the fire line
Falling the burning snag

It fanned sparks down like shooting stars
Over the dry woods, starting spot-fires
Flaring in wind up Skagit valley
From the Sound.
Toward morning it rained.
We slept in mud and ashes,
Woke at dawn, the fire was out,
The sky was clear, we saw
The last glimmer of the morning star.

THE MYTH

Fire up Thunder Creek and the mountain—
troy's burning!
The cloud mutters
The mountains are your mind.
The woods bristle there,
Dogs barking and children shrieking
Rise from below.

Rain falls for centuries
Soaking the loose rocks in space
Sweet rain, the fire's out
The black snag glistens in the rain
& the last wisp of smoke floats up
Into the absolute cold
Into the spiral whorls of fire
The storms of the Milky Way
"Buddha incense in an empty world"
Black pit cold and light-year
Flame tongue of the dragon
Licks the sun

The sun is but a morning star

LeRoi Jones 1934—

SCENARIO VI

. . . and I come out of it
with this marvelous yellow cane
in my hand, yellow cashmere jacket
green felt pants & green boater . . . & green &
black clack shoes, polished & fast, jiggling
in the wings . . . till Vincente says "rollllem"
& I jiggle out on the stage, hands in my pockets,
the cane balanced delicately under my arm, spinning
& clack clack clacking across the bare sunday clothesline
tilting the hat to avoid the sun & ginergerly missing
the dried branch I had put there yesterday.

The motion of the mind! Smoooooth; I jiggle
& clack stomping one foot & the clothesline swings.
Fabulei Verwachsenes. Ripping this one off
in a series of dramatic half-turns I learned
many years ago in the orient; Baluba:
"The power to cloud men's minds" &c., which
I'm sure you must have heard about, doodle-doo.

& then I'm sitting in this red chair, humming,
feet still pecking at the marble floor, the
line motionless with only the tiniest leaf
on the dead branch waving, slowly; With a red background,
& I can't see anything, only hear this raspy 1936 voice
singing in german a very groovy love song; to me.

There's a train whistle too. In and out like this.
When out the open window of early spring, sharp
browns & greens fuzzy through the shade
& a fence somehow too bleak to describe, or even
be made sad by.

From *Preface to a Twenty Volume Suicide Note* 1961.

& I'm not even breathing hard. Tapping my feet
so nicely, the cane too, on the red marble. No
echo, that's distant thunder for these early summer storms,
cools off the whole scene too. But waiting
for my next cue, Vincente comes over, lights my cigarette,
We make a date for next wednesday, at the rainbow hut,
& he has a fabulous cigarette holder. & he pats
my cane-hand & says, "you do it up, baby". I'm on again.

Sylvia has come out in her smashing oranges & jewelry,
she has her mouth wide & I can hear her listening to
my feet clackings for her deep beauty doesn't include
rhythm. But we make it in great swirls out to the terrace,
which overlooks Sumer . . . & the Indus river, where next
week probably all kinds of white trash will ride in
on stolen animals we will be amazed by.

Ishmael Reed 1938—

I AM A COWBOY IN THE BOAT OF RA

"The devil must be forced to reveal any such physical evil (potions, charms, fetishes, etc.) still outside the body and these must be burned."
—RITUALE ROMANUM, *published 1947, endorsed by the coat of arms and introduction letter from Francis Cardinal Spellman*

I am a cowboy in the boat of Ra,
sidewinders in the saloons of fools
bit my forehead   like   O
the untrustworthiness of Egyptologists
Who do not know their trips. Who was that
dog-faced man? they asked, the day I rode
from town.

School marms with halitosis cannot see
the Nefertiti fake chipped on the run by slick
germans, the hawk behind Sonny Rollins' head or
the ritual beard of his axe; a longhorn winding
its bells thru the Field of Reeds.

I am a cowboy in the boat of Ra. I bedded
down with Isis, Lady of the Boogaloo, dove
down deep in her horny, stuck up her Wells-Far-ago
in daring midday get away. "Start grabbing the
blue," i said from top of my double crown.

I am a cowboy in the boat of Ra. Ezzard Charles
of the Chisholm Trail. Took up the bass but they
blew off my thumb. Alchemist in ringmanship but a
sucker for the right cross.

I am a cowboy in the boat of Ra. Vamoosed from
the temple i bide my time. The price on the wanted
poster was a-going down, outlaw alias copped my stance

From *The New Black Poetry*, ed. Clarence Major 1969.

and moody greenhorns were making me dance; while my
mouth's
shooting iron got its chambers jammed.

I am a cowboy in the boat of Ra. Boning-up in
the ol West i bide my time. You should see
me pick off these tin cans whippersnappers. I
write the motown long plays for the comeback of
Osiris. Make them up when stars stare at sleeping
steer out here near the campfire. Women arrive
on the backs of goats and throw themselves on
my Bowie.

I am a cowboy in the boat of Ra. Lord of the lash,
the Loup Garou Kid. Half breed son of Pisces and
Aquarius. I hold the souls of men in my pot. I do
the dirty boogie with scorpions. I make the bulls
keep still and was the first swinger to grape the taste.

I am a cowboy in his boat. Pope Joan of the
Ptah Ra. C/mere a minute willya doll?
Be a good girl and
Bring me my Buffalo horn of black powder
Bring me my headdress of black feathers
Bring me my bones of Ju-Ju snake
Go get my eyelids of red paint.
Hand me my shadow
I'm going into town after Set

I am a cowboy in the boat of Ra
look out Set here i come Set
to get Set to sunset Set
to unseat Set to Set down Set
usurper of the Royal couch
imposter RAdio of Moses' bush
party pooper O hater of dance
vampire outlaw of the milky
way

BEWARE : DO NOT READ THIS POEM

tonite , thriller was
abt an ol woman , so vain she
surrounded herself w/
    many mirrors

it got so bad that finally she
locked herself indoors & her
whole life became the
    mirrors

one day the villagers broke
into her house , but she was too
swift for them . she disappeared
    into a mirror

each tenant who bought the house
after that , lost a loved one to
    the ol woman in the mirror :
    first a little girl
    then a young woman
    then the young woman/s husband

the hunger of this poem is legendary
it has taken in many victims
back off from this poem
it has drawn in yr feet
back off from this poem
it has drawn in yr legs

back off from this poem
it is a greedy mirror
you are into this poem . from
    the waist down
nobody can hear you can they ?
this poem has had you up to here
    belch

From *Soulscript*, ed. June M. Jordan 1970.

this poem aint got no manners
you cant call out frm this poem
relax now & go w/ this poem
move & roll on to this poem
do not resist this poem
this poem has yr eyes
this poem has his head
this poem has his arms
this poem has his fingers
this poem has his fingertips

this poem is the reader & the
reader this poem

statistic : the us bureau of missing persons reports
that in 1968 over 100,000 people disappeared
leaving no solid clues
nor trace only
a space in the lives of their friends

Jim Rosenberg 1947—

RICHARD HOFSTADTER & MICHAEL WALLACE A DOCUMENTARY HISTORY OF AMERICAN VIOLENCE

numbers of employees them
in post expected this quarter Urban Race Riots in
CXII

Bacon's Rebellion
late eighteenth century and a common
protests rose often enough to of violence

No royal governor was largely true such action as
of the 1780's destructiveness development
In a somewhat effect. He

Ohio, lately arrived, and
next fell neck. James Harper party of squatters times fired
upon before
of Robinson gentleman that of a similar
occupied nowhere
could be regarded as distinctively to
In addressing paragraphs crowd cheered this distinguished

followed by enlightened excitement of coming so the whole

the
eleven years old towards us, from the stringent federal law deep
political self-confidence
the frequent riots it
each each other from time

to Cripple hardly nation
even those with after the Shays' Rebellion some secret American
soul is

First published as a broadside in Berkeley, 1971.

the stability if one suddenly entire

the

of of course were killed they could get over the fence
saw the people on
discharge his revolver

Nassau, Prince of Orange, defeated James II at of the
States with the Irish

riots in of a parade control of the
urged their parishioners came out in to harass the ensuing fight
by final attack

nothing incompetency of
refusal of the

Irish immigrants arrived seaboard cities early 1830's some
groups New York to
courses by robbing the nineteenth resort to professional grave
Dr. William
into the next newly to
entered the hospital some additional corpses discovered

(Composed entirely by chance events using random numbers and a used IBM Selectric typewriter ribbon. Each event extracted one to four consecutive words.)

Ray YoungBear 1951—

FOUR POEMS

1. RIVERTHOUGHT

the turtle with eyes
shining
like wet stones,
drank
the sunlight while my
thoughts
felt her hands, shaping
the
sand into an otter
sleeping
through rain, inside this
darkness
where sometimes, i hear
my
brothers and sisters, stir
and
call out, finally waking us.

2. HARD TIMES

the crow cleaned his feet
against
the snowy branch, and once in
awhile
my head disappeared under
this
wing, my teeth bringing out
the
corn, i hid from the others.

Here first published.

3. QUIET HILL

the fox's eye blinked with
the
frost shooting a little ways
from
his whiskers to the hills,
where
the leaves fall, making
me
aware of each drop,
and
listening to barks, now
turning
the other way, i will be safe—
but
tonight, my stomach will
remember
the chickens and then i'll
know
that it was worth it to kill
for
the small ones asleep, faraway.

4. A TIME TO HIDE

the bear had been up for
a
couple of days, not sleeping,
not
knowing, of the sky and how
it
has turned grey, telling us
to
move and lose time, by
trying
to forget his sad paws
rubbing
the blood of his son, over
his
body, at this nearing winter.

A Chronological List of Authors

To the Virginian Voyage
Christopher Marlowe 1564-1593
The Passionate Shepherd to His Love
William Shakespeare 1564-1616
Sonnets
Thomas Campion 1517-1620
Hark, All You Ladies that do sleep
Barnabe Barnes 1569-1609
Sonnets from Parthenophil and Parthenophe
John Davies 1569-1626
Sonnets from Gulling Sonnets
John Donne 1572-1631
The Canonization
A Lecture upon the Shadow
Sonnets from Divine Poems 1633: Holy Sonnets
Ben Jonson 1572-1636
An Ode. To Himself
Robert Herrick 1591-1674
The Hock-Cart, or Harvest Home
Corinna's Going a-Maying
George Herbert 1593-1633
The Holdfast Sin
Prayer (I)
The Holy Scriptures (I)
The Answer
John Milton 1608-1674
Lycidas
On the Morning of Christ's Nativity
On the Detraction Which Followed upon My Writing Certain Treatises
To the Lord General Cromwell, May 1652
On the Late Massacre in Piedmont
On His Blindness
On His Deceased Wife
Abraham Cowley 1618-1667
The Praise of Pindar (*Horace*)
Andrew Marvell 1621-1678
An Horatian Ode upon Cromwell's Return from Ireland
To His Coy Mistress
The Nymph Complaining for the Death of Her Faun
John Dryden 1631-1700
The Tenth Pastoral. Or, Gallus (*Virgil*)
Juana de Asbaje 1651-1695
Crimson lute that comest in the dawn
Green enravishment of human life
Jonathan Swift 1667-1745
The Humble Petition of Frances Harris, Who Must Starve, and Die a Maid If It Miscarries
Alexander Pope 1688-1744
Solitude. An Ode
The Lamentation of Glumdalclitch, for the Loss of Grildrig—A Pastoral
Duke upon Duke
Thomas Gray 1716-1771
Ode on the Death of a Favourite Cat, Drowned in a Tub of Gold Fishes
William Collins 1721-1759
Ode to Evening
William Blake 1757-1827
The Crystal Cabinet
The Mental Traveller
"Let the Brothels of Paris be opened
from Tiriel
Robert Burns 1759-1796
John Barleycorn. A Ballad
The Prayer of Holy Willie, a Canting, Hypocritical Kirk Elder
William Wordsworth 1770-1850
Strange fits of passion have I known
Lucy Gray; or, Solitude
The world is too much with us; late and soon

A Chronological List of Authors

Colonus' Praise (*Sophocles*)
Crazy Jane on God
For Anne Gregory
Colonel Martin

Enrique González Martínez 1871-1952
Wring the Swan's Neck

Robert Frost 1874-1963
A Servant to Servants
After Apple-Picking

William Carlos Williams 1883-1963
Idyl I (*Theocritus*)
This Is Just to Say
A Unison
From The Wanderer: A Rococo Study
An Elegy for D. H. Lawrence
Sonnet in Search of an Author

Ezra Pound 1885—
Marvoil
from Homage to Sextus Propertius
from The Cantos
Ballad of the Goodly Fere
"This Monument Will Outlast" (*Horace*)

T. S. Eliot 1888-1965
The Love Song of J. Alfred Prufrock

John Crowe Ransom 1888—
Captain Carpenter

e e cummings 1894-1962
the Cambridge ladies who live in furnished souls
unnoticed woman from whose kind large flesh
O It's Nice To Get Up In,the slipshod mucous kiss
the dirty colours of her kiss have just
Thou in whose swordgreat story shine the deeds
"next to of course god america i
Space being(don't forget to remember)Curved
helves surling out of eakspeasies per(reel)hapsingly
nothing false and possible is love

Federico García Lorca 1899-1936
Ballad of the Moon, Moon
The Ballad of the Sleepwalker

Pablo Neruda 1904—
Ode to My Socks

Langston Hughes 1902-1967
Ballad of the Moon, Moon (*Lorca*)
The Ballad of the Sleepwalker (*Lorca*)

Samuel Beckett 1906—
Crimson lute that comest in the dawn (*Asbaje*)
Green enravishment of human life (*Asbaje*)
Wring the Swan's Neck (*González Martínez*)

Louis MacNeice 1907-1963
Solvitur Acris Hiems (*Horace*)

W. H. Auden 1907—
In Memory of W. B. Yeats

Theodore Roethke 1908-1963
from Meditations of an Old Woman

W. R. Rodgers 1909-1969
A Last Word

Miguel Hernández 1910-1942
War

Dylan Thomas 1914-1953
Sonnets from Altarwise by Owl-Light
Ballad of the Long-Legged Bait

John Berryman 1914-1972
Sonnets from Berryman's Sonnets

William Stafford 1914—
Believing What I Know
At Our House
So Long

Robert Duncan 1919—
A Poem Beginning with a Line by Pindar

Denise Levertov 1923—
   Hypocrite Women
   In Mind
Robin Blaser 1925—
   Seventh Olympic Hymn (*Pindar*)
Frank O'Hara 1926-1966
   Ode to Willem de Kooning
   Ode on Lust
Allen Ginsberg 1966—
   America
Robert Creeley 1926—
   I Know a Man
   Not Now
   The Friends
Robert Bly 1926—
   Ode to My Socks (*Neruda*)
John Ashbery 1926—
   Definition of Blue
James Wright 1927—
   War (*Hernández*)
W. S. Merwin 1927—
   Count Arnaldos (*Spanish*)
   Lanzarote (*Spanish*)
   The Mooress Morayma (*Spanish*)
   The Moorish King Who Lost Granada (*Spanish*)
   Death and the Lover (*Spanish*)
Gary Snyder 1930—
   Second Shaman Song
   My clutch and your clutch
   John Muir on Mt. Ritter
   Sourdough mountain called a fire in
Gregory Corso 1930—
   Zizi's Lament
Sylvia Plath 1932-1963
   Lady Lazarus
R. G. Barnes 1932—
   Father of heaven, after squandered days (*Petrarch*)
   A white doe appeared to me over green (*Petrarch*)
LeRoi Jones 1934—
   Scenario VI
Ted Berrigan 1934—
   from The Sonnets
Andrew Hoyem 1935—
   Spook Sheep (*Nerval*)
   Golden (*Nerval*)
   The Wanderer (*Old English*)
Ishmael Reed 1938—
   I Am A Cowboy In The Boat Of Ra
   beware : do not read this poem
Tom Clark 1941—
   Five A.M. on East Fourteenth
   I'm out to eat
Jim Rosenberg 1947—
   Richard Hofstadter & Michael Wallace A Documentary History of American Violence
Ray YoungBear 1951—
   riverthought
   hard times
   quiet hill
   a time to hide

Index of Authors, Titles, First Lines, and Metrical Forms